POQUOSON FAMILIES

VOLUME I

THE FORREST FAMILY

OF THE
POQUOSON DISTRICT YORK COUNTY VIRGINIA

Compiled by
Albert James Willett, Jr.

HERITAGE BOOKS
2016

HERITAGE BOOKS
AN IMPRINT OF HERITAGE BOOKS, INC.

Books, CDs, and more—Worldwide

For our listing of thousands of titles see our website
at
www.HeritageBooks.com

Published 2016 by
HERITAGE BOOKS, INC.
Publishing Division
5810 Ruatan Street
Berwyn Heights, Md. 20740

Copyright © 2001 Albert James Willett, Jr.

All rights reserved. No part of this book may be reproduced or transmitted in any form or by any means, electronic or mechanical, including photocopying, recording or by any information storage and retrieval system without written permission from the author, except for the inclusion of brief quotations in a review.

International Standard Book Numbers
Paperbound: 978-0-7884-5739-5
Clothbound: 978-0-7884-1808-2

This volume is dedicated to the memory of

JESSIE FAY FORREST
1919-2000

POQUOSON FAMILIES, VOLUME I:
THE FORREST FAMILY
OF THE POQUOSON DISTRICT,
YORK COUNTY, VIRGINIA

TABLE OF CONTENTS

PREFACE:	i
CHAPTER ONE: Abraham Forrest (c1780-c1865) of Mathews County	1
CHAPTER TWO: Thomas Humphrey Forrest (c1800-c1846) of Poquoson	9
CHAPTER THREE: Abraham Forrest (1812-c1873) of Poquoson	138
CHAPTER FOUR: Henry Harry Forrest (1818-1904) of Mathews and Poquoson	149
CHAPTER FIVE: Henry Nathaniel Forrest (1814-c1880) of Poquoson	199
CHAPTER SIX: Thomas Humphrey Forrest (1835-1913) of Poquoson	222
BIBLIOGRAPHY of published works concerning Poquoson District, York County Virginia	232
ACKNOWLEDGEMENTS	238
POQUOSON GRADUATES OF THE VIRGINIA MILITARY INSTITUTE	241
INDEX:	242

PREFACE

This volume is a single surname study of the Forrest family of Messick, Poquoson, York County, Virginia. As such, most female lines have not been followed to more than one generation. It is the editor's intent to publish a separate single surname study of the Holloway family, and to follow that with a general study of the remaining Messick, Poquoson families which were published in the original *Poquoson Watermen*, 1988.

Because the following family history is an expanded 2nd edition and based on the previous volume of *Poquoson Watermen*, it has not been felt necessary to cite the original volume.

A word about locations. Most census records only identify that a person lived in Poquoson. The census generally does not mention Messick, Jeffs, or any of the other Post Office addresses of Poquoson. When identifying where a family resided, the editor has had to rely on what has been reported by descendants.

A word about dates. Our ancestors were not as precise in recording dates as we are today. There must be a myriad of errors in a work of this type. Old records are often recorded in a handwriting in which it is difficult to determine if a "1" or a "7" was meant. Many court records and other official vital records are faded, smudged, or otherwise difficult to discern. Many of the years of birth or marriage are computed from a census record that says a person was of a particular age when the census was taken. Thus all single year dates need to be considered as reasonably correct, but plus or minus one year. Sometimes, records simply contradict each other and can never be reconciled. In such a case, the normal assumption is that the record which is nearest the event is most likely the most reliable. But, errors occur, memories fade, sometimes the person giving the information is not the closest of kin, and is only guessing at the age or dates that are being recorded.

FOR THE RECORD: The editor makes no claim to perfection. What is produced here is an assemblage of birth, marriage, death data, oral family traditions, written but maybe unpublished family histories, extracts of census and vital records that often are confusing, conflicting and open to varying interpretations. What is presented here is a best effort to understand and assemble the available data. The editor takes sole responsibility for the final product and leaves it to future research to clarify any errors, omissions, or mistakes that may have inadvertently been repeated or made.

Census records are transcribed as they appeared to various transcribers, but the editor has brought in a few cases some uniformity to the way the census data is transcribed. Many of the census records are smudged, faded, water-stained. This may lead to errors in transcription. However, every reasonable effort has been made to produce in type what was written by hand but at the same time a small degree of uniformity has been artificially asserted so that the census records can be more easily compared to one another. Not every item of data has been transcribed from the various census records; the only census data that is included in this volume is that census data that helps define the various families.

Handwritten records have been transcribed as close as possible as type permits. There are a few exceptions. Often the census will say a wife is "keeping house". This has been has transcribed as "keep house" in order to keep from running over into another line when the information is not critical. Also, there has been a certain amount of uniformity brought to the transcribed census records, and often a relationship is typed in that does not appear in the original record.

Abbreviations are kept to a minimum in this volume. The following are the only abbreviations used by the editor:

    B = born
    M = married
    D = died
    Sic = Latin for "as it is written"
    NR = Not Recorded
    Daug = daughter
    Y. M. B. = York County Marriage Book

Expect errors. In a work of this scope and size, with numerous sources for data, there are bound to be mistakes. Every effort has been made to compare data and note discrepancies by circulating the original drafts of various sections of this volume to those most interested and often most directly descended from a particular branch of the family. Every census record was consulted which seemed even remotely possible to be connected to this extended family. Every census record that was found to pertain to this extended family has been extracted and cited. Published works, whether newspaper articles, obituaries, or biographies, have been consulted and abstracted. Every effort has been made to ascribe data taken from previously published sources. But in some cases, either in the distant past, or more recent but careless present, a citation has been lost while the quote or data has been retained. It has been felt more important to present the data that has been collected than to exclude data because it was not fully documented or properly cited. The goal of this volume is to point a future researcher to the records or locale where further information can be found thus saving them time and effort to fully document their own line. In this respect, I believe the following work will be found useful.

The index is not an every-name index. The index is abbreviated and lists only those names as listed in CAPITAL letters in the "Heading" of a narrative section, and those names which have the surname CAPITALIZED under the "List of Children" section. This index leads the researcher only to descendants of the subject of this volume or to those who married into the family. Also it has the advantage of never listing the same person more than twice, once as a child, and then again as the adult head of a family. This index leads anyone searching for information to only that data connected to the genealogical purpose of this volume.

Accuracy: this work does not present itself as perfect. At the same time, what is presented is not "plausible" genealogy, but the results of numerous contributors both living and deceased. Information has been gleaned from numerous printed, manuscript, Bible Record, Vital Record, and oral history sources and thus each source will have to be weighted to determine its degree of accuracy and trustworthiness.

As best as type can reproduce the written word, each census record, abstract, or transcript is as close to the original as type permits. Brackets [ ] are used when information has been inserted in an original record, usually to clarify what is being said.

Italics are used to list the names and ages of persons who are only listed by age groupings in the 1790-1840 census records. In thes 1790-1840 census records, only the name of the head of the household is listed in the original record. These early census records cite only the sex and approximate age of those being counted. Whenever other sources, such as, later census records, Bible Records, family history, oral history make it possible, the name of the wife and children are listed in *italics* beside the age and sex groupings.

If there is a Question Mark (?) behind a date, the date is estimated.

If there is a Star (*) behind a date, the date does not agree with the year range as applied to the 1790-1840 census records. However, do not expect all records to agree in every respect. Census takers make mistakes; the person giving the census taker the information can be mistaken; a mark meant for one age grouping may be entered in the one before or after its proper place. What is important is that the records taken as a whole are in reasonable agreement with what is otherwise known are inferred.

Any year date, which is not prefaced by a month and day, can be expected to be correct with plus (+) or minus (-) one year. Do not expect all dates as recorded to agree with each other. Even those dates graven on tombstones are notorious for the errors graven into the stone. This is because such dates are only as accurate as the memory of the person who provided the information. Particularly when the elderly outlive their contemporaries such dates are often the best guess of the person writing the obituary or providing the stone carver with information. The dates as recorded in the various records need to be balanced against the sum total of all known and available data.

Underlining is used to bring attention to the fact that a particular surname is "as written" in an original record. This has the same meaning as the Latin "sic" which is also used to denote that a record is "as" originally written. Usually this is used for the surname where one record will spell <u>Forest</u> with only one "r" while another record concerning the same individual or family will spell the surname <u>Forrest</u> with two "rr"s. In the same way, some census records spell the <u>Holloway</u> surname as <u>Holoway</u>. When original records are being directly cited by the editor, the original spelling is maintained.

Nicknames are generally listed after the Christian name from which they derive. However, some nicknames have no relationship to a given name and are normally listed after the first Christian name.

A researcher may come across the following Latin or common abbreviations when doing research in wills and other documents:

a.a.s	died in the year of their age = anno aetitis suae (i.e., 86 year of, or died in year 86 of his/her life)
d.s.p	died without issue = decessit sine prole legitima
d.s.p.l	died without legitimate issue = decessit sine prole mascula supesita
d.s.p.m.s	died without surving male issue = decessit sine prole mascula supersita
d.s.p.s	died without surviving issue = decessit sine prole supersita
d. unm	died unmarried
d.v.p.	died in the lifetime of his father = decessit vita patris
d.v.m.	died in the lifetime of his mother decessit vita matris
Et Al	and others = et alia
Inst	present month = instans
Liber	book or volume
Nepos	grandson
Nunc	Nuncapative will, an oral will, written by a witness
Ob	he/she died = obit
Relict	widow or widower = relicta/relictus
Sic	so or this, exact copy as written
Testes	witnesses
Utl	late = ultimo
Ux or vs	wife = uxor
Viz	namely - videlicet

In a work of this size there are bound to be errors. Having said that, every effort has been made to reduce the number of errors that occur and to ensure that the data presented is as reflected in the original records. Often, ages from one census to another do not agree; names change slightly as the census taker did his best to record what was probably told to him in a heavy Elizabethan accent. Whenever there is any doubt, the editor recommends that a researcher return to the original record.

Conventions:
Census records are copied as close to the original entry as type permits, and as closely as possible to the original entry. Thus often a census record will say that so-in-so is a son of the head of the household, when they are actually the grandson or in some cases the stepson of the head of the household. In this case, the census record is copied "as is".

No attempt has been made to copy every data entry in a census record. The researcher is referred to the original if more detail is sought. Thus, depending on the census record, additional data can be obtained as to whether or not the person can read or write, owns or rents, is single or has been married. Also, the exact day a census record was taken is normally listed at the top of each census sheet. To give uniformity to census data that was not recorded in a uniform manner some of the data from certain census records is reordered. In a few instances, data is inserted which is not in the original, i.e., a relationship that is not recorded in the original. Generally, this has been denoted by brackets [ ] around the inserted material.

An entry typed into the census data line as "m-39" means that the couple had been "married" "39 years".

An entry typed into the census data line of the wife as 5-4 (always behind the wife's name line), means that 5 children were born to her and that 4 are still living as of the date the census was taken.

Census records taken 1790 to 1840 only list the head of the household. However, names and ages have been placed beside these census records whenever possible to show that the census record reflects the particular family as it is known to us in the present. The "added" names and ages are placed in *italics* to show that they are only conjectural but based on research from other records.

Multiple sources have been used to establish relationships. Each researcher is referred to as many source documents as possible so that they can determine when future data becomes available if the relationships as given in this volume are actually as presented.

Names are often fluid. "Weston" Cemetery on Poquoson Avenue is the correct designation. However, the cemetery is more commonly known by most residents as the "Western" Cemetery. This difference of name for the same cemetery probably arose because Poquoson also has an "Eastern" Cemetery. In this volume, the more common usage of Western is used to designate the Weston Cemetery.

> Albert James Willett, Jr.
> Topping, Virginia
> May 1, 2001

CHAPTER ONE
THE ABRAHAM FORREST FAMILY
OF MATHEWS AND POQUOSON

FOR THE RECORD: The Forrest name is very ancient in Gloucester County, Virginia. Henry Forrest was born about 1623, and married about 1645, Elizabeth [Cheesman]. In 1658, Henry patented land in Gloucester County, Virginia. His sons were John and Edmund. John Forrest married Anne Long and had Abraham Forrest (b abt 1690, Gloucester) who later settled in Amelia County, Virginia.

FOR THE RECORD: One oral tradition has been handed down that Reginald Forrest recalled that Thomas Humphrey ("Tom Tit") Forrest (b 1832/1835) called Robert James Forrest "cousin". There is a slim chance that Henry Nathaniel Forrest and Tom Tit Forrest may be nephews of Abraham Forrest below.

FT.1a
ABRAHAM FORREST and (UNKNOWN)
Of Mathews County, Virginia

Abraham Forrest was born circa 1780, in the northern portion of (then) Gloucester County which after 1790, became Mathews County, Virginia. This date of birth agrees with the 1830 York county census, where it shows Abraham was born between 1780-1790.

NOTE: Abraham Forrest may be a son of George Forrest, the Revolutionary War veteran whose pension is on record. Note that the emphasis her is on "may be". However, the naming patterns of the known sons of Abraham Forrest do not match those of George Forrest, nor are any of his sons named George. However, deducting solely from census records, it appears that Abraham Forrest had two sons who are otherwise unknown by descendants of Abraham Forrest and either of who may have been named George.

It is thought that Abraham Forrest married 1st about 1798 (wife's name unknown, but possibly a Hudgins). If the traditional brother relationship between Thomas Humphrey and Abraham is correct, and that Henry Harry is their half-brother, then this first wife would have presumably died about 1815.

Children of Abraham Forrest and his 1st wife:

1. Thomas Humphrey FORREST: b abt 1800 (1790-1800), Mathews County, Virginia; m 1st abt 1821, Mary Weston (b 1805; d abt 1838); m 2nd abt 1839, Mrs. Martha ("Patsy") A. (Rollins) Quinn (b 1802; living 1860), the widow of James Quinn; d 1846, in York County, Virginia. See next FT.1.1.

2. (male) FORREST: b abt 1806. Inferred from the 1820 Mathews County, Virginia census.

3. Abraham FORREST: b February 15, 1812, Mathews County, Virginia; m 1st in York County, Virginia, November 23, 1837, Susan Callis (b abt 1807; d before 1840); m 2nd abt 1842, Mary ("Polly") Emily (b January 1, 1822; d January 31, 1866, buried Western Cemetery); resided in Poquoson, Virginia; d on December 4, 1873, age 61 years, 2 months, 8 days. See next FT.1.3.

FT.1b
ABRAHAM FORREST and MARY
Of Mathews County, Virginia, and Poquoson District, York County, Virginia

Abraham Forrest married (possibly as his 2nd wife) about 1815, Mary ("Polly") (b 1778, Mathews County, Virginia; d abt 1855). Abraham was an oysterman (1850), and a turner (1860).

In 1810, Abraham Forrest is not listed as the head of a household in the Mathews County, Virginia census.

Abraham Forrest served in the War of 1812. At the time, he was still a resident of Mathews County, Virginia. Abraham served as a Private in the 61st Regiment of the Virginia Militia under the command of Colonel Levin Gayle (Abraham's son, Thomas H. Forrest, served in the same 61st Regiment Militia but in a different company). Abram Forrest served for two days in Captain Bailey Diggs' Company (Pay Roll Accounts). He served for six days (on March 10 and 11, May 12, and from May 27 until May 31, 1813) days in Captain Christopher Tompkins' Company of Rifle Volunteers (Muster Rolls). Abram Forrest served for four months and 15 days from 1813 until 1815 in Captain Thomas Teagle Todd Tabb's Company.

In 1820, Abraham Forrest and family are listed in the Mathews County, Virginia census, as follows:

```
1 male    26-45  1775-1794  Abraham   age 40  b 1780
1 female  26-45  1775-1794  Mary      age 42  b 1778
1 male    0-10   1810-1820  Abraham   age 8   b 1812
1 male    0-10   1810-1820
1 male    0-10   1810-1820  Henry H.  age 2   b 1818
1 male    0-10   1810-1820
```

In 1826, Abraham Forrest sold land that was in Mathews County, Virginia, to William Brooks, Jr. This same property had previously been part of the John Hudgins estate, so it might be that Abraham Forrest's 1st wife was a Hudgins.

NOTE ON RELATIONSHIPS: In 1846, Mary Langley Hudgins of Mathews County, Virginia, married Samuel Rollins of Poquoson. She is the daughter of Bailey Hudgins. Bailey Hudgins' sister married William Brooks, Jr. Bailey Hudgins is the son of Anthony Hudgins, who is the son of William Hudgins.

Evidently, about or soon after 1826, Abraham Forrest and family moved from Mathews County, Virginia, across the York River to Poquoson, York County, Virginia.
In 1830, Abraham Forrest and family are listed in the York County, Virginia census, page 438, as follows:

```
1 male    40-50  1780-1790 Abraham age 50  b 1780
1 female  40-50  1780-1790 Mary    age 52* b 1778
1 male    10-15  1815-1820
1 male    10-15  1815-1820 Henry H. age 12 b 1818
1 female   5-10  1820-1825
1 female   0-5   1825-1830 Nancy   age 4?  b 1826
```

In 1840, Abraham Forrest and family are listed in the York County, Virginia census, page 311, as follows:

```
1 male    50-60  1780-1790 Abraham age 60  b 1780
1 female  50-60  1780-1790 Mary    age 62* b 1778
1 male    20-30  1810-1820 Henry H. age 22 b 1818
1 female  10-15  1825-1830 Nancy   age 14? b 1826
1 female  10-15  1825-1830
```

In 1850, Abraham Forrest and family are listed in the York County, Virginia census, page 345, dwelling 33-33, as follows:

```
Forrest Abraham       head   70 Mathews Co
                             Oysterman
        Polly         wife   72 Mathews Co
        Jno. H.       gson   18 Mathews Co
        Wm. T.        gson   16 Mathews Co
        Robert        gson   14 Mathews Co
```

In February 1854, Abraham Forrest filed for a pension based on his service in the War of 1812, as follows:

> State of Virginia, Mathews County, to wit, on this 21st day of Feby 1854, personally appeared before me, a Justice of the Peace, in and for the county and State aforesaid, Abraham Forrest age 69 years; now a resident of the county of York, formerly a resident of the county of Mathews and State of Virginia, who being duly Sworn according to law, declared that he is the identical Abraham Forrest who was a Soldier in the company commanded by Capt. Bailey Diggs in 61 Regt of Virginia Militia in the war with Great Britain, declared by the United States on the 18th day of June, 1812. That he entered the Service at the commencement of the war as a militia man and continued in Service at the whole war, that is to say he was not out all the time in active Service but he was out whenever it was necessary for him to be on duty when ever his officers called on him. He served in the early part of the war under Capt. Bailey Diggs; he afterwards left that company and joined the Rifle Company, which was first commanded by Christopher Tompkins and afterwards by Capt. Thomas Tabb. He never received any written discharge but was discharged as all the rest of the militia of this county that is at the end of the war they were dismissed from further Service. He is willing to receive for the time he served that is to Say whatever the pay rolls of the two said companies will Show that is on file in Washington. He makes this declaration for the purpose of obtaining the bounty land to which he may be entitled to under the act Granting bounty land to certain officers and soldiers who have been engaged in the

military Service of the United States passed September 28th 1850.

  Test.   His
  D. G. Foster Abraham (x) Forrest
           Mark

  Mathews County State of Virginia, to wit:
  Sworn to and subscribed before me this day and year above written. And I hereby certify, that I believe the said Abraham Forrest to be the identical man who serve as aforesaid, and he is of the age stated and is a man of good character. Given under my hand and seal, the 21st day of February, 1854.

         SSSS
    W. G. Lane, JP, S Seal S
         SSSS

  Evidently, Abraham Forrest received 80 acres of bounty land based on the above claim, which he subsequently disposed of as is evident by another claim under an act that increased the amount of acreage a soldier could claim:

  State of Virginia, County of York
  On this 24st day of April 1855, personally appeared before me, a Justice of the Peace, within and for the County and State aforesaid, Abraham Forrest age 71 years; a resident of said County and State, who being duly Sworn according to law, declares that he is the identical Abraham Forrest who was a Private in the Company commanded by Captain T. T. Tabb in the Regt of Virginia Militia commanded by Lieut. Col. Levin Gayle in the war with Great Britain, declared on the 18th day of June, 1812, and continued in actual service in said war for a term of at least 14 days; that he has heretofore made application for bounty land under act of

September 28th, 1850 (to which he now refers for particulars of his service) upon which has received a land warrant for 80 acres, No. ____ which he has legally disposed of, and cannot return.

He makes this declaration to obtain the bounty land to which he may be entitled under the act of Congress approved the third day of March, 1855. He further declares that he has not received nor applied for bounty land under this or any other Acts of Congress, except as above stated.

W. L. Matleute of York Town, Va., is hereby authorized to prosecute this my claim, and to receive any warrant which may be issued hereon.

His
Abraham (x) Forrest (Seal)
Mark

Mathews County State of Virginia, to wit:

Sworn to and subscribed before me this day and year above written. And I hereby certify, that I believe the said Abraham Forrest to be the identical man who serve as aforesaid, and he is of the age stated and is a man of good character. Given under my hand and seal, the 21st day of February, 1854.

SSSS
W. G. Lane, JP, S Seal S
SSSS

Hinde Holloway certified that he knew the claimant.

In 1860, Abraham <u>Forest</u> was enumerated in the household of James Martin in the Post Office Halfway House, York County, Virginia census, dwelling 79-79, as follows:

Martin	James		head	39	oysterman
	Nancy		wife	34	
	Hester		daughter	13	
	Pauline		daughter	9	
	Andrew		son	7	
Forest	Abraham		NR	78	turner

The Forrest surname is spelled with only one "R" in the 1850 York County census. Abraham Forrest was most likely the father-in-law of James Martin.

Abraham Forrest died sometime after June, 1860 (after the 1860 York County census was taken), in York County, Virginia.

> NOTE: Mrs. Jessie Forrest thought that Abraham died in 1865.

Children of Abraham Forrest and his 2nd wife, Mary ("Polly"):

4. Henry ("Long Henry") Harry FORREST: b September 22, 1818, Mathews County, Virginia; m Polly Rogers Simpson (b 1819, Accomac County, Virginia; d September 4, 1904, age 85 years, buried Western Cemetery, Poquoson); d August 18, 1897, and is buried in the Western Cemetery. See next FT.1.4.

5. (son) FORREST: b abt 1819 [Mathews County, Virginia]; living abt age 1 in the 1820 Mathews County census; living abt age 11 in the 1830 York County census; unknown what became of him after that date.

6. (daughter) FORREST: b abt 1823 [Mathews County, Virginia]; living abt age 17 in the 1840 census; unknown after that date.

7. Nancy/Ann FORREST: b [abt] 1826; possibly the Nancy Forrest who married about 1845, James Martin. In 1860, Abraham Forrest was living in the James and Nancy Martin household.

CHAPTER TWO
THE THOMAS HENRY FORREST FAMILY
POQUOSON DISTRICT, YORK COUNTY, VIRGINIA

FT.1.1a
THOMAS HUMPHREY FORREST and MARY WESTON
Of Mathews County, Virginia
And Poquoson, York County, Virginia

Thomas Humphrey Forrest was born about 1800 (between 1790-1800 according to the 1830 census), Mathews County, Virginia.

NOTE: Joe Frank Bunting stated that Thomas Humphrey Forrest was a half brother of Henry Harry Forrest.

Thomas H. Forrest had military service during the War of 1812 in the Mathews County, Virginia, Militia, as did his father Abraham. Thomas H. Forrest was a private in Capt. Christopher T. Lewis' Company of the 61st Regiment of Virginia Militia. The 61st Regiment was commanded by Colonel Levin Gayle during the years 1813-1815. Thomas served for 5 months, and 12 days. Later, Thomas Forrest was a farmer and a waterman; he attended the Methodist Church.

Thomas Forrest married 1st about 1821, Mary Weston (b 1805; d abt 1838 or 1839).

NOTE: The known Thomas Humphrey Forrest and Mary Weston children are listed as being born in Mathews County, with the single exception of their last child together, Martha Ann who was born in York County. Possibly Mary (Weston) Forrest died in childbirth. It is more likely, that they moved to York County before 1830 (as they are listed in the 1830 York County census), and perhaps returned to Mathews County soon afterwards. Another possibility is that Mrs. Mary (Weston) Forrest returned home to Mathews County to the care of her mother for the birth of her children, but in fact did live continuously in York County.

In 1830, Thomas H. Forrest and family are listed in the York County, Virginia census, page 429, as follows:

```
1 male    30-40  1790-1800  Thomas    age 30? b 1800
1 female  20-30  1800-1810  Mary      age 25  b 1805
1 male     5-10  1820-1825
1 male     5-10  1820-1825
1 male     5-10  1820-1825
1 female   0-5   1825-1830  Mary J.   age 2  b 1828
1 female   0-5   1825-1830  Sarah M.  age 1  b 1829
```

1. (son) FORREST: b abt 1821 (1820-1825) (1830 York County census); living abt age 9 in 1830; unknown after that date.

2. (son) FORREST: b abt 1824 (1820-1825) (1825-1830) (1830, 1840 York County census); living abt age 6 in 1830 York County census; living abt age 16 in 1840; unknown after that date.

3. (son) FORREST: b abt 1826 (1810-1820) (1830, 1840 York County census); living abt age 4 in 1830 census; living abt age 14 in 1840 census; unknown after that date.

4. Mary Jeanette FORREST: b 1828 (1825-1830); m 1st abt 1865, William H. Weston (b 1828, Mathews County, Virginia); m 2nd Littleton W. Watkins; she was a midwife. Her name was pronounced as "Jean Eddy", and "Jane Eddie." Jane Eddy died in January, 1905, and is buried in the Western Cemetery, Poquoson.

5. Sarah ("Sally") Margaret FORREST: b 1829 (b 1825-1830) (1830-1835); m abt 1853, John Bonaparte Huggett (b 1825, Mathews County,

Virginia; d 1889, buried Western Cemetery); d 1886, buried Western Cemetery, Poquoson.

6. John Henry FORREST: b January 7, 1832, Mathews County, Virginia; on July 27, 1850, he was enumerated with his grandfather, Abraham Forrest (1850 York County census, dwelling 33-33); on July 29, 1850, his stepbrother, John H. Forrest (actually Quinn), age 14, was enumerated with his widowed mother (1850 York County census, dwelling 44-44); m 1st abt 1851, Louisa Weston (b 1835), the daughter of John and Margaret (Banks) Weston of Mathews County, Virginia; m 2nd January 1, 1876, Mary Ann Holloway (b March 24, 1854; d April 27, 1900), age 22, the daughter of John Holloway and Frances (Dixon) Holloway; oysterman (1860); d January 19, 1894, buried Forrest Road Cemetery. See next FT.1.1.6.

7. William Thomas ("Tom Toad") FORREST: b December 7, 1833, Mathews County, Virginia; on July 27, 1850, he was enumerated with his grandfather, Abraham Forrest (1850 York County census, dwelling 33-33); m abt 1853, Ann (Nancy) Page; d May 2, 1909, buried Western Cemetery. See next FT.1.1.7.

8. Robert James ("Captain Bob") FORREST; b December 25, 1836, Mathews County, Virginia; on July 27, 1850, he was enumerated with his grandfather, Abraham Forrest (1850 York County census, dwelling 33-33); m 1st Mary Frances Weston; m 2nd Ann Deborah Holloway, widow of William Carmines, Jr; d May 14, 1907, buried Western Cemetery. See next FT.1.1.8.

9. Martha Ann FORREST: b 1839 (or 1838 according to the 1850 census) (1835-1840) York County, Virginia; she is possibly the Ann Forrest, age 12, who was enumerated with the George Page family on July 26, 1850 (1850 York County census, dwelling 21-21); m abt 1856, William Wesley Page (b 1836), the son of William Page and Rachel Messick; d between 1872

[birth of last son] and when the 1880 census was taken. See next FT.1.1.9.

FT.1.1b
THOMAS HUMPHREY FORREST and MARTHA A. QUINN
Of Poquoson, York County, Virginia

Thomas Forrest married 2nd about 1839, Mrs. Martha ("Patsy") A. (Rollins) Quinn (b 1802, York County), the daughter of Joseph Rollins and Mary S., and the widow of James Quinn. Mrs. Martha Quinn bought to this marriage several stepchildren.

Thomas was a farmer and waterman, and a Methodist.

He is not mentioned in the 1835 Processing Records of York County, however, he was mentioned in the 1844 Processing Record.

In 1840, Thomas H. Forrest and family are listed in the York County, Virginia census, page 311 (listed before his father, Abraham), as follows:

```
1 male    30-40  1800-1810  Thomas         age 40? b 1800
1 female  30-40  1800-1810  Martha         age 38  b 1802
1 female  20-30  1810-1820
1 female  15-20  1820-1825
1 male    10-15  1825-1830  Joseph QUINN, age 11
1 female   5-10  1830-1835  Mary J.        age 12* b 1828
1 female   5-10  1830-1835  Sarah M.       age 11* b 1829
1 male     5-10  1830-1835  Benjamin QUINN, age 6
1 male     5-10  1830-1835  John H.        age 8   b 1832
1 male     5-10  1830-1835  Wm. T.         age 7   b 1833
1 male     0-5   1835-1840
1 male     0-5   1835-1840
1 male     0-5   1835-1840  John QUINN, age 4
1 male     0-5   1835-1840  Robert         age 4   b 1836
1 female   0-5   1835-1840  Ann            age 2   b 1838
```

Thomas Humphrey Forrest died in 1846, in Messick, Poquoson District, York County, Virginia.

THE FORREST FAMILY

In 1850, [Mrs.] Martha Forrest and family are listed in the York County, Virginia census, page 345B, dwelling 44-44, taken on July 29/30, 1850, as follows:

Forrest	Martha	head	45	York County
[QUINN]	Joseph	son	21	York County
[QUINN]	Rebecca	daughter	18	York County
[QUINN]	Benjamin	son	16	York County
[QUINN]	Jno. H.	son	14	York County
	Ann	daughter	12	York County
	S. E.	daughter	8	York County
	Abraham	son	6	York County

In 1850, the orphaned children of Thomas Forrest are listed with their grandfather, Abraham Forrest in the York County, Virginia census, page 345, dwelling 33-33, taken on July 29, 1850, as follows:

Forrest	Abraham	head	70	Mathews Co Oysterman
	Polly	wife	72	Mathews Co
	Jno. H.	gson	18	Mathews Co
	Wm. T.	gson	16	Mathews Co
	Robert	gson	14	Mathews Co

In 1860, Martha <u>Forest</u> is listed as the head of household in the Post Office Halfway House, York County, Virginia census, dwelling 90-90, as follows:

<u>Forest</u>	Martha	head	58
Quinn	John	son	24
Quinn	Silvester	NR	17
Forrest	Abn.	son	14

The Forrest surname is spelled with only "R" in the 1860 census.

The following are the children of Martha (Rollins) Quinn and stepchildren of Thomas Forrest. They are erroneously listed as Forrest children in 1850 York County census, page 345B, dwelling 44-44. See *York County,*

Virginia, Guardian Book 1823-1846 page 246, for additional information.

    A. Joseph J. QUINN (stepson): b 1829 (or 1830), York County (1830-1835); oysterman (1850). In 1840 listed with his stepfather Thomas H. Forrest.
    B. Mary O. QUINN (stepdaughter): b abt 1831.
    C. Rebecca I. QUINN (stepdaughter): b 1832, York County, Virginia (or 1831), York County.
    D. Benjamin F. QUINN (stepson): b 1834, York County, Virginia (1835-1840). In 1840 listed with stepfather Thomas H. Forrest.
    E. John Harwood QUINN: (stepson): b 1836. (1835-1840) In 1840 listed with stepfather Thomas H. Forrest.

The following are children of Thomas Humphrey Forrest by his 2nd wife, Mrs. Martha A. ("Patsy") (Rollins) Quinn:

10. Sarah Sylvester ("Toss") FORREST: b 1841 or 1842 (possibly the S. E., age 8, listed in the 1850 York County census); m abt 1862, Thomas Curtis Page (b 1838); no children; left her property to namesake niece, Sarah Sylvester ("Toss") Forrest, who married Robert Meade Watkins.

11. Abraham FORREST: b December 7, 1842 (1844 according to the 1850 census; 1846 according to the 1860 census), Messick, York County, Virginia; m in Messick, York County, Virginia, on March 16, 1865, Sarah Elizabeth Topping (b November 17, 1845), the daughter of John Topping and Martha Dixon; d in Messick, on February 11, 1894, buried Western Cemetery. See next FT.1.1.11.

FT.1.1.6a
JOHN HENRY FORREST and LOUISA WESTON
Of Poquoson District, York County, Virginia

John Henry Forrest was born on January 7, 1832, in Mathews County, Virginia. John Henry Forrest was orphaned in 1846, when his father, Thomas Forrest, died in Messick, Poquoson District, York County, Virginia.

In 1850, Jno. H. Forrest, age 18, was listed in the household of his grandfather, Abraham Forrest, in the York County, Virginia census, page 345, dwelling 33-33.

John Henry Forrest married 1st about 1851, Louisa Weston (b 1835), the daughter of John and Margaret (Banks) Weston, originally of Mathews County, Virginia, but before 1850 residents of Poquoson, York County. Louisa Weston was the sister of Mary Weston who was the first wife of Robert James Forrest, brother to John Henry Forrest.

> NOTE: Mrs. Tillie Weston believed that John H. Forrest's 1st wife was Louisa Weston (subsequent research has fully supported her opinion).

In 1860, Jno. H. <u>Forest</u> and family are listed in the Post Office Halfway House, York County, Virginia census, dwelling 51-51, as follows:

Forest	Jno. H.	head	27	VA
			oysterman	
	Louisa	wife	23	VA
	Polly	daughter	6	VA
	Martha	daughter	3	VA
	Rosanna	daughter	7/12	VA
Banks	William	NR	25	
			sailor inland	
Banks	Mary	NR	19 farm hand	

The war came closer each day - the Poquoson men and boys knew who to fight for - and where to join up. In late May and early June, 1861, almost every able bodied "*Bull Islander*" joined the local Nelson Guards Virginia Militia, which later became the 32d Virginia Infantry, C.S.A. It may seem strange to us, that none of the Poquoson men opted to join the Union Army but a "foreign" and "Yankee" force was occupying Fort Monroe, and an increasing number of Union foraging parties were depleting the livestock, wooden fence rails were disappearing from the countryside, crops were being destroyed or confiscated. At the best, these goods were paid for, at the worse, Union cavalry troops simply raided and plundered "*Secess*" farms and homes.

There must have been a lot of war talk going around the small insular Poquoson community. Hard decisions affecting the future livelihood of Poquoson families were being contemplated by good hardworking men who knew next to nothing about war. As of June 3, 1861, many of these decisions had been made, because on that date in Williamsburg, Colonel Benjamin S. Ewell enlisted a reasonably large group of Poquoson volunteers for an one year tour of duty in Company F, ("Nelson Guards") of the 32nd Virginia Infantry Regiment. These June 3, 1861, volunteers were:

    Robert C. Claviers, 30, Virginia, oysterman
    James M. Firman, 32, York County, sailor
    Charles Firth, 23, York County, fisherman
    George W. Firth, 29, York County, fisherman
    Henry [Nathaniel] Forrest, 44, Baltimore, sailor
    Robert James Forrest, 24, Messick, sailor
    Wilton Holloway, 35, York County, oysterman
    Donard Insley, 24, York County, oysterman
    William Collona Joynes, 16, (Hampton)
    Moses Martin, 30, York County, sailor
    Robert W. McGee, 26, Chesterfield County, Barkeeper
    Robert M. Robertson, 18, York County, sailor inland
    John P. Thomas, 20, York County, sailor
    Solomon Wainwright, 20, York County, sailor
    Steven Wesley Ward, 19, York County, sailor

Henry Watkins, 22, York County, sailor

NOTE: Many of the above listed were the Poquoson friends and neighbors of John Henry Forrest.

Originally, there were just 24 privates enlisted, four officers and nine Non-Commissioned Officers for a total of 37 men in Company F. By June 14, twenty-one new privates had been enlisted bringing the total 32nd Virginia Infantry, Company F to just 58 (*32nd Virginia Infantry*, page 38). Why John Henry Forrest waited until February 1, 1862, to enlist at Ship's Point, York County, in Company B, 115th Virginia, is unknown. Perhaps, as one a little older than the average soldier and with the responsibility of three small children and a wife to support, the decision to join was postponed as long as possible.

However, Private John Henry Forrest was at the defense of Yorktown, a participant in the Battle of Williamsburg, and the subsequent retrograde movement of the Confederate Army to the Chickahominy River.

The 32nd and 115th Virginia were at the Seven Days battles in the defense of Richmond, but although they stood to and were ready to do their duty, and although the battles swirled close around them, somehow the brunt of an attack never fell to their lot. At one point, they stood shoulder to shoulder at Malvern Hill while death and destruction swirled all around them, but again they were untouched. After a relatively quiet summer's campaign on the Peninsula and before the gates of Richmond, the 32nd was dispatched to the Northern Virginia theater of war.

On September 6, the 32nd Virginia marched out of their bivouac and forded the Potomac River at White's Ferry, in water up to their chests, and entered the state of Maryland. By September 7 they were at Frederick, Maryland. General Lee had three objectives: to take

Harper's Ferry, to gather new recruits in Maryland, and to take the war to northern soil.

The attempt to take Harper's Ferry resulted in several battles. On September 14, 1862, a battle was fought at Crampton's Gap in Maryland. The Confederates at the gap were outnumbered and gave way. Captain Wynne and the Nelson Guard were on the other side of South Mountain expecting an Union attack, which fortunately, for them, never came. Further to the east, the Union troops at Harper's Ferry surrendered to General Jackson's force, and on September 16, 1861, the 32nd Virginia crossed back over the Potomac River, marched through Harper's Ferry, and on to Halltown, 4 miles west of Harper's Ferry (*32nd Virginia Infantry*, page 89).

By daybreak September 17, the 32nd Virginia had reached Botelier's Ford on the Potomac at Shepherd's Town opposite Sharpsburg. At this time, John Henry Forrest's regiment was part of Semmes' Brigade, McLaws' Division, and was assigned a position on Lee's left flank at Sharpsburg. For most of the morning, the 32nd Virginia had a relatively protected position in the West Woods. All morning there was a constant rattle of shot and shell, but most of the fighting took place just across the road and centered around the cornfield were so many from both sides died in charges and countercharges. Then the word was passed to the 32nd Virginia to clear the Federals from their front and push them back into their own lines. The word was passed, and the 32nd came charging out of the West Woods and crossed the open farmland, around the hayracks to their front, and kept their charge up until they passed the Nicodemus farm house and barns and reached the fences on the farthest side of the farm.

As the Confederate soldiers emerged from the woods, they were met by volleys of Union fire. As the Confederate emerged from the woods and began their charge across the open farmland, Captain Wynne was hit by a "minnie" ball over his right eye, and died. Colonel Montague's horse was hit; several other 32nd soldiers were hit. The 32nd Virginia Regiment advanced steadily towards the Federal soldiers until they were near the Alfred Poffenberger farmhouse, and finally the Confederate Infantry stopped and opened fire on the Federal forces that, at this time, were behind and protected by a stone wall. Bob Forrest was the color bearer that day and led the brigade's charge driving the Federals from the Nicodemus Barn and farmyard. The 32nd Virginia had advanced 300 yards in front of the rest of the Confederate Army and were now taking an enfilating fire from their exposed forward position.

The battle shifted away from the 32nd Virginia to the main road, and the soldiers of the 32nd Virginia were left to hug the ground they had taken for the remainder of that day. The 32nd Virginia had gone into action with 158 officers and men; at the end of the day, 15 were killed, among them John Sidney Freeman of Company I, and 57 wounded. Private Moses Martin of Company F was seriously wounded, and although we have no record of it, his wounds were probably thought to be fatal. Sergeant William Gibbs of Company F lost an arm.

That evening the 32nd Regiment was pulled back from its exposed forward position. However, Captain Stores asked (and received) permission to take a file of men back over the morning's battlefield and tend and recover those so seriously wounded that they had been left on the battlefield. On his mission, Captain Stores met General Lee astride his horse Traveler. General Lee was looking over the battlefield trying to decide whether or not to send Stonewall Jackson's Corps against the Federal troops on the next day. After personally reconnoitering the battlefield, General Jackson advised against such an undertaking and Lee did not order the renewal of the battle on the morrow.

Later Colonel Montague would say of that day,

"... I am gratified to be able to say that, after the enemy had been driven from his position and our portion of the fight had ceased, every man was at his post except the killed and wounded, not a single man gave back or straggled to the rear ... Nor do I think a single one got behind his company until the fight was over ..." (*32nd Virginia Infantry*, page 94)

On the following day, General Lee had his battered army hold the positions they had held as evening brought an end to the battle. Lee fully expected a renewal of the Federal attack; instead General McClelland hesitated, and General Lee took the opportunity to cross his Army back over the Potomac River into the safety of the northern Virginia countryside.

Later, in September, 1862, there was a reorganization of the Confederate units and the 32nd Virginia regiment was transferred to Corse's Brigade, General Pickett's Division, General Longstreet's I Corps.

John Henry Forrest was promoted to 4th Corporal on October 1, 1862. His muster roll record shows that his new salary was $46.00, an increase of $13.00 over previous salary. Pickett's Division was ordered north (eventually to gain immortality at Gettysburg on July 3, 1863). However, the 32nd VA regiment was detached and ordered to stay behind at Petersburg to serve as Provost Guard until Lee's army returned from the northern campaign.

During the summer of 1863, while the threat of attack around Petersburg was remote, John Henry Forrest may have been granted a furlough; or maybe he just took the opportunity to slip home. At any rate, as was the habit of Confederate soldiers from Poquoson, John Henry attempted to cross the Federal lines and return home for a brief visit, perhaps also with an official purpose of recruiting replacements for the much depleted ranks of the 32nd Virginia. Instead, on July 24, 1863, Corporal John Henry was captured at Yorktown by the Federals along with his brother, Robert James (Bob). His company officer had him declared a "deserter" on July 24, 1863. John Henry and his brother appear on the Union Prisoner of War list that states they were "Rebel Deserters" captured July 24, 1863. Most likely they were given the opportunity by the Federal command to swear allegiance to the Union. If they did so, they would be immediately released on parole and permitted to return home. Regardless of the reason for their capture, they were decidedly unrepentant Rebels, and they obviously refused the offer and so were transported northward to a prisoner of war camp. They were being held at the guard house on July 24, 1863, at Fort Henry, Maryland, and then forwarded the next day to the Prisoner of War camp at Fort Delaware, Delaware. Fort Delaware also held many Confederate prisoners from the Battle of Gettysburg. Most likely, John Henry and Robert James heard of the terrible price Virginians paid on that third day at Gettysburg when Pickett's Division made their valiant charge.

On September 26, 1863, after two months as prisoners of war, John Henry Forrest and Robert James Forrest were released after taking an oath of allegiance to the United States and permitted to return home together. For them, and many others, the War of Northern Aggression was at an end. Other Bull Islanders came home in 1864; yet a few Poquoson men had the high honor to be still with General Lee when he surrendered at Appomattox. It is hard for us to imagine the terrible price the Confederate soldiers had to pay. Many were stricken with disease and died without going into battle. Others paid the supreme sacrifice to their country on the battlefield. Still others were wounded, recovered from their wounds but sent home as invalids; still others campaigned day after day, hungry and ragged, did their duty as best their fatigued and over-wrought bodies would allow, were captured and eventually were paroled to return home. All would carry the physical and emotional effects of campaigning to their grave; many a veteran's grave was dug much earlier than would have been necessary if these men had not given their country their utmost effort in the face of battle, wounds, disease, and the deliberating effects of arduous campaigns.

A FAMILY TRADITION: There is an interesting story told about John Henry Forrest coming home from the war with a bag of gold coins. The family story has it that when someone questioned him about his sudden wealth and land buying sprees, John Henry clammed up and remained close-mouthed to his grave. According to Deanna Hunt's brother, Dwight, he heard someone in the family suggest that John Henry may have gotten the gold from a dead Yankee payroll courier. Unfortunately, at this point, it's just all speculation.

In 1870, Jno. H. <u>Forest</u> and family are listed in the Poquoson Township, York County, Virginia census, dwelling 108-115, as follows:

Forest	Jno. H.	head	38	VA farmer
	Louisa	wife	33	VA keep house
	Mary F.	daughter	15	VA
	Martha	daughter	12	VA
	Frank L.	son	6	VA
	Joanna	daughter	4	VA
	Nowida	daughter	8/12	VA

Children of John Henry Forrest and his first wife, Louisa Weston:

1. Mary ("Polly") F. FORREST: b May 1, 1854 (according to the 1850 census), York County, Virginia; m in Nansemond County, Virginia, on August 29, 1872, Gilbert B. Insley (b October 11, 1949; d December, 1938, buried Forrest Cemetery, Poquoson), the son of Gilbert Insley and Harriet Holloway; d 1925, buried Forrest Cemetery, Poquoson. See next FT.1.1.6.1.

2. Martha Louise FORREST: b May 1, 1857, York County, Virginia; m in York County on November 7, 1875, James Holloway (b February 28, 1845), and son of John and Sarah Holloway; d December 15, 1939, both buried Forrest Road Cemetery. See next FT.1.1.6.2.

3. Rosanna FORREST: b 1859, York County, Virginia. She was age 7 months at the 1860 York County census, but not listed in the 1870 York County census. Rosanna is not remembered in Messick, and may have died young.

4. Frank Lee FORREST: b July 11, 1863, York County, Virginia; m November 25, 1883, Emma Hopkins (b October 1, 1865; d March 8, 1930), the daughter of Edward and Amelia Hopkins; d February 13, 1945, both buried Forrest Road Cemetery, Poquoson. See next FT.1.1.6.4.

5. Joanna FORREST: b April, 1868, York County, Virginia; m February 19, 1884, Oliver Cromwell ("Crummie") Topping (b December, 1859), the son of John and Harriett Topping. See next FT.1.1.6.5.

6. Nowida ("Novada") Lulu FORREST: b February 22, 1870, York County, Virginia. She was 8 months old when the 1870 census was taken on September 20, 1870; m 1st December 31, 1891, Josiah Freeman, the son of J. Wesley and Hester Freeman; m 2nd Lorenzo P. Topping (b March 15, 1866; d October 2, 1949), the son of Josiah F. Topping and Augusta D. White Freeman; d August 8, 1943, buried Carmine-Phillips Cemetery.

7. Charles W. FORREST: b July 15, 1872, York County, Virginia; m April 30, 1890, Sallie (Pattie C. in 1910) Saunders (b March 8, 1871; d December 19, 1950), the daughter of William and Margaret (Moore) Saunders; d April 13, 1925, both buried Tabernacle Churchyard. See next FT.1.1.6.7.

FT.1.1.6b
JOHN HENRY FORREST and MARY ANN HOLLOWAY
Of Poquoson District, York County, Virginia

John H. Forrest married 2nd at John Holloway's in Poquoson on January 1, 1876, Mary Ann Holloway (b March 24, 1854; d April 27, 1900), age 22, the daughter of John and Frances (Dixon) Holloway. John Forrest was a fisherman (1850) and oysterman (1860).

| JOHN HENRY FORREST | MARY ANN (HOLLOWAY) FORREST |

In 1880, J. H. Forrest and family are listed in the Poquoson District, York County, Virginia, census, dwelling 220-220, as follows:

```
Forrest  J. H.        head      48 farmer
         Mary         wife      25 keep house
         Robt. T.     son        3 at home
         H. S.        son        1 at home
         Lula         daughter  19 at home
```

```
            Frank              son        15 at home
            Chas.              son         7 at home
            Joanna             daughter   13 at home
```

John Henry Forrest died on January 19, 1894, Poquoson, Virginia, and is buried in the Forrest Road Cemetery, Poquoson.

In 1900, John Henry Forrest's oldest son, Robert T. Forrest, was the head of a household that included his brothers and sisters as listed in the Poquoson, York County, Virginia census, dwelling 489-497, as follows:

```
Forrest  Robert T., head     Jan 1877 23 VA s
         Henry S., bro.      Feb 1879 21 VA s
         William B., bro.    Sep 1880 19 VA s
         Mary V., sister     Apr 1882 18 VA s
         John T., bro.       Apr 1884 16 VA s
         Rhoda, sister       Dec 1887 12 VA s
         Lloyd, brother      Mar 1890 10 VA s
```

Children of John Henry Forrest and 2nd second wife, Mary Ann Holloway:

8. Robert T. FORREST: b December 27, 1877, York County, Virginia; unmarried; in 1910, he was residing with his brother Henry S. Forrest; d December 24, 1966. See next FT.1.1.6.8.

9. Henry Stephen FORREST: b September 27, 1878, York County, Virginia; m 1st on June 17 1901, Mattie Evans (b September 22, 1876; d July 11, 1909), the daughter of George D. and Jane Evans; in 1910, he was a widow and head of a household which consisted of his brother Robert (b December 27, 1877); m 2nd March 9, 1911, Edna Louise Saunders (b April 22, 1893; d January 23, 1968), the daughter of William and Edith (Carmines) Saunders; d December 11, 1964. See next FT.1.1.6.9.

10. William B. ("Bill Dan") FORREST: b September, 1881, York County, Virginia (1880 as recorded in the 1900 York County census,

dwelling 489-497); m May 25, 1901, Martha Firth (b 1885). See next FT.1.1.6.10.

11. Mary ("Mollie") V. FORREST: b April, 1882, York County, Virginia; m Alonzo F. Moore, the son of J. W. and Rebecca Moore.

12. John Thomas FORREST: b April 29, 1884, York County, Virginia; m April 21, 1906, Annie Virginia Saunders (b April 15, 1887; d January 17, 1975), the daughter of William and Edith (Carmines) Saunders; d February 17, 1958. See next FT.1.1.6.12.

13. Rhoda FORREST: b December, 1887 York County, Virginia; m George W. Moore, the son of Starkey and Virginia Moore.

14. Lloyd FORREST: b March 1, 1890, York County, Virginia; m December 20, 1913, Annie Forrest Watkins, the daughter of Robert Mead and "Toss" Watkins. See next FT.1.1.6.14.

15. Benjamin T. FORREST: b January 1, 1886, York County, Virginia; d January 15, 1894, buried in the Forrest Road Cemetery, Poquoson, Virginia.

FT.1.1.6.1
MARY F. FORREST and GILBERT B. INSLEY
Of Messick, Poquoson District, York County

Mary ("Polly") F. Forrest was born on May 1, 1854 (according to the 1850 census).
Miss Mary F. Forrest married in Nansemond County, Virginia, on August 29, 1872, Gilbert B. Insley (b October 11, 1949; d December, 1938, buried Forrest Cemetery, Poquoson), the son of Gilbert Insley and Harriet Holloway.
In 1880, Gilbert Ainsley, Jr., and family are listed in his father's household in the Poquoson District, York County, Virginia census, dwelling 154-154, as follows:

Ainsley	Gilbert	head	63	VA	farm
	Harriet	wife	56	VA	keep house
	Allice	daughter	19	VA	
	Ella Lee	daughter	14	VA	
	Gilbert Jr.	son	21	VA	laborer
	Mary	wife	21	VA	
	Gilbert C.	son	6/10	VA	

FOR THE RECORD: The spelling of the surname as Ainsley is taken from the 1880 census record.

They were also listed in the 1880 census near Rescue, Newport District, Isle of Wight County, Virginia County census, dwelling 343-354, where he was an oysterman.

In 1900, Gilbert B. Insley and family are listed in the York County, Virginia census, dwelling 493-501, as follows:

Insley	Gilbert B.	head	Nov 1849	50	m-28	
	Mary F.	wife	Jul 1853	46	10-8	
	Gilbert L.	son	Oct 1877	22	s	
	John S.	son	Sep 1880	19	s	
	Mahala L.	daughter	Oct 1882	17	s	
	Sarah E.	daughter	Sep 1886	13	s	
	Margaret M.	daughter	Aug 1888	11	s	
	Mary R.	daughter	Mar 1895	5	s	
	Lloyd F.	son	Feb 1898	2	s	

In 1910, Gilbert B. Insley and family are listed in the York County, Virginia census, dwelling 247-253, as follows:

Insley	Gilbert B.	head	58	m-1	34	
	Mary F.	wife	58	m-1	34	10-8
	Mary R.	daughter	14	s		
	Lloyd	son	12	s		

Gilbert Insley died on December 15, 1938, and is buried in the Forrest Cemetery, Poquoson, York County.
(*Poquoson Waterman*, page 261).

1. William J. INSLEY: b June 17, 1875, York County, Virginia; m in Poquoson on November 11, 1896, Millie E. Pauls (b March 16, 1879; d August 30, 1950, buried Eastern Cemetery); d December 23, 1938, buried Eastern Cemetery, Poquoson.

2. Gilbert ("Gib") C./L. INSLEY: b December, 1879, York County, Virginia; m December 21, 1901, Ella R. Insley (b 1883); d November 24, 1924, in a bus-train accident along with his son Gilbert E. Insley; they were residents of York County, Virginia.

3. John Sydney INSLEY: b September 11, 1880, York County, Virginia; m in York County on September 28, 1901, Lucy Saunders (b May, 1854; d March 11, 1951, buried Tabernacle United Methodist Churchyard, Poquoson), age 17, the daughter of William and Edith (Carmines) Saunders. John was a boatman (1901); d December 15, 1942, buried Tabernacle United Methodist Churchyard, Poquoson.

4. Mahala Louise INSLEY: b October, 1882, York County, Virginia; m in Poquoson on June 28, 1904, Authur Wilson, age 23, the son of Rodulphus and Lucy Wilson (*Marriage Record No. 1, 1854-1928, York County*, page 62, line 24).

5. Sarah E. INSLEY: b September, 1886, York County, Virginia; m in Poquoson on October 20, 1906, Benjamin Freeman, age 22, the son of Wesley and Hester Freeman (*Marriage Record No. 1, 1854-1928, York County*, page 67, line 59).

6. Margaret M. INSLEY: b August, 1888, York County, Virginia; m in Poquoson, on July 1, 1907, William Shederick ("Shed") Saunders (b June, 1889), the son of William and Edith (Carmines) Saunders.

7. Mary R. INSLEY: b March, 1895, York County, Virginia.

8. Lloyd F. INSLEY: b February, 1898, York County, Virginia.

FT.1.1.6.2
MARTHA LOUISE FORREST and JAMES HOLLOWAY
Of Poquoson, York County, Virginia

Martha Louise Forrest was born on May 1, 1857, York County, Virginia.

Miss Martha Louise Forrest married in York County on November 7, 1875, James Holloway (b February 28, 1845), and son of John and Sarah Holloway (*Marriage Record No.1, 1854-1928, York County*, page 14, line 20). They resided in York County, Virginia.

In 1900, James Holloway and family are listed in the York County, Virginia census, dwelling 305-312, as follows:

Holloway	James	head	Feb 1845	55	m-22
	Martha L.	wife	Jan 1857	43	9-3
	Mary E.	daughter	Aug 1879	20	s
	Martha L.	daughter	Nov 1882	17	s
	Josiah	son	Sep 1889	11	s

James Holloway died on June 1, 1908, and is buried in the Forrest Cemetery, Forrest Road, Poquoson.

In 1910, Martha L. Holloway and family are listed in the York County census, dwelling 259-266, as follows:

Holloway	Martha L.	head	54 wd	9-3	VA VA VA
	Josiah	son	20 s		VA VA VA

Mrs. Martha Louise (Forrest) Holloway died d December 15, 1939, and both she and her husband are buried in the Forrest Road Cemetery, Poquoson.

(*Book of Remembrance*, Poquoson Library, Family Group Sheet, page 343; *Colonial Cousins*, 1940, page 69).

1. Mary Elizabeth ("Lizzie") HOLLOWAY: b August 22, 1879, York County, Virginia; m Jefferson Phillips.

2. Martha Lucy HOLLOWAY: b November 20, 1882, York County, Virginia; m Wade Hampton Whitson.

3. Joseph ("Josiah") HOLLOWAY: b September 2, 1889, York County, Virginia; m November, 1913, Mary (Mamie") Elizabeth Edwards (b July 12, 1894, York County), the daughter of Franklin Edwards and Sarah Elizabeth Moore.

FT.1.1.6.4
FRANK LEE FORREST and EMMA HOPKINS
Of Poquoson, York County, Virginia

Frank Lee Forrest was born on July 11, 1863, York County, Virginia, the son of John Henry Forrest and Louisa Weston. Obviously, Frank Lee Forrest was named after his father's commanding officer, Captain Frank Lee, of the Lee Guards, 32nd Virginia Infantry, C.S.A. Captain Frank Lee had been transferred to Stevenson's Division, Army of the Mississippi, and had died at Vicksburg, Mississippi, in 1863.

Frank Lee Forrest married in 1883, Emma Hopkins (b October 1, 1866; d March 8, 1930), the daughter of Edward and Amelia Hopkins. They resided in Poquoson, Virginia.

In 1900, Frank L. Forrest and family are listed in the Poquoson Magisterial District, York County, Virginia census, dwelling 302-309, as follows:

Forrest	Frank L.	head	Jul 1864	35 VA
	Emma	wife	Oct 1865	34 10-8
	Sallie E.	daughter	Jan 1885	15 VA
	Vergie V.	daughter	Sep 1886	13 VA
	Frank L.	son	Feb 1888	12 VA
	John B.	son	Sep 1889	10 VA
	Lemuel E.	son	Apr 1891	9 VA

Amelia H.	daughter	Aug 1892	7 VA
Margaret	daughter	May 1895	5 VA
Thomas L.	son	Jun 1899	11/12 VA

In 1910, they lived on the "Main Poquoson Road to Barrel Factory" and next door to his brothers, William B. Forrest and Charles W. Forrest.

In 1910, Frank L. Forrest and family are listed in the Poquoson Township, York County, Virginia census, dwelling 253-259, as follows:

Forrest	Frank L.	head	46	VA m-1
	Emma	wife	45	VA m-1
	children: 14 born – 12 living			
	John B.	son	30	VA s
	Lemuel E.	son	18	VA s
	Amelia H.	daughter	17	VA
	Maggie A.	daughter	14	VA
	Laurens	son	10	VA
	Viola	daughter	6	VA
	Ethel	daughter	5	VA
	Pearl	daughter	1 6/12	VA

Frank L. Forrest died on February 13, 1945, and both he and his wife are buried in the Forrest Road Cemetery.

1. Sallie E. FORREST: b January, 1885, York County, Virginia; m 1st December 29, 1905, Willis W. Freeman, the son of E. R. and Emma S. Freeman; m 2nd after 1925, Daniels; buried in Parklawn Cemetery, Hampton, Virginia.

2. Mary Virginia ("Virgie") FORREST: b September 7, 1886, York County, Virginia; m November 28, 1903, Leroy Forrest (b December, 1882), the son of William H. and Sallie Forrest. See next FT.1.4.2.6.

3. Frank Lee FORREST (Jr.): b February 20, 1888, York County, Virginia; m June 10, 1925, Dorothy Riggins (b March 27, 1903; d July 28, 1951), the daughter of H. and P. Riggins; d

March 25, 1948, both buried at Emmaus Churchyard, Poquoson.

4. John Bunyan FORREST: b September, 1889, York County, Virginia; m July 18, 1920, Beulah Firth (b September 2, 1900); d 1963, age 74. See next FT.1.1.6.4.4.

5. Lemuel E. FORREST: b April, 1891, York County, Virginia; m before 1919, Ann Alethia Nurvey (b 1888; d 1960, York County, Virginia); d 1985, buried in the Parklawn Memorial Cemetery, Hampton, Virginia

6. Amelia H. FORREST: b August, 1892, York County, Virginia; m January 4, 1910, William T. Hunt, the son of William H. Hunt and Sallie Topping.

7. Margaret ("Maggie") A. FORREST: b May, 1895, York County, Virginia; m Hilary Garner, Sr; d August, 1970, buried in the Parklawn Cemetery, Hampton, Virginia.

8. Thomas Laurens FORREST: b June 6, 1899, York County, Virginia; d May 7, 1945, buried Forrest Road Cemetery.

9. Viola FORREST: b 1903, York County, Virginia; m November 13, 1920, George Enoch Freeman, the son of Noah and Lovedy Freeman.

10. Ethel FORREST: b December 29, 1904, York County, Virginia; m Thomas Deans, Sr.

11. Edith FORREST: b January 13, 1907, York County, Virginia; m Richard Spencer Jones (b March 28, 1908; d July 17, 1993).

12. Pearl FORREST: b 1908, York County, Virginia; m Wilton Wilson.

13. Louise FORREST (twin): b abt 1909, York County, Virginia; died as infant before 1910.

14. John FORREST (twin): abt 1909, York County, Virginia; died as infant before 1910.

15. John B. FORREST: b abt 1912, York County, Virginia; m Beulah Firth, the daughter of Frank and Van Forrest Firth.

FT.1.1.6.4.4
JOHN BUNYAN FORREST and BEULAH FIRTH
Of York County, Virginia

John Bunyan Forrest was born on September, 1889, York County, Virginia.
John Bunyan Forrest married on July 18, 1920, Beulah Firth (b September 2, 1900).
John Bunyan Forrest died in 1963, age 74.

1. Talmadge Bunyan FORREST: b July 11, 1921; m Sarah Martin.

2. John Bunyan FORREST, Jr: b May 8, 1923; m Dorothy Roger.

3. Jack Nathan FORREST: b January 10, 1927; m Jean Ray Burcher.

4. Ann Temple FORREST: b April 13, 1932; m Eugene Hunt.

FT.1.1.6.5
JOANNA FORREST and OLIVER CROMWELL TOPPING
Of Poquoson, York County, Virginia

Joanna Forrest was born on April, 1868.

Miss Joanna Forrest married in York County on February 19, 1884, Oliver Cromwell Topping (b in December, 1859, in York County, Virginia) (*Marriage Record No. 1, 1854-1928, York County*, page 28, line 5). He was an oysterman (1884).

In 1900, Oliver C. Topping and family are listed in the York County, Virginia census, dwelling 303-310, as follows:

Topping	Oliver C.	head	Dec 1859	40	m-16		
	Johannah	wife	Apr 1868	32	3-3		
	Sarah L.	daughter	Jul 1889	10	s		
	Hattie	daughter	Sep 1892	7	s		
	John O.	son	Mar 1897	3	s		

In 1910, Oliver C. Topping and family are listed on the "Road running from the Main Poquoson Road to Barrel Factory, Bennett's Creek in the York County, Virginia, census, dwelling 256-262, as follows:

Topping	Oliver C.	head	51		m-1 27			
	Joannah	wife	47		m-1 27	5-5		
	Hattie	daughter	16	s		VA	VA	VA
	John O.	son	13	s		VA	VA	VA
	Lulu M.	daughter	7	s		VA	VA	VA
	Grayson	son	4	s		VA	VA	VA

1. Sarah L. TOPPING: b July, 1889, York County, Virginia; d 1946.

2. Hattie TOPPING: b September, 1892, York County, Virginia.

3. John Oliver TOPPING: b March 29, 1897, York County, Virginia; m July 3, 1919, Luenette (" Nettie") Estelle Jenkins, age 19 (b June 10, 1902, Warwick County, Virginia).

4. Lulu M. TOPPING: b 1903, York County, Virginia.

5. Charles Grayson TOPPING: b 1906, York County, Virginia; m February 13, 1926, Amelia Firman, age 17, the daughter of Moody and Virginia Firman (*Marriage Record No. 1, 1854-1928, York County*, page 28, line 5); d 1970.

FT.1.1.6.7
CHARLES W. FORREST and SALLIE CLYDE SAUNDERS
Of Poquoson, York County

Charles W. Forrest was born on July 15, 1872, in York County, Virginia.

Charles W. Forrest married on April 30, 1891, Sallie (Pattie C. in 1910) Clyde Saunders (b March 8, 1871; d December 19, 1950), the daughter of William and Margaret (Moore) Saunders.

In 1900, Charles W. Forrest and family are listed in the Poquoson Magisterial District, York County, Virginia census, dwelling 301-308, as follows:

Forrest	Charles W.	head	Jul 1872	27	VA
	Sallie C.	wife	Jun 1871	28	6-4
	Robert C.	son	Mar 1892	8	VA
	Maud L.	daug	Feb 1895	5	VA
	William H.	son	Oct 1896	3	VA
	Leroy P.	son	Feb 1900	3/12	VA

In 1910, they lived on the "Main Poquoson Road to the Barrel Factory."

In 1910, Charles W. Forrest and family are listed in the Poquoson Township, York County, Virginia census, dwelling 251-257, as follows:

Forrest	Charles W.	head	37	VA m-1	
	Sallie C.	wife	38	VA m-1	7-5
	Robert C.	son	18	VA	
	Maud L.	daug	15	VA	
	William H.	son	13	VA	
	Roy P.	son	10	VA	

Leon[e]   daug   8 VA

In 1920, Charles Forrest and family are listed in the Poquoson Township, York County, Virginia census, dwelling 123-125, as follows:

Forrest Charles   head   47 VA
         Sallie C.   wife   47 VA
         Leon[e]   daug   17 VA

Charles W. Forrest died on April 13, 1925, and both he and his wife are buried in the Tabernacle Churchyard, Poquoson, Virginia.
(*Book of Remembrance*, Poquoson Library, Family Group Sheet, page 211).

1. Robert Claytor FORREST: b March 1, 1892, York County, Virginia; m December 7, 1912, Mary Augusta Topping, the daughter of Lorenzo P. Topping and Rosanna V. Hopkins. See next FT.1.1.6.7.1.

2. Charles Franklin FORREST: b July 23, 1893, York County, Virginia; d October 25, 1894.

3. Maud Louise FORREST: b February 25, 1895, York County, Virginia; m December 24, 1912, William Thomas Hopkins (b March 3, 1890), the son of G. E. and Ellen Hopkins. See next FT.1.1.6.7.3.

4. William Henry FORREST: b October 25, 1896, York County, Virginia; m December 23, 1915, Eva Constance Cox, the daughter of John Rosser and Octavia Susan Cox (b May 7, 1898; d October 6, 1978); d October 3, 1975. See next FT.1.1.6.7.4.

5. Leroy Thaupe FORREST: b February 7, 1900, York County, Virginia; m April 7 1918, Emma Page (b August 25, 1897), the daughter of Skidmore Page and Estelle Ree Insley; d May 1, 1955. See next FT.1.1.6.7.5.

6. Fannie Leone FORREST: b March 21, 1902, York County, Virginia; m December 24, 1921, Talmadge M. Watkins (b November 16, 1901; d March 21, 1971, buried Smith Cemetery, Poquoson), the son of Braxton Watkins and Emma Moore; d February 20, 1962, buried Smith Cemetery, Poquoson.

    1. Oren WATKINS: m Robert Floyd Holloway.

FT.1.1.6.7.1
ROBERT CLAYTOR FORREST and MARY AUGUSTA TOPPING
Of York County

Robert Claytor Forrest was born on March 1, 1892, in York County.

Robert Claytor Forrest married on December 7, 1912, Mary Augusta Topping (b January 28, 1894; d March 6, 1968). The daughter of Lorenzo P. Topping and Rosanna V. Hopkins.

In 1920, Clada Forrest and family are listed in the Poquoson Township, York County, Virginia census, dwelling 240-242, as follows:

Forrest	Clada	head	24	VA
	Mary	wife	24	VA

    (remainder not copied)

Robert Claytor Forrest died on June 9, 1966.

(*Thomas James, Clerk of Kingston Parish, 1783-1796, Ancestry and Descendants, 1653-1951*, Elizabeth Hogg Ironmonger, 1961, page 318; *Book of Remembrance*, Poquoson Library, Family Group Sheet, page 228).

    1. Robert Hartness FORREST: b September 9, 1913, York County, Virginia; m May 3, 1931, Virginia Lewis (b July 9, 1919, Pitt County, North Carolina), the daughter of Herbert Raymond Lewis and Effie Alberta Corey. See next FT.1.1.6.7.1.1.

2. Mary Virginia FORREST: b October 8, 1915, York County, Virginia; m December 24, 1932, Vernon Page.

3. Sallie Lucille FORREST: b February 19, 1921, York County, Virginia; m Vernon Watkins.

4. Lorenzo Charles FORREST (twin): b October 8, 1924, York County, Virginia; m in North Carolina on August 21, 1952, Mary Etta Calitri (b December 11, 1904, North Carolina).

5. Edith Charlene FORREST (twin): b October 8, 1924, York County, Virginia; m December 24, 1944, Wallie Gene White.

6. Nellie Gray FORREST: b November, 1927, York County, Virginia; m June 19, 1948, Thomas Benton Rollins.

FT.1.1.6.7.1.1
ROBERT HARTNESS FORREST and VIRGINIA LEWIS
Of York County, Virginia

Robert Hartness Forrest [Sr.] was born on September 9, 1913, York County, Virginia.

Robert Hartness Forrest married on May 3, 1931, Virginia Lewis (b July 9, 1919, Pitt County, North Carolina), the daughter of Herbert Raymond Lewis and Effie Alberta Corey.

1. Robert Hartness FORREST, Jr: b April 14, 1942, York County; m Alma Carol Messick (b July 31, 1944, York County), the daughter of Thomas Wesley Messick and Alma Elizabeth Moore.

    1. Robert Brian FORREST: b May 8, 1962, York County.

    2. Melanie Ann FORREST: b March 15, 1964, York County.

FT.1.1.6.7.3
MAUD LOUISE FORREST and WILLIAM THOMAS HOPKINS
Of Poquoson, York County, Virginia

Maud Louise Forrest was born on February 25, 1895, York County, Virginia.

Miss Maud Louise Forrest married on December 24, 1912, William Thomas Hopkins (b March 3, 1890), the son of G. E. and Ellen Hopkins.

William Hopkins was a farmer.

(*Freeman Forebears*, page 35; *The Hopkins Family of Virginia*, page 244; *Book of Remembrance*, Poquoson Library, page 355).

1. William Eldridge HOPKINS: b October 21, 1913, in York County; m December 19, 1931, Maynie ("Mamie") Dryden Moore (b May 2, 1916, York County), the daughter of Leven James Moore and Etna Dryden Milloway.

2. Louise Forrest HOPKINS: b August 18, 1919, in York County; m June 19, 1937, Thomas A. Dorsey.

3. Charles Wesley HOPKINS: b August 22, 1925, in York County; m September 15, 1951, Betty Gray Mills (b May 28, 1928, Seaford, York County, Virginia), the daughter of Charles Wesley Mills and Mary Madeline Sparrow.

FT.1.1.6.7.4
WILLIAM HENRY FORREST and EVA CONSTANCE COX
Of Poquoson, York County, Virginia

William Henry Forrest, was born on October 25, 1896, York County, Virginia.

William Henry Forrest married December 23, 1915, Eva Constance Cox (b May 7, 1898; d October 6, 1978), the daughter of John Rosser and Octavia Cox.

William Henry Forrest died October 3, 1975.

1. Vernell FORREST: b August 9, 1920, Poquoson, Virginia; m William Leonard Ackiss (d December 10, 1989); d February 2, 1994. See next FT.1.1.6.7.4.1.

2. William Hugh FORREST, Sr: b December 17, 1925, Poquoson, Virginia; m October 15, 1945, Coretta Dawson Moore (b November 21, 1926, Poquoson, Virginia); d September 9, 1994. See next FT.1.1.6.7.4.2.

FT.1.1.6.7.4.1
VERNELL FORREST and WILLIAM LEONARD ACKISS

Vernell Forrest was born on August 9, 1920, Poquoson, Virginia.

Miss Vernell Forrest married William Leonard Ackiss (d December 1, 1989).

Mrs. Vernell (Forrest) Ackiss died February 2, 1994.

1. William Leonard ACKISS (Jr.): b June 27, 1944; m June 24, 1967, Linda Holt (b July 15, 1948).

    1. Tommy ACKISS: b August 15, 1969.

2. David Lansing ACKISS: b April 2, 1950; m 1st Chris (divorced); m 2nd Ann Nicalas (b July 15, 1962).

    1. Claire ACKISS: b December 3, 1991.

FT.1.1.6.7.4.2
WILLIAM HUGH FORREST and CORETTA DAWSON MOORE
Of Poquoson, Virginia

William Hugh Forrest was born on December 17, 1925, Poquoson, Virginia.

William Hugh Forrest married October 15, 1945, Coretta Dawson Moore (b November 21, 1926, Poquoson, Virginia), the daughter of James Harry Moore and Isabel Vandelia Dawson.

William worked in administration at NASA. Coretta attended Emmaus School - Ruth Cox was her teacher.

William Hugh Forrest died on September 9, 1994.

1. Vandelia Lee FORREST: b October 2, 1947, Riverside Hospital, Newport News, Virginia; m September 5, 1964, Harry Calvin Forrest (b December 7, 1945), the son of James Osborne Forrest, Jr., and Mary Virginia Jarvis. See next under husband's name FT.1.1.8.1.7.1.2.

2. William Hugh FORREST, Jr: b October 29, 1948, Riverside Hospital, Newport News, Virginia; m August 20, 1971, Betty Ann Bloxom (b November 9, 1952, Poquoson, Virginia). See next FT.1.1.6.7.4.2.2.

3. Mark Leaven FORREST: b November 26, 1955, Riverside Hospital, Newport News, Virginia; m April 8, 1978, Kim Laurene Riddick (b December 31, 1959). See next FT.1.1.6.7.4.2.3.

4. Kurt Moore FORREST: b February 8, 1968, Riverside Hospital, Newport News, Virginia.

FT.1.1.6.7.4.2.2
WILLIAM HUGH FORREST, JR. and BETTY ANN BLOXOM

William Hugh Forrest, Jr., was born on October 29, 1948, Poquoson, Virginia.

William Hugh Forrest, Jr., married on August 20, 1971, Betty Ann Bloxom (b November 9, 1952, Poquoson, Virginia), the daughter of Marvin B. and Irella (Lawson) Bloxom.

1. Mary Ilene FORREST: b March 11, 1972, Virginia; m April 25, 1998, Christopher Aaron Stephen (b December 8, 1973).

2. Rachel Anne FORREST: b October 20, 1977, Virginia.

FT.1.1.6.7.4.2.3
MARK LEAVEN FORREST and KIM LAURENE RIDDICK

Mark Leaven Forrest was born on November 26, 1955, Poquoson, Virginia.

Mark Leaven Forrest married on April 8, 1978, Kim Laurene Riddick (b December 31, 1959).

1. Kymberly Ann FORREST: b July 20, 1981.

2. Kory Laurene FORREST: b February 23, 1985.

FT.1.1.6.7.5
LEROY THAUPE FORREST and EMMA PAGE
Of York County, Virginia

Leroy Thaupe Forrest was born on February 7, 1900, York County, Virginia.

Leroy Thaupe Forrest married on April 7, 1918, Emma Page (b August 25, 1897), the daughter of Skidmore Page and Estelle Ree Insley.

Leroy Forrest died on May 1, 1955.

THE FORREST FAMILY

(*Book of Remembrance*, Poquoson Library, Family Group Sheet, page 224).

1. Roy Wilbur FORREST: b October 1, 1923, York County; m Anna Cecilia Martin. See next FT.1.1.6.7.5.1.

2. Pauline FORREST: b April 13, 1925, York County; m January 21, 1943, Joseph Sidney Cross.

3. William Thomas FORREST: b October 28, 1927, York County; m May 8, 1946, Emily Virginia Insley. See next FT.1.1.6.7.5.3.

4. Maylon Page FORREST: b July 25, 1932; unmarried; enlisted and served as Sergeant in Company B, 76th Tank Battalion, Korea; d December 1, 1952, in Korea, and is buried in the Western Cemetery.

FT.1.1.6.7.5.1
ROY WILBUR FORREST and ANNA CECILIA MARTIN

Roy Wilbur Forrest was born on October 1, 1923, York County.
Roy Wilbur Forrest married Anna Cecilia Martin.

1. Bonnie Faye FORREST: b December 7, 1938, Messick, Poquoson District, York County, Virginia; m Edward Sinclair Holloway; member of Tabernacle Methodist Church; d August 23, 1999, age 60, and is buried in the Parklawn Cemetery, Hampton, Virginia.

2. Linnie Lee FORREST: m Richard Wood of Poquoson.

FT.1.1.6.7.5.3
WILLIAM THOMAS FORREST
And EMILY VIRGINIA INSLEY

William Thomas Forrest was born on October 28, 1927, York County.

William Thomas Forrest married on May 8, 1946, Emily Virginia Insley.

1. Emily Jean FORREST: b September 25, 1947; m March 30, 1962, Charles Macon Southall, III (Emily was 14); resides Smith Street, Poquoson. See next FT.1.1.6.7.5.3.1.

2. Judith Lane FORREST: b March 16, 1952; m April 26, 1974, Robert K. Stewart. See next FT.1.1.6.7.5.3.2.

3. Ann Thomas FORREST: b January 23, 1960; m September 12, 1977, Charles J. Johnson. See next FT.1.1.6.7.5.3.3.

FT.1.1.6.7.5.3.1
EMILY JEAN FORREST and CHARLES MACON SOUTHALL

Emily Jean Forrest was born on September 25, 1947.

Miss Emily Jean Forrest married March 30, 1962, Charles Macon Southall, III (Emily was 14); resides Smith Street, Poquoson.

1. Charles Thomas SOUTHALL: b November 8, 1965.

2. David Sidney SOUTHALL: b November 26, 1968.

FT.1.1.6.7.5.3.2
JUDITH LANE FORREST and ROBERT K. STEWART

Judith Lane Forrest was born on March 16, 1952.

Miss Judith Lane Forrest married on April 26, 1974, Robert K. Stewart.

1. Stacey Annette STEWART: b October 20, 1975.

2. William Keith STEWART: b July 22, 1979.

FT.1.1.6.7.5.3.3
ANN THOMAS FORREST and CHARLES J. JOHNSON

Ann Thomas Forrest was born on January 23, 1960.

Miss Ann Thomas Forrest married September 12, 1977, Charles J. Johnson.

1. Kimberley Ann JOHNSON: b April 2, 1978.

FT.1.1.6.8
ROBERT T. FORREST
Of Poquoson, York County, Virginia

Robert T. Forrest was born on December 27, 1877, York County, Virginia. He was unmarried.

In 1900, Robert T. Forrest was the head of a household, which included his brothers, and sisters as listed in the Poquoson, York County, Virginia census, dwelling 489-497, as follows:

Forrest	Robert T.	head	Jan 1877	23 VA s
	Henry S.	brother	Feb 1879	21 VA s
	William	brother	Sep 1880	19 VA s
	Mary F.	sister	Apr 1882	18 VA s
	John T.	brother	Apr 1884	16 VA s
	Rhoda	sister	Dec 1887	12 VA s
	Lloyd	brother	Mar 1890	10 VA s

In 1910, Robert T. Forrest was residing with his brother Henry S. Forrest.

Robert T. Forrest died on December 24, 1966.

FT.1.1.6.9a
HENRY STEPHEN FORREST and MATTIE EVANS
Of Poquoson, York County, Virginia

Henry Stephen Forrest was born on September 27, 1878, York County, Virginia.

Henry Stephen Forrest married 1st on June 16, 1901, Mattie Evans (b September 22, 1876; d July 17, 1909), the daughter of George D. and Jane Evans.

In 1910, Henry S. Forrest was a widow and head of a household in the Poquoson, York County, Virginia census, dwelling 267-274, as follows:

Forrest	Henry S.	head	32	VA	widower
	Robert	brother	34	VA	single

Children of Henry Stephen Forrest and his 1st wife, Mattie Evans:

1. Lue Ceal FORREST: b March 1, 1902, York County, Virginia; d May 4, 1904.

2. Mary ("Mamie") Margaret FORREST: b September 4, 1903, York County, Virginia; m circa 1923, Milton J. Hoffman (b February 15, 1903; d December 13, 1938); d October 22, 1961, buried Western Cemetery, Poquoson.

    1. Mary Milton HOFFMAN:

3. Maywood FORREST: b October 12, 1905, York County, Virginia; m Sarah Newton.

FT.1.1.6.9b
HENRY STEPHEN FORREST and EDNA LOUISE SAUNDERS
Of Poquoson, York County, Virginia

Henry Stephen Forrest married 2nd March 9, 1911, Edna Louise Saunders (b April 22, 1893; d January 23, 1968), the daughter of William and Edith (Carmines) Saunders.
Henry S. Forrest died on December 11, 1964.
Children of Henry Stephen Forrest and his 2nd wife, Edna Louise Saunders:

4. Gladys Louise FORREST: b February 22, 1913; d September 6, 1913.

5. Henry Stephen FORREST, Jr: b May 22, 1919; m Roselyn Wilson (b October 23, 1918). See next FT.1.1.6.9.5.

6. Orville H. FORREST: b November 29, 1929; m Lois Hall (b October 12, 1934). See next FT.1.1.6.9.6.

FT.1.1.6.9.5
HENRY STEPHEN FORREST, JR., and ROSELYN WILSON

Henry Stephen Forrest, Jr., was born on May 22, 1919.

Henry Stephen Forrest married Roselyn Wilson (b October 23, 1918).

1. Daniel Wilson FORREST: b October 8, 1941.

2. Henry Stephen FORREST, III: b July 7, 1947.

FT.1.1.6.9.6
ORVILLE H. FORREST and LOIS HALL

Orville H. Forrest was born on November 29, 1929.

Orville H. Forrest married Lois Hall (b October 12, 1934).

1. Dana Kay FORREST: b June 9, 1960; m August 23, 1993, Joseph M. Zadodny (b December, 1958).

    1. Eva C. ZADODNY: b March 16, 1998.

FT.1.1.6.10
WILLIAM B. FORREST and MOLLIE L. FIRTH
Of Poquoson, York County, Virginia

William B. Forrest was born in September, 1881, Virginia (1880 according to the 1880 York County census, dwelling 489-497), Virginia.

William B. Forrest married on May 25, 1901, Martha ("Matt"/"Mollie") L. Firth (b 1885), the daughter of George W. Firth and Charlotte Insley.

In 1910, they lived on the "Main Poquoson Road to the Barrel Factory" (1910 York County, Virginia, census, dwelling 252-258).

In 1910, William B. Forrest and family are listed in the Poquoson Township, York County, Virginia census, dwelling 252-258, as follows:

```
Forrest  William B.  head      28  VA  m-1
         Mollie L.   wife      25  VA  m-1 5-3
         Mary T.     daughter   5  VA
         Felton      son        3  VA
         Helen S.    daughter   2  VA
         Lloyd       brother   18  VA
```

In 1920, William Forrest and family are listed in the Poquoson Township, York County, Virginia census, dwelling 238-240, as follows:

```
Forrest  William   head      37  VA
         Mattie    wife      35  VA
         Mary      daughter  14  VA
         Felton    son       12  VA
         Hellen    daughter  11  VA
         Nanie     daughter   8  VA
```

1. Mary T. FORREST: b 1905, York County, Virginia; m John Gibson Reveley, Jr; removed to Smithfield, Virginia; retired school teacher; d March 25, 2000, Smithfield, Virginia. See next FT.1.1.6.10.1.

2. Felton FORREST: b 1907, York County, Virginia; m abt 1927, Catherine.

3. Helen S. FORREST: b 1908, York County, Virginia; m John Benjamin Graham, the son of William and "Jicie" Lee Graham.

4. Nannie FORREST: b December 14, 1911, York County, Virginia; m John Elwood Forrest, the son of John Andrew and Alice (Rollins) Forrest; living 2000.

5. Cecelia FORREST: b abt 1921, York County, Virginia; m abt 1940, Richard Prince; resides (2000) Toano, James City County, Virginia.

FT.1.1.6.10.1
MARY T. FORREST and JOHN GIBSON REVELEY, JR.
Of Smithfield, Isle of Wight County, Virginia

Mary T. Forrest was born in 1905, York County, Virginia.

Miss Mary T. Forrest married John Gibson Reveley, Jr. They removed to Smithfield, Virginia. She is a retired schoolteacher.

Mrs. Mary T. (Forrest) Reveley died on March 25, 2000, Smithfield, Virginia.

1. Marianne REVELEY: m Christison; of (2000) Cleveland, Tennessee.

2. John Gibson REVELEY, III: of (2000) Virginia Beach, Virginia; m Betty.

3. William Forrest REVELEY: of (2000) New Kent County, Virginia; m Madeline.

FT.1.1.6.12
JOHN THOMAS FORREST and ANNIE VIRGINIA SAUNDERS
Of Poquoson, York County, Virginia

John Thomas Forrest was born on April 29, 1884, the son of John Henry Forrest and Mary Ann Holloway.

John Thomas Forrest married in the Big Bethel area in the Parsonage home of the Rev. W. R. Keefe on April 21, 1906, to Annie Virginia Saunders (b April 15, 1887; d January 17, 1975), the daughter of William and Edith (Carmines) Saunders.

| JOHN THOMAS FORREST | ANNIE V. (SAUNDERS) FORREST |

John Thomas Forrest died on February 17, 1958, and is buried in the Parklawn Cemetery, Hampton, Virginia.

1. Henry Vernon FORREST: b August 6, 1907, Poquoson, York County, Virginia; m by the Rev. W. L. Burks at Tabernacle parsonage on February 27, 1928, Evelyn Louise Phillips (b April 9, 1907; d January 19, 1998), the daughter of Henry Jefferson and Mary Lizzie (Holloway) Phillips; d September 24, 1974. See next FT.1.1.6.12.1.

2. William Otis FORREST: b March 19, 1910, Poquoson, York County, Virginia; m on October 15, 1932, Pearl Forbes of Hampton (b July 19, 1914; d January 1, 1993); d May 5, 1994, buried Parklawn Cemetery, Hampton, Virginia. See next FT.1.1.6.12.2.

3. Fannie Virginia FORREST: b January 20, 1913, Poquoson, York County, Virginia; m on February 8, 1930, Roland Randolph Rollins (b February 28, 1908), the son of William Manning and Priscilla Bell (Chesser) Rollins. See next FT.1.1.6.12.3.

4. John Magruder FORREST: b January 4, 1915, Poquoson, York County, Virginia; m Esta Smith of Shreveport, Louisiana; d March 25, 1989. See next FT.1.1.6.12.4.

5. Mary Lorene FORREST: b March 12, 1919, Poquoson, York County, Virginia; m on October 13, 1940, Buford Raymond Hunt of East Bend, North Carolina (b September 2, 1913; d November 22, 1994). See next FT.1.1.6.12.5.

6. Edith Florence FORREST: b February 11, 1921, Poquoson, York County, Virginia; m on April 28, 1940, to Thomas Elliott Steele of Charlotte, North Carolina (b November 26, 1919; d May 25, 1985). See next FT.1.1.6.12.6.

7. Benjamin Franklin FORREST: b May 8, 1923; m Jeanne Miller of Newport News; d November 29, 1975. See next FT.1.1.6.12.7.

8. Donald Lee FORREST, Sr: b December 3, 1930; m on November 16, 1950, Ida Sue Rollins, the daughter of Thomas Jefferson Rollins, Jr., and Agatha Ward (b February 17, 1935; d July 17, 1972); d September 17, 1969. See next FT.1.1.6.12.8.

FT.1.1.6.12.1
HENRY VERNON FORREST and EVELYN LOUISE PHILLIPS
Of Poquoson, Virginia

Henry Vernon Forrest was born on August 6, 1907, in Poquoson, Virginia.

Henry Vernon Forrest married by the Rev. W. L. Burks at Tabernacle parsonage on February 27, 1928, Evelyn Louise Phillips (b April 9, 1907; d January 19, 1998), the daughter of Henry Jefferson and Mary Lizzie (Holloway) Phillips.

Henry Vernon Forrest died on September 24, 1974, and is buried in the Parklawn Cemetery, Hampton, Virginia.

1. Marilyn Louise FORREST: b September 2, 1935; m 1st on July 6, 1952, Jack Royall; m 2nd on November, 1958, Robert Ferguson (deceased); m 3rd April 2, 1988, Warren Nichols.

   1. Martha Louise FERGUSON: b August 7, 1959; m on September 6, 1987, Robert Gerard Williams (divorced).

      1. Kathryn Louise WILLIAMS: b December 21, 1988.

FT.1.1.6.12.2
WILLIAM OTIS FORREST and PEARL FORBES

William Otis Forrest was born on March 19, 1910, Poquoson, York County, Virginia.

William Otis Forrest married on October 15, 1932, Pearl Forbes of Hampton (b July 19, 1914; d January 1, 1993).

WILLIAM OTIS FAMILY
(Photograph courtesy of Deanna Hunt)

William Otis Forrest died May 5, 1994, and is buried in the Parklawn Cemetery, Hampton, Virginia.

1. Clarice Jean FORREST: b December 24, 1933; m Herbert Green (divorced).

    1. Michael GREEN: b July 5, 1955.

    2. Mark GREEN: b July 13, 1962.

2. William Otis FORREST, Jr: b July 30, 1935; d October 14, 2000.

3. Edward Spencer FORREST: b April 2, 1937.

4. Thomas Ward FORREST: b July 16, 1944; m June 21, 1969, Diane Williams of Hampton, Virginia.

    1. Elizabeth FORREST: m Michael Jennings.

    2. Shelly FORREST: m June 22, 1996, James H. Helms.

    3. Emily FORREST: m June 25, 1998, Aaron M. Pritchett.

    4. Anne Virginia FORREST:

FT.1.1.6.12.3
FANNIE VIRGINIA FORREST
And ROLAND RANDOLPH ROLLINS
Of Poquoson, York County, Virginia

Fannie Virginia Forrest was born on January 20, 1913, Poquoson, York County, Virginia.

Miss Fannie Virginia Forrest married on February 8, 1930, Roland Randolph Rollins (b February 28, 1908), the son of William Manning and Priscilla Bell (Chesser) Rollins.

**ROLAND RANDOLPH ROLLINS
And FANNIE VIRGINIA FORREST
(Photograph courtesy of Deanna Hunt)**

1. Janet Sue ROLLINS: b November 13, 1931; m 1st James Robins of Mathews County, Virginia (divorced); m 2nd Roy Cross; resides (1998) in Fayetteville, Georgia.

    1. James ROBINS, Jr: b September 3, 1951.

    2. Neal ROBINS: b March 26, 1955.

    3. Roy CROSS, Jr: b June 15, 1959.

    4. Edward CROSS: b January 13, 1962.

    5. Debra CROSS: b February 21, 1964.

2. William Randolph ROLLINS: b March 22, 1933; m Lucille Batten of Hampton, Virginia.

    1. Rhonda ROLLINS: b December 12, 1955.

    2. Melanie ROLLINS: b March 1, 1961.

3. Barbara Ann ROLLINS: b August 24, 1934; m Waymond Sellers (divorced); resides (2000) in Poquoson, Virginia.

    1. Timothy SELLERS: b May 7, 1958.

    2. Randy SELLERS: b March 16, 1961.

    3. Neil SELLERS: b June 25, 1972.

4. Jack Nathan ROLLINS: b July 3, 1939; m 1st Judith Harrell (divorced); m 2nd Susan Townsend; resides (1998) in Gloucester, Virginia.

    1. Robert ROLLINS: b February 12, 1960.

2. Scott ROLLINS: b June 17, 1968.

3. Shawn ROLLINS: b June 30, 1964.

5. Judith Fae ROLLINS: b October 7, 1940; m Norman Neil, Sr. (divorced).

1. Norman NEIL, Jr: b November 2 1960.

2. Tina Ann NEIL: b November 3, 1964.

FT.1.1.6.12.4
JOHN MAGRUDER FORREST and ESTA SMITH
Of Hampton, Virginia

John Magruder Forrest was born on January 4, 1915, Poquoson, Virginia.
John Magruder Forrest married Esta Smith of Shreveport, Louisiana.
John Magruder Forrest died on March 25, 1989, and is buried in the Parklawn Memorial Park, Hampton, Virginia.

1. David Neil FORREST: b July 21, 1945; m Sharon Mann of Hampton, Virginia; resides (2001) Hampton, Virginia.

1. Chris FORREST: b June 14, 1971.

2. Greg FORREST: b November 13, 1973.

3. Andrea FORREST: b June 3, 1976.

FT.1.1.6.12.5
MARY LORENE FORREST and BUFORD RAYMOND HUNT
Of Poquoson, York County, Virginia

Mary Lorene Forrest was born on March 12, 1919, Poquoson, Virginia.

Miss Mary Lorene Forrest married at the Emmaus Baptist parsonage, Poquoson, by the Rev. N. D. Blackman on October 13, 1940, to Buford Raymond Hunt of East Bend, North Carolina (b September 2, 1913; d November 22, 1994), the son of George W. and Naomi (Jackson) Hunt. Mary Lorene Forrest is a 1936 graduate of Poquoson High School and a 1938 graduate of Newport News Business College, Newport News, Virginia.

November 19, 1943
MARY (FORREST) and BUFORD RAYMOND HUNT
(Photograph courtesy of Deanna Hunt)

In 1934, Buford Hunt enlisted as a private in the Army Air Corps. From January, 1934, until March, 1940, he was assigned to Langley Field, Virginia, as an Air Mechanic. It is interesting to note that in a letter he wrote on May 15, 1937 while traveling to West Point and the Catskills Mountains, he saw the dirigible *Hindenberg* at Lakehurst, New Jersey. March and April, 1940, found him assigned to McDill Field, Florida, as an Assistant Crew Chief. From 1940 until 1945, he was stationed in Florida as an aircraft inspector, except for a six-month tour of duty in the Panama Canal. During World War II, he traveled from air base to air base, mostly on the west coast of Florida. Shortly after the war ended, he did a 16-month tour of duty in West Germany. He returned to Langley Field and, in 1955, after 21 years of service, retired from the Air Force with the rank of Warrant Officer. Buford Hunt immediately went to work for NASA, in Hampton, Virginia, and retired from NASA in 1983.

1. Deanna Elaine HUNT: b November 20, 1943, at Dale Mabry Field, Tallahassee, Florida; graduated June, 1963, from Poquoson High School; 1964-1973, worked as civilian employee at Fort Monroe and then, in 1975, transferred to Langley Air Force Base; on May 28, 1999, retired from the 1st Medical Group, Langley Air Force Base, Virginia, after 33 years of Civil Service.

2. Buford Dwight HUNT: b October 18, 1947, in Newport News, Virginia; m 1st on August 16, 1969, to Donna Lee White (divorced); m 2nd on July 17, 1976, Cathy Arlene McBride (b September 20, 1949), the daughter of Robert H. and Peggy (Wheeler) McBride of Hampton, Virginia; resides in Yorktown, Virginia. See next FT.1.1.6.12.5.2.

3. Mary Susan HUNT: b September 5, 1951, Hampton, Virginia; June, 1969, graduated from Poquoson High School; m on August 18, 1973, David Lee Shifflett (b June 10, 1951) of Elkton, Virginia; May, 1971, graduated from Chowan College with an Associates Degree in Education; May, 1973, graduated from Campbell University, North Carolina, with a Bachelor's

Degree in Elementary Education. See next FT.1.1.6.12.5.3.

FT.1.1.6.12.5.2a
BUFORD DWIGHT HUNT and DONNA LEE WHITE
Of Poquoson, Virginia

Buford Dwight Hunt was born on October 18, 1947, in Newport News, Virginia. In June, 1965, he graduated from Poquoson High School; June, 1974, he graduated from Campbell University with a Bachelor's Degree in Geology.

Buford Dwight Hunt married 1st on August 16, 1969, to Donna Lee White (divorced).

FT.1.1.6.12.5.2b
BUFORD DWIGHT HUNT and CATHY ARLENE MCBRIDE
Of Yorktown, Virginia

Buford Dwight Hunt married 2nd on July 17, 1976, Cathy Arlene McBride (b September 20, 1949), the daughter of Robert H. and Peggy (Wheeler) McBride of Hampton, Virginia. They reside in Yorktown, Virginia.

1. Robert Graham HUNT: b October 20, 1979, Newport News, Virginia; June, 1998, graduated from Poquoson High School.

2. Todd Forrest HUNT: b January 7, 1987, Hampton, Virginia.

FT.1.1.6.12.5.3
MARY SUSAN HUNT and DAVID LEE SHIFFLETT
Of Poquoson, Virginia

Mary Susan Hunt was born on September 5, 1951, Hampton, Virginia. She is a June, 1969, graduate from Poquoson High School, Poquoson, Virginia.

Miss Mary Susan Hunt married on August 18, 1973, David Lee Shifflett (b June 10, 1951), the son of Norris V. and Lucille (Morris) Shifflett of Elkton, Virginia; May, 1971, graduated from Chowan College with an Associates Degree in Education; May, 1973, graduated from Campbell University with a Bachelor's Degree in Elementary Education.

    1. Kimberly Ann SHIFFLETT (twin): b July 17, 1977, Newport News, Virginia; June, 1995, Honor Graduate from Poquoson High School; May 15, 1999, graduated from Virginia Tech with a Bachelor's Degree in Psychology; resided (1999) Roanoke, Virginia; m on September 18, 1999, Mark Dorsey Hoback (b July 9, 1976) of Roanoke, Virginia, the son of Jacob D. and Ellouise (Conner) Hoback; resides (2000) Richmond, Virginia.

    2. Heather Marie SHIFFLETT (twin): b July 17, 1977, Newport News, Virginia; June, 1995, Honor Graduate from Poquoson High School; May 15, 1999, graduated from Virginia Tech with a Bachelor's Degree in Psychology; m on November 18, 2000, Daniel Wilson Hogge (b July 4, 1974) of Gloucester, Virginia, the son of Wilson M. and Jean (Darnell) Hogge; resides (2000) Yorktown, Virginia.

FT.1.1.6.12.6
EDITH FLORENCE FORREST
And THOMAS ELLIOTT STEELE
Of Poquoson, Virginia

    Edith Florence Forrest was born on February 11, 1921, Poquoson, Virginia. Edith Florence Forrest is a 1937 graduate of Poquoson High School.
    Miss Edith Florence Forrest was married at the Monument Lodge, Yorktown, Virginia, by the Rev. A. J. Renforth, on April 28, 1940, to Thomas Elliott Steele (b November 26, 1919; d May 25, 1985), the son of James Cardwell and Elizabeth Inez (Merritt) Steele. Thomas Steele was originally from Rock Hill, South Carolina, but later of Charlotte, North Carolina.

THOMAS AND EDITH (FORREST) STEELE
(Photograph courtesy of Deanna Hunt)

Mrs. Edith (Forrest) Steele resides (1998) in Hampton, Virginia.

1. Betsy Marie STEELE: b September 15, 1941; m 1st Leon Martin; m 2nd Richard Graham; m 3rd John Baron; d November 24, 1993. See next FT.1.1.6.12.6.1.

2. Robert Elliott STEELE (twin): b July 5, 1944; m 1st on July 23, 1965, Nancy Lee Evans (divorced before 1975); m 2nd on June 23, 1975, to Jeanine Tracy. See next FT.1.1.6.12.6.2.

3. Ronald Ervin STEELE (twin): b July 5, 1944; m 1st on October 2, 1965, to Mary Susan Williams (divorced March, 1974); m 2nd on March 26, 1982, to Doris Jean Graham. See next FT.1.1.6.12.6.3.

4. John Thomas STEELE [Sr.]: b June 10, 1952; m 1st in 1971, to Debra Hope Phillips (divorced); m 2nd to Jacque Niehouse (divorced); resided (1998) in Hampton, Virginia; d April 11, 2001.

    1. John Thomas STEELE, Jr: b August 28, 1972.

FT.1.1.6.12.6.1
BETSEY MARIE STEELE

Betsy Marie Steele was born September 15, 1941.
Miss Betsy Marie Steele married 1st Leon Martin.
Mrs. Betsy Marie (Steele) Martin married 2nd Richard Graham.
Mrs. Betsy Marie (Steele, Martin) Graham married 3rd John Baron; d November 24, 1993.

1. Danny Lee MARTIN:

2. David MARTIN:

3. Ginger GRAHAM:

4. John BARON:

FT.1.1.6.12.6.2
ROBERT ELLIOTT STEELE

Robert Elliott Steele (twin) was born on July 5, 1944. He is a June, 1962, graduate of Poquoson High School.
Robert Elliott Steele married 1st on July 23, 1965, Nancy Lee Evans (divorced before 1975).
Robert Elliott Steele married 2nd on June 23, 1975, to Jeanine Tracy. They reside (1998) in Gloucester, Virginia.

1. Tina Margaret STEELE: b November 2, 1966.

2. Kory Lee Elliott STEELE: b February 3, 1977.

FT.1.1.6.12.6.3
RONALD ERVIN STEELE

Ronald Ervin Steele (twin) was born July 5, 1944. He is a June, 1962, graduate of Poquoson High School.
Ronald Ervin Steele married 1st on October 2, 1965, to Mary Susan Williams (divorced March, 1974).
Ronald Ervin Steele married 2nd on March 26, 1982, to Doris Jean Graham. They reside in Hampton, Virginia.

1. Sharon Ellen STEELE: b May 23, 1966; m on October 2, 1993, Allen Outlaw.

    1. Christopher Tyler OUTLAW: b January 1, 1993.

2. Paul Edward STEELE: b March 20, 1969.

FT.1.1.6.12.7
BENJAMIN FRANKLIN FORREST and JEANNE MILLER

Benjamin Franklin Forrest was born on May 8, 1923.
Benjamin F. Forrest married Jeanne Miller of Newport News, Virginia.
Benjamin F. Forrest died on November 29, 1975, and is buried in the Parklawn Memorial Park, Hampton, Virginia.

1. Nancy Jeanne FORREST: b September 11, 1951; m 1st Jonathan Montgomery (divorced); m 2nd Steven Schott.

    1. Ryan MONTGOMERY:

66 POQUOSON FAMILIES

    2. Jessica MONTGOMERY: m February 2, 2000, Jason L. Green.

    3. Kylene SCHOTT:

2. John Braden FORREST: b May 25, 1953.

FT.1.1.6.12.8
DONALD LEE FORREST, SR., and IDA SUE ROLLINS

Donald Lee Forrest, Sr., was born on December 3, 1930.

IDA SUE (ROLLINS) AND DONALD LEE FORREST, SR.
KEVIN AND DONNIE, JR.
(Courtesy of Deanna Hunt)

Donald Lee Forrest, Sr., married at the Trinity Church, Messick, Poquoson, Virginia, on

November 16, 1950, Ida Sue Rollins, the daughter of Thomas Jefferson Rollins, Jr., and Agatha Ward (b February 17, 1935; d July 17, 1972).

Donald Lee Forrest, Sr., died on September 17, 1969, and is buried in the Parklawn Cemetery, Hampton, Virginia.

1. Donald Lee FORREST, Jr: b September 28, 1951; m on October 26, 1972, Ellen Sue Moore (b September 30, 1954). They reside in Poquoson, Virginia.

    1. Donald Lee FORREST, III: b September 29, 1974.

    2. Christina Sue FORREST: b August 17, 1976.

2. Kevin D. FORREST: b April 24, 1952.

3. Cathy Susan FORREST: b July 18, 1961; m 1st on January 12, 1979, Curtis Warren Shaw, Sr. (divorced); m 2nd on May 18, 1994, to Norman E. Neil, Jr. (b November 2, 1960), the son of Judy (Rollins) and Norman E. Neil, Sr.

    1. Curtis Warren SHAW, Jr: b July 30, 1979.

    2. Jennifer Adelle SHAW: b August 9, 1981.

4. Candace Maureen FORREST: b July 13, 1964; m on July 23, 1982, to Michael Evans.

    1. Raven Nicole EVANS: b December 30, 1987.

    2. Sarah Lacy Sue EVANS: b December 26, 1991.

FT.1.1.6.14
LLOYD FORREST and ANNIE FORREST WATKINS
Of Poquoson, York County, Virginia

Lloyd Forrest was born on March 1, 1890, York County, Virginia.

Lloyd Forrest married December 20, 1913, Annie Forrest Watkins, the daughter of Robert Mead and "Toss" Watkins.

In 1920, Lloyd Forrest and family are listed in the Poquoson Township, York County, Virginia census, dwelling 237-239, as follows:

Forrest	Lloyd	head	28	VA
	Annie	wife	25	VA
	Henry	son	4	VA

1. Henry FORREST: b September 7, 1915, York County, Virginia; m Lavinia Joyner; d June 5, 1954.

    1. Brenda FORREST:

    2. Paige FORREST:

2. Annie Jeannette FORREST: m John W. Cross.

3. Robert FORREST: m Nancy; d December 25, 1997.

FT.1.1.7
WILLIAM THOMAS FORREST and NANCY PAGE
Of Poquoson, York County, Virginia

William Thomas ("Tom Toad") Forrest [Sr.] was born on December 7, 1833, in Mathews County, Virginia.

William Thomas Forrest married in 1853, Ann (Nancy) Page (b January 31, 1833; d April 16, 1905, buried Western Cemetery). He was a farmer (1870).

In 1870, Wm. T. Forrest and family are listed in the Poquoson Township, York County, Virginia census, dwelling 132-139, as follows:

Forrest	Wm. T.	head	36	farmer
	Nancy	wife	34	keep house
	Mary J.	daughter	9	
	William Jr.	son	7	
	Robert J.	son	4	
	Dolly E.	daughter	2	
Freeman	Jesse	NR	14	
				oyster catcher

In 1880, Wm. Forrest and family are listed in the Poquoson District, York County, Virginia census, dwelling 142-142, as follows:

Forrest	Wm.	head	47	retail grocer
	Nancy	wife	46	keep house
	Wm. Jr.	son	17	at sea
	Robt.	son	15	at home
	Dolly	daughter	13	at home
	John	son	9	at home

In 1900, William T. Forrest and family are listed in the Poquoson Magisterial District, York County census, dwelling 476-480, as follows:

Forrest	William T.	head	Nov 1833 66 VA	m-39
	Nancy	wife	Jan 1833 67 VA	5-5
477-481	Sarah D.	head	Mar 1868 32 VA	wd.
	Hattie	daughter	Mar 1893 7 VA	

William Forrest died on May 2, 1909, and is buried in the Western Cemetery.

1. Mary Jane FORREST: b 1861, York County, Virginia; m February 29, 1879, Henry Cole Huggett (b November, 1857; d March 19, 1894), the son of Josiah M. and Matilda Huggett; buried Trinity Churchyard.   See next FT.1.1.7.1.

2. William Thomas FORREST (Jr.): b June 5, 1863, York County, Virginia; m 1st June 15, 1881, Sarah Wesley Hopkins (b December 11, 1864; d June 5, 1892) (divorced before 1884); m 2nd on December 28, 1884, Buena Vista Quinn (divorced before 1887); m 3rd January 23, 1889, Sarah L. Winder; m 4th January 23, 1899, his previous 2nd wife, Buena Vista Quinn; removed to Surry County, Virginia; buried at Bacon's Castle Church; d October 10, 1934. See next FT.1.1.7.2.

3. Robert ("Bob Toad") James FORREST: b November 28, 1865, York County, Virginia; m December 28, 1884, Elizabeth Ann Huggett, the daughter of John and Sally Huggett; d April 13, 1936. See next FT.1.1.7.3.

4. Dolly E. FORREST: b April, 1868, York County, Virginia; m in Poquoson on April 14, 1888, John Thomas Messick (b May 13, 1867; d November 17, 1900), the son of Wesley and Indiana Messick. See next FT.1.1.7.4.

5. John Andrew FORREST: b July 9, 1871, York County, Virginia; m May 2, 1891, Alice Geneva Rollins (b July 25, 1872; d April 4, 1964), the daughter of James and Susan (Rollins) Taylor; d August 26, 1941. See next FT.1.1.7.5.

FT.1.1.7.1
MARY JANE FORREST and HENRY COLE HUGGETT
Of Poquoson, York County, Virginia

Mary Jane Forrest was born in 1861, York County, Virginia.

Miss Mary Jane Forrest married on February 29, 1879, Henry Cole Huggett (*Marriage Record No. 1, 1854-1928, York County*, page 19, line 15).

Henry Huggett died on March 19, 1894, age 39 years, and four months, and is buried in the Trinity Church Cemetery, Poquoson.

In 1900, (Mrs.) Mary Huggett was the head of a household in York County, Virginia, census, dwelling 478-486, as follows:

Huggett	Mary,	wd. head	Mar 1862	38	VA
	William M.	son	Dec 1879	20	VA
	Sadie E.	daughter	Oct 1882	17	VA
	Bessie J.	daughter	Nov 1888	11	VA
	Matilda A.	daughter	Jan 1890	10	VA
	Henry J.	son	Feb 1893	7	VA

1. William M. HUGGETT: b December, 1879, York County, Virginia; m in 1902, Elizabeth (b 1885, Virginia).

2. Sadie E. HUGGETT: b October, 1882, York County, Virginia.

3. Bessie J. HUGGETT: b November, 1888, York County, Virginia.

4. Matilda A. HUGGETT: b January, 1890, York County, Virginia.

5. Henry J. HUGGETT: b February, 1893, York County, Virginia.

FT.1.1.7.2a
WILLIAM THOMAS FORREST and SARAH WESLEY HOPKINS
Of Poquoson, York County, Virginia

William Thomas Forrest (Jr.) was born on June 5, 1863, York County, Virginia.

William Thomas Forrest married 1st on June 15, 1881, Sarah Hopkins (b December 11, 1864; d June 5, 1892). They were divorced before 1884. No children.

FT.1.1.7.2b
WILLIAM THOMAS FORREST and BUENA VISTA QUINN
Of Poquoson, York County, Virginia

William Forrest married 2nd on December 28, 1884, Buena Vista Quinn (b December 16, 1868; d February 28, 1938, buried in the Bacon's Castle Church Cemetery, Surry County, Virginia).

They were divorced before 1887. Mrs. Buena Vista (Quinn) Forrest married 2nd Henry Forrest of Poquoson. There where no children by this marriage. See next FT.1.3.12a.

FT.1.1.7.2c
WILLIAM THOMAS FORREST and SARAH LANEY WINDER
Of Poquoson, York County, Virginia

William Forrest married 3rd on January 23, 1889, Sarah Laney Winder. In 1900, Sarah D. Forrest, widow [sic] was the head of a household which consisted of her two daughters.

Children of William Thomas Forrest and his 3rd wife, Sarah Laney Winder:

1. Hattie A. FORREST: b March 18, 1893; m April 16, 1910, Fred T. Carmines, the son of John Daniel and Annie D. Carmines; d January 14, 1947, and is buried in the Western Cemetery, Poquoson.

2. Hester J. FORREST: b April, 1896.

FT.1.1.7.2d
WILLIAM THOMAS FORREST and BUENA VISTA QUINN
Of Poquoson, York County,
And Surry County, Virginia

William Forrest married 4th January 23, 1899, his previous 2nd wife, Buena Vista (Quinn) Forrest. They removed to Surry County, Virginia.

William Forrest died on October 10, 1934, and is buried at Bacon's Castle Church, Surry County, Virginia, in the old church cemetery beside his wife and three of his children.

Children of William Thomas Forrest and his 4th wife, Buena Vista Quinn:

3. Leamond Lankford FORREST: b March 12, 1899; d March 8, 1949, buried Bacon's Castle Church Cemetery.

4. Alma Lee FORREST: b October 30, 1902; d November 10, 1902, buried Bacon's Castle Church Cemetery.

5. Benjamin T. FORREST: b August 16, 1907; d November 19, 1907, buried Bacon's Castle Church Cemetery.

FT.1.1.7.3
ROBERT JAMES FORREST and ELIZA ANN HUGGETT
Of Poquoson, York County, Virginia

Robert ("Bob Toad") James Forrest (II) was born on November 28, 1865, York County, Virginia.

Robert James Forrest married on December 28, 1884, Eliza Ann Huggett (b March 8, 1866; buried Western Cemetery), the daughter of John and Sally Huggett.

In 1900, Robert J. Forrest and family are listed in the Poquoson Township, York County, Virginia census, dwelling 475-483, as follows:

Forrest	Robert J.	head	Jun 1867	33	VA
	Eliza E.	wife	Jan 1866	34	VA
		8 children 6 living			
	William C., son		Feb 1885	15	VA
	Winnie C.	daughter	Sep 1889	10	VA
	Pearlie J., daughter		Oct 1891	9	VA
	Floyd	son	Dec 1894	5	VA
	Maggie	daughter	Jun 1897	3	VA
	John H.	son	Nov 1899	6/12	VA

In 1910, Robert J. Forrest and family are listed in the Poquoson Township, York County, Virginia census, dwelling 15-16, as follows:

Forrest	Robert J.	head	47	VA m-1	
	Lira E.	wife	44	VA m-1 9-8	
	Winnie	daughter	20	VA s	
	Lloyd	son	15	VA	
	Maggie	daughter	13	VA	
	John A.	son	11	VA	(A. = sic)
	Nannie	daughter	9	VA	
	Alvon N.	son	4	VA	

In 1920, Robert J. Forrest and family are listed in the Poquoson Township, York County, Virginia census, dwelling 39-41, as follows:

Forrest	Robert J.	head	54	VA
	Eliza A.	wife	54	VA
	Winnie C.	daughter	29	VA
	John H.	son	18	VA
	Nanie L.	daughter	17	VA
	Alfred N.	son	13	VA

Robert Forrest died on April 13, 1936, and is buried in the Western Cemetery, Poquoson.

1. William Crosby FORREST: b February 9, 1885, York County, Virginia; m May 29, 1909, Martha Martin (b 1893), the daughter of George and Annie F. Martin; d March 25, 1963, buried Parklawn Memorial Park, Hampton.

2. Winnie Colber FORREST: b September 9, 1890, York County, Virginia; m December 21,

1920, Mary Chrystine Carmines (b September 15, 1903), the daughter of John C. and Effie H. Carmines; d November 18, 1958, buried Western Cemetery.

3. Pearle J. FORREST: b October, 1891, York County, Virginia; m April 12, 1909, Henry Essie Watkins (b May 12, 1889; d December 17, 1941, buried Western Cemetery, Poquoson), the son of Eddie Lee and Lizzie Bunting Watkins.

4. Floyd M. FORREST: b December, 1894, York County, Virginia; m 1st Naomi Holloway (b November 13, 1900; d February 3, 1930, buried Western Cemetery, Poquoson); m 2nd Margie Rowe; buried Peninsula Memorial Park, Hampton.

    1. Flossie FORREST: m Osborn Evans.

5. Sally Margaret ("Maggie") FORREST: b December 22, 1897, York County, Virginia; m September 15, 1916, Harry Hopkins, the son of George E. and Sarah E. Hopkins; d May 15, 1938, buried Western Cemetery, Poquoson.

6. John Henry ("Buck") FORREST: October 6, 1900 (November, 1899), York County, Virginia; m July 20, 1922, Lavina Forrest, the daughter of John Samuel and Martha (Chesser) Forrest; d July 3, 1981, buried Parklawn Memorial Park, Hampton, Virginia. See next FT.1.1.7.3.6.

7. Nannie FORREST: b February 28, 1901, York County, Virginia; m Hunter Riggins; d December 28, 1978, buried Peninsula Memorial Park, Hampton.

8. Alvon (Alfred) N. FORREST: b 1906, York County, Virginia; m Ruby Diggs of Mathews County, Virginia; resided Mathews County, Virginia; d October 22, 1993, in Mathews County, Virginia, and is buried in the Gwynn's Island Cemetery, Mathews County, Virginia. See next FT.1.1.7.3.8.

FT.1.1.7.3.6
JOHN HENRY FORREST and LAVINA FORREST

John Henry ("Buck") Forrest was born on October 6, 1900 (November, 1899), York County, Virginia.

John Henry Forrest married July 20, 1922, Lavina Forrest, the daughter of John Samuel and Martha (Chesser) Forrest.

John Henry Forrest died July 3, 1981, and is buried in the Parklawn Memorial Park, Hampton, Virginia.

1. Elizabeth Ann FORREST: b September 17, 1926; m Mack C. Burcher; d February 13, 1992. See next FT.1.1.7.3.6.1.

2. Robert Samuel FORREST: b March 16, 1930; m 1st in December, 1950, Peggy Grace Lee (b July 30, 1929; d July 1, 1964); m 2nd Lou Stubbs. See next FT.1.1.7.3.6.2.

FT.1.1.7.3.6.1
ELIZABETH ANN FORREST and MACK C. BURCHER

Elizabeth Ann Forrest was born September 17, 1926.

Miss Elizabeth Ann Forrest married Mack C. Burcher.

Mrs. Elizabeth Ann (Forrest) Burcher died February 13, 1992.

1. Amy Carol BURCHER: m Christopher Robinson.

    1. Courtney Anne ROBINSON:

    2. Ashley Carol ROBINSON:

2. John Barry C. BURCHER: m Dee.

    1. Tyler BURCHER:

FT.1.1.7.3.6.2
ROBERT SAMUEL FORREST

Robert Samuel Forrest was born March 16, 1930.

Robert Samuel Forrest married 1st in December, 1950, Peggy Grace Lee (b July 30, 1929; d July 1, 1964).

Robert Samuel Forrest married 2nd Lou Stubbs.

1. Robert Craig FORREST: b September 9, 1952.

    1. Brandon FORREST:

    2. Travis FORREST:

    3. Ashley FORREST:

    4. Zachery FORREST:

2. Carmen Lee FORREST: b July 30, 1957; m David Melton.

    1. Clinton MELTON:

    2. Derek MELTON:

3. Elizabeth Ann FORREST: b June 19, 1960; m David Brian Roberts.

    1. Heidi ROBERTS:

    2. Brady ROBERTS:

FT.1.1.7.3.8
ALVON N. FORREST and RUBY DIGGS
Of Mathews County, Virginia

Alvon (Alfred) N. Forrest was born in 1906, York County, Virginia. He is listed as Alfred N. Forrest in the 1920 census.

Alvon N. Forrest married Ruby Diggs of Mathews County, Virginia. They resided in Mathews County, Virginia.

Alvon N. Forrest died on October 22, 1993, in Mathews County, Virginia, and is buried in the Gwynn's Island Cemetery, Mathews County, Virginia.

1. Betty Ann FORREST: b abt 1936, Mathews County, Virginia; resides Remlik, Middlesex County, Virginia.

2. Sally FORREST: b abt 1938, Mathews County, Virginia; m "Sweet Pea" Hugate; resides in New Point, Mathews County, Virginia.

3. Robert H. FORREST: b abt 1940, Mathews County, Virginia; resides Crew, Nottaway County, Virginia.

4. Naomi FORREST: b abt 1942, Mathews County, Virginia; m David "Day Boy" Hudgins; resides Mathews County, Virginia.

5. Diane FORREST: b abt 1944, Mathews County, Virginia; resides Deltaville, Middlesex County, Virginia.

FT.1.1.7.4
DOLLY E. FORREST and JOHN THOMAS MESSICK
Of Messick, York County, Virginia

Dolly E. Forrest was born on April, 1868, York County, Virginia.

Miss Dolly E. Forrest married in Poquoson on April 14, 1888, John Thomas Messick (b May 13, 1867; d November 17, 1900), the son of

Wesley and Indiana Messick (*Marriage Record No. 1, 1854-1928, York County*, page 34, line 14).

In 1900, John T. Messick and family are listed in the Poquoson Magisterial District, York County, Virginia census, dwelling 479-487, as follows:

Messick	John T.	head	May 1868	32	m-13
	Dolly E.	wife	Apr 1868	32	3-3
	Minnie B.	daughter	May 1889	11	s
	John T.	son	Jan 1891	9	s
	Lettie J.	daughter	Nov 1898	1	s

John Thomas Messick died on November 17, 1900, and is buried in the Western Cemetery.

In 1910, Dolly E. Messick and family are listed in the York County, Virginia census, dwelling 22-23, as follows:

Messick	Dolly E.	head	42	wd.	3-3
	Lettie J.	daughter	11	s	
	John T.	son	18	m-1	
	Elizabeth A.	daughter	20	m-1	

In her old age, Dolly ("Mammy") Messick, widow, resided in a little house on the east side of Messick Road, beside the house of Lelia Ann Martin, widow.

As a winter storm was coming on, Dolly Messick went down to the marsh to look for her cows. She was caught in the storm and drowned in a shallow sinkhole in the Big Marsh in 1910.

1. Minnie B. (P.) MESSICK: b January 11, 1888; m in Poquoson on November 26, 1904, William E. Powell, age 19, the son of John R. and Ellen Powell (*Marriage Record No. 1, 1854-192, York County*, page 63, line 39); d February 7, 1957, buried Western Cemetery, Poquoson.

   1. Pauline M. POWELL: b 1906, York County, Virginia.

2. Minnie E. POWELL: b December 25, 1908, York County, Virginia; d January 26, 1909, buried Western Cemetery, Poquoson.

2. John Thomas MESSICK (Jr.): b January, 1891; oysterman (1910); m 1st at Jeffs in York County on March 12, 1910, Elizabeth Holloway (b 1890), age 19, the daughter of Robert and Lizzie A. Holloway (*Marriage Record No. 1, 1854-1928, York County*, page 72, line 13); m 2nd in York County on December 24, 1917, Deniza Insley, age 18, the daughter of Gilbert and Ella Insley (*Marriage Record No. 1, 1854-1928, York County*, page 85, line 71).

1. Mary E. MESSICK: b 1910; d 1918, buried Western Cemetery, Poquoson.

3. Lettie Jane MESSICK: b December 22, 1899; m William Hope Forrest (b February 5, 1892; d December 3, 1966, buried Western Cemetery); d December 1, 1958, buried Western Cemetery. See next under her husband's listing FT.2.8.1.

FT.1.1.7.5
JOHN ANDREW FORREST and ALICE GENEVA ROLLINS
Of Poquoson, York County, Virginia

John Andrew Forrest was born on July 9, 1871, York County, Virginia.

John Andrew Forrest married on May 2, 1891, Alice Geneva Rollins (b July 25, 1872; d April 24, 1964, buried Western Cemetery), the daughter of James Taylor and Susan Rollins.

In 1900, John A. Forrest and family are listed in the Poquoson, York County, Virginia census, dwelling 414-422, as follows:

Forrest	John A.	head	Jul 1871	28	m-9
	Alice G.	wife	Jul 1872	28	3-3
	Lillie B.	daughter	Feb 1892	8	
	Mollie E.	daughter	Oct 1893	6	
	Lloyd	son	Feb 1899	1	

In 1910, John A. Forrest and family are listed in the Poquoson, York County, Virginia census, dwelling 141-146, as follows:

Forrest	John A.	head	38 VA	m-18
	Alice G.	wife	37 VA	7-7
	Lillie B.	daughter	18 VA	
	Mollie J.	daughter	15 VA	
	Lloyd	son	11 VA	
	Beamon T.	son	9 VA	
	Gladwyn H.	son	6 VA	
	Nellie G.	daughter	4 VA	
	Warren S.	son	2 VA	

John A. Forrest died on August 26, 1941, and is buried in the Western Cemetery, Poquoson, Virginia.

(*Ancestry and Descendants of Peter B. Smith... 1738-1984*, Robert Ellerson White, n. d., page 42).

1. Lillie Beatrice FORREST: b May 25, 1890 (February 11, 1892), York County, Virginia; m March 23, 1911, Lemuel V. Forrest (b May 25, 1890; d November 11, 1978. See next FT.1.1.8.1.5.

2. Mollie Jane FORREST: b October 14, 1891 (1894), York County, Virginia; m 1st William Taylor Freeman (b August 2, 1891; d January 2, 1946), the son of W. and Virginia Freeman; m 2nd William James Insley, the son of Littleton and Virginia Insley; d November 11, 1980, buried Western Cemetery, Poquoson. See next FT.1.1.7.5.2.

3. Lloyd FORREST: b February 23, 1899, York County, Virginia; m November 3, 1917, Mary Emma Carmines (b June 15, 1899; d January 20, 1980), the daughter of John Daniel and Annie Dora (Watkins) Carmines; d October 22, 1983. See next FT.1.1.7.5.3.

4. Beamon Taylor FORREST: b September 16, 1901, York County, Virginia; m December 22,

1928, Dorothy Alexander Garrett (b February 15, 1905) of Newport News, Virginia; d January 4, 1901, and is buried in the Western Cemetery, Poquoson. See next FT.1.1.7.5.4.

5. Gladwyn Hartley FORREST: b July 7, 1904, York County, Virginia; m 1st January 7, 1929, Juanita Barnett; m 2nd March 17, 1945, Mrs. Margaret Adelaide Brady Mingee (b December 5, 1912); d December 23, 1973. See next FT.1.1.7.5.5.

6. Nellie Geneva FORREST: b April 30, 1906, York County, Virginia; m April 30, 1927, Henry Milton Forrest, the son of Henry Thomas and Carrie (Freeman) Forrest.

7. Warren Smith FORREST: b March 1, 1908, York County, Virginia; m Hettie Leone Forrest (b September 7, 1913; d June 28, 1991, and is buried in the Western Cemetery, Poquoson), the daughter of Cornelius and Sadie Forrest; d January 17, 1992, and is buried in the Western Cemetery, Poquoson. See next FT.1.1.7.5.7.

8. John Elwood FORREST: b July 21, 1911, York County, Virginia; m on December 30, 1930, Nannie Forrest, the daughter of William ("Bill Dan") and Martha ("Matt") Forrest. See next FT.1.1.7.5.8.

FT.1.1.7.5.2a
MOLLIE JANE FORREST and WILLIAM TAYLOR FREEMAN

Mollie Jane Forrest was born October 14, 1891 (1894), York County, Virginia.
Miss Mollie Jane Forrest married 1st William Taylor Freeman (b August 2, 1891; d January 2, 1946), the son of W. and Virginia Freeman.

Children of Mollie Jane Forrest and her 1st husband, William Taylor Freeman:

1. Wade Forrest FREEMAN: b April 26, 1913, York County, Virginia; m 1st Gladys Whitfield; m 2nd Frances Jenkins (b November 7, 1920); d December 14, 1980. See next FT.1.1.7.5.2.1.

2. Joseph Elvin ("Ned") FREEMAN: b March 18, 1915, York County, Virginia; m 1st July 1, 1939, Edith Walters (d August 23, 1974); m 2nd Florence Holloway. See next FT.1.1.7.5.2.2.

FT.1.1.7.5.2b
MRS. MOLLIE JANE (FORREST) FREEMAN
And WILLIAM JAMES INSLEY

Mrs. Mollie Jane (Forrest) Freeman married 2nd William James Insley, the son of Littleton and Virginia Insley.

Mrs. Mollie Jane (Forrest, Taylor) Insley died on November 11, 1980, and is buried in the Western Cemetery, Poquoson, Virginia.

FT.1.1.7.5.2.1a
WADE FORREST FREEMAN and GLADYS WHITFIELD

Wade Forrest Freeman was born on April 26, 1913, York County, Virginia.

Wade Forrest Freeman married 1st Gladys Whitfield

Children of Wade Forrest and his 1st wife, Gladys Whitfield:

1. Mollie Mae FREEMAN: b March 3, 1942; m November 16, 1971, Thomas Michael Hampker (b March 19, 1942).

    1. Mollie Katherine HAMPKER: b July 5, 1973.

    2. Christopher Michael HAMPKER: b July 23, 1977.

FT.1.1.7.5.2.1b
WADE FORREST FREEMAN and FRANCES JENKINS

Wade Forrest Freeman married 2nd Frances Jenkins (b November 7, 1920).

Wade Forrest Freeman died on December 14, 1980.

Child of Wade Forrest Freeman, Sr., and his 2nd wife, Frances Jenkins:

    2. Wade Forrest FREEMAN, Jr: b August 15, 1954.

FT.1.1.7.5.2.2a
JOSEPH ELVIN FREEMAN and EDITH WALTERS

Joseph Elvin ("Ned") Freeman was born on March 18, 1915, York County, Virginia.

Joseph Elvin Freeman married 1st July 1, 1939, Edith Walters (d August 23, 1974).

    1. Joseph Elvin FREEMAN, Jr: b May 20, 1942; m June 2, 1961, Frances S. Holloway.

        1. Joseph Elvin FREEMAN, III: b February 16, 1965.

        2. Yvette Holloway FREEMAN: b March 12, 1970.

FT.1.1.7.5.2.2b
JOSEPH ELVIN FREEMAN and FLORENCE HOLLOWAY

Joseph Elvin Freeman married 2nd Florence Holloway.

FT.1.1.7.5.3
LLOYD FORREST and MARY EMMA CARMINES

Lloyd Forrest was born on February 23, 1899, York County, Virginia.

Lloyd Forrest married November 3, 1917, Mary Emma Carmines (b June 15, 1899; d January 20, 1980, and is buried in the Western Cemetery, Poquoson), the daughter of John Daniel and Annie Dora (Watkins) Carmines.

Lloyd Forrest died on October 22, 1983, and is buried in the Western Cemetery, Poquoson.

1. Wallace Jerome FORREST: b May 19, 1918; m Elsie Lorraine Moore; d February 13, 1981.

2. Annie Geneva FORREST: b July 13, 1920; m August 25, 1937, Carroll Davis Mann, Sr.

3. Rosanna ("Anne") Sue FORREST: b December 1, 1929; m March 24, 1951, John Bunyan Hollingsworth, Jr.

4. Lloyd FORREST, Jr:

FT.1.1.7.5.4
BEAMON TAYLOR FORREST
And DOROTHY ALEXANDER GARRETT

Beamon Taylor Forrest was born on September 16, 1901, York County, Virginia.

Beamon Taylor Forrest married on December 22, 1928, Dorothy Alexander Garrett (b February 15, 1905) of Newport News, Virginia.

Beamon Taylor Forrest died on January 4, 1991, and is buried in the Western Cemetery, Poquoson.

1. Beamon Taylor FORREST (Jr.): b May 5, 1934; m August 29, 1959, Joyce Ann Miller (b January 4, 1937).

    1. Tammy Ann FORREST: b May 15, 1963; m May 18, 1985, Joe Lee Swofford, Sr. (b September 22, 1960).

    2. Beamon Taylor FORREST (III): b November 29, 1965; m January 7, 1989, Sarah Melissa Frost (b November 5, 1968).

FT.1.1.7.5.5a
GLADWYN HARTLEY FORREST and JUANITA BARNETT

Gladwyn Hartley Forrest was born on July 7, 1904, York County, Virginia.
Gladwyn Hartley Forrest married 1st on January 7, 1929, Juanita Barnett.

Child of Gladwyn Hartley Forrest and his 1st wife, Juanita Barnett:

1. Gladwyn Hartley FORREST, Jr: b July 25, 1931.

FT.1.1.7.5.5b
GLADWYN HARTLEY FORREST
And Mrs. MARGARET A. B. MINGEE

Gladwyn Hartley Forrest married 2nd March 17, 1945, Mrs. Margaret Adelaide Brady Mingee (b December 5, 1912).
Gladwyn Hartley Forrest died on December 23, 1973.

Children of Gladwyn Hartley Forrest and Margaret A. B. Mingee:

2. John Andrew FORREST: b March 18, 1946; m April 11, 1969, Kathyrn Louise Plotz (b January 27, 1946).

1. Thomas Warren FORREST: b November 27, 1970.

3. Robert Claytor FORREST: b November 9, 1948; m May 2, 1970, Joyce Hudgins.

4. Marie Annette FORREST: b September 11, 1954; m April 19, 1980, George Kautz.

    1. Kelly Nicole KAUTZ: b November 3, 1981.

FT.1.1.7.5.7
WARREN SMITH FORREST and HETTIE LEONE FORREST

Warren Smith Forrest was born on March 1, 1908, York County, Virginia.

Warren Smith Forrest married Hettie Leone Forrest (b September 7, 1913; d June 28, 1991, and is buried in the Western Cemetery, Poquoson), the daughter of Cornelius and Sadie Forrest.

Warren S. Forrest died on January 17, 1992, and is buried in the Western Cemetery, Poquoson.

1. Viola Mae FORREST: b February 11, 1936, Poquoson, Virginia; m Edward Earl Tyndall, Jr. (b July 16, 1932); d February 22, 2001, age 65, Poquoson, Virginia.

    1. Carole TYNDALL: m James W. Jones, Jr., of (2001) Poquoson.

    2. Patricia TYNDALL: m Randy R. Hill of (2001) Hampton, Virginia.

2. Warren Smith FORREST, Jr: b March 12, 1937; m 1st June, 1958, Ann Carol Anderson (divorced before 1982); m 2nd August 20, 1982, Sylvia J. Chestnut.

3. Judith Lynne FORREST: b September 28, 1945; m 1st April 6, 1974, Ernest John Leduc; m 2nd July 14, 1979, Clarence Thomas Arehart.

FT.1.1.7.5.8
JOHN ELWOOD FORREST and NANNIE FORREST

John Elwood Forrest was born on July 21, 1911, York County, Virginia.

John Elwood Forrest married on December 30, 1930, Nannie Forrest, the daughter of William ("Bill Dan") and Martha ("Matt") Forrest.

1. Nancy Lee FORREST: b March 1, 1937; m November 13, 1971, Nelson Arthur Betts.

2. Linda Layne FORREST: b August 29, 1939; m June 10, 1962, Guy Wilson Moorman, Sr.

FT.1.1.8a
ROBERT JAMES FORREST and MARY FRANCES WESTON
Of Messick, Poquoson District, York County

Robert James (Captain Bob) Forrest was born on December 25, 1836, in Mathews County, Virginia.

Robert James Forrest married 1st on March 13, 1858, Mary Frances Weston (b September 30, 1833, Mathews County, Virginia; d May 12, 1883, Messick, York County, Virginia, buried Western Cemetery), the daughter of John and Margaret Banks Weston, originally of Mathews County, Virginia.

In 1860, Robt. J. Forrest and family are listed in the Post Office Halfway House, York County, Virginia census, dwelling 134-134, as follows:

```
Forrest   Robt. J.   head    23   sailor inland
          Mary       wife    26
          Lemuel     son     1
```

When the Civil War came to the Peninsula, Robert James Forrest was one of the earliest of the Poquoson boys to enlist on June 3, 1861, in Company I, 32d Virginia Infantry, along with many of the other Poquoson boys. The 32nd Virginia was at the evacuation of Yorktown, and the Seven Days battles around Richmond. In mid-August the 32nd Virginia was ordered to join the Army of Northern Virginia. They marched through Hanover Junction, Rapidan Station, Culpeper Courthouse, Fauquier White Sulphur Springs, Gainesville, Bull Run. Now on September 3, 1862, they were at Leesburg, were John French White wrote, "... How the Ladies received us by waving their handkerchiefs as we marched through ..." (Jensen, page 83).

At this time, Robert Forrest's 32nd Regiment was a member of Semmes Brigade, McLaw's Division under General James Longstreet. The 32nd marched north from Leesburg, and on September 6, the regiment crossed the Potomac River into Maryland. At this point, General Longstreet's Corps was at Boonsboro, while McLaw's Division was at Middletown. McLaw was ordered south to take possession of Maryland Heights overlooking Harper's Ferry. Semmes Brigade was left at Brownsville to guard the South Mountain passes. On September 14, as the Federal troops attempted to force Crampton's Gap, Montague placed Company I, 32nd Virginia under Captain Stores and position them at the eastern base of the gap. Most of the fighting for Campton's Gap was borne by other units; but the 32nd Virginia was on alert, unsure who was winning the fight for the gap (the Federals won). Then when the Federals at Harper's Ferry surrendered to General Stonewall Jackson's soldiers on September 16, orders came for the 32nd to march through Harpers Ferry, stopping in bivouac at Halltown. It was 1 AM of that morning of September 17. The 32nd was aroused from their too short rest and ordered to make haste for Sharpsburg, Maryland.

General Jackson had left Harper's Ferry and rushed to Sharpsburg, Maryland, arriving about midday. Jackson deployed his troops in the woods on the Confederate west flank and immediately came under repeated Federal assault. After fierce fighting in the West Woods, and the cornfield, the Yankees were prevailing and driving General Jackson's Confederates from their place on the battle field. The Confederate left wing of Lee's Army was near collapsing. McLaw's men of the 32nd Virginia had now arrived at Boteler's Ford at Shepherdstown, Virginia, opposite Sharpsburg, Maryland. Wounded Confederates were streaming past the now resting position of 32nd and continuing into the relative safety of northern Virginia and the security of the rear echelons. The 32nd Virginia was ordered to ford the Potomac River, and march by the double quick. They passed Dunker Church, kept moving beyond Barksdale's Mississippi brigade, keeping the West Woods to their right. Just at they were approaching their assigned position, Barkdales'

Mississippi brigade were ordered to charge into and through the woods. John Parham, 32nd Virginia, remembered:

> "... Their fire was so steady and so severe that it looked like a whirlwind was passing through the leaves on the ground and woods. I remarked to Captain Coke, on my left, 'to look; was not that the grandest sight he ever saw.' He said, 'Yes, John, it is grand; but look in our front, my boy, and see what we have to face'" (Jensen, page 90).

General Semmes commanded, 'By company into line!' followed by 'Forward into line!' and so the 32nd Virginia came to the support of Jackson's battered line. As they moved forward into the open, Captain Wynne was hit by a minie ball just about the right eye, and fell down dead. Colonel Montague's horse was hit, pitching the Colonel to the ground. Sergeant Darius Moreland of Company I was the first enlisted man to die; several 32nd men were wounded. The regiment advanced until it was on the Alfred Pottenberger farm. With the Federals barely 75 yards away, Colonel Montague finally gave the order to commence firing. Robert Forrest was the flag bearer, "minnie" balls were churning the ground in front of him up. The flag was shot through seventeen times, the flagstaff cut into twice during the attack, but Robert always recovered it. His clothing was bloodied and shot through, but amazingly he survived the day without a scratch. Semmes gave the order to charge and the 32nd swept past the Alfred Pottenburger farm, through a skirt of woods that extended to the west of the West Woods, and on to the open fields of the Nicodemus Farm. They came within 150 yards of a stone fence behind which the Federals were making a determined stand. They were being fired on by both small arms and artillery from the front and their right was exposed to Federal batteries in the Miller cornfield area across the road. General J. E. B. Stuart rode up and asked Montague if his boys could take the Federal batteries to their right; however, the 32nd Virginia was nearly out of ammunition and severely the fighting had depleted their strength. General Stuart then rode off to Barksdale's Missisippi brigade with the same request. McLaw's Division suffered 40% casualties that day, as did the York Rangers. Only the Texas Division suffered more casualties that day (80% casualties).

ROBERT JAMES FORREST
(From original tintype in possession of Mrs. Jessie Forrest)

In 1870, Robt. J. Forrest and family are listed in the Poquoson Township, York County, Virginia census, dwelling 160-169, as follows:

Forrest	Robt. J.	head	34	VA	oysterman
	Mary F.	wife	37	VA	keep house
	Lemuel	son	11	VA	
	Emma J.	daug	8	VA	
	Robert L.	son	5	VA	
	Mary A.	daug	1	VA	
Amory	Mary	NR	16	VA	

In 1880, Robt. J. Forrest and family are listed in the Poquoson District, York County, Virginia, census, dwelling 90-90, as follows:

Forrest	Robt. J.	Head	43	farmer
	Mary F.	wife	46	keep house
	Emma	daug	18	at home
	Robt. S.	son	13	at home
	Mary A.	daug	12	at home
	Maggie	daug	8	at home
	Annie M.	daug	6	at home

Children by 1st wife, Mary Frances Weston:

1. Lemuel Mansfield Duncan FORREST: b December 9, 1858, Messick, York County, Virginia; m in Messick, Poquoson, York County, Virginia, on January 22, 1880, Missouri Hall Watkins (b October 26, 1858; d December 21, 1935, buried Western Cemetery), daughter of Henry and Sarah Anne (Linton) Watkins (*Marriage Record No. 1, 1854-1928, York County*, page 11, line 202); d May 24, 1930, buried Western Cemetery, Poquoson. See next FT.1.1.8.1.

2. Emma A. FORREST: b April 23, 1861, Messick, York County, Virginia; m May 7, 1881, John W. Rollins, son of Samuel and Matilda F. Rollins (Marriage Record No.1, 1854-1928, York County, page 13, line 290); d December 1, 1884, in childbirth in Messick; d. s. p.

3. Sarah FORREST: b July 23, 1864; d August 12, 1864; d. s. p.

4. Robert Lee FORREST: b August 27, 1865, Messick, York County, Virginia; m in York County, on January 22, 1885, Melissa Virginia Holloway (b April 16, 1865, Messick; June 26, 1946, Hampton, Virginia, buried Western Cemetery), daughter of Elias Rosser and Susan Amory Holloway *(Marriage No. 1, 1854-1928, York County*, page 17, line 485); d December 8, 1940. See next FT.1.1.8.4.

5. Mary Adlena FORREST: b May 4, 1868, Messick, York County, Virginia; m July 28, 1887, Thomas James Quinn, son of Joseph and Mary E. Quinn *(Marriage Record No. 1, 1854-1928, York County*, page 20, line 614); d October 21, 1935, buried Western Cemetery.

6. Margaret ("Maggie") Sylvester ("Toss") FORREST: b September 30, 1871, Messick, York County, Virginia; her family called her "Maggie," but in the Messick community she was always known as "Toss"; m June 18, 1894, Henry White, son of Wise Henry and Elizabeth White *(Marriage Record No. 1, 1854-1928, York County*, page 29, line 1042); d December 17, 1926, buried Western Cemetery.

7. Annie Marie FORREST: b April 11, 1874, Messick, York County, Virginia; m December 28, 1903, John A. White (b May 3, 1865; d February 11, 1923, buried Western Cemetery), son of Wise Henry and Elizabeth White *(Marriage Record No. 1, 1854-1928, York County*, page 42, line 355); d February 1, 1937, buried Western Cemetery.

FT.1.1.8b
ROBERT JAMES FORREST and ANN DEBORAH HOLLOWAY
Of Messick, Poquoson District, York County

"Captain Bob" Forrest married 2nd in Messick on January 31, 1886, Ann Deborah Holloway, daughter of Robert Holloway and

Harriett (Ryder) Carmines, and the widow of William Carmines, Jr.

Robert Forrest was a member of the Poquoson Board of Supervisors from 1900 until 1904.

In 1900, Robert J. Forrest and family are listed in the Poquoson Magisterial District, York County, Virginia census, dwelling 323-331, as follows:

```
Forrest  Robert J.  head  Dec 1836  63  widower
         Mary F.    daug  Apr 1874  26
         John T.    son   Jan 1890  10
```

Robert Forrest died on May 14, 1907, and is buried in the Western Cemetery, Poquoson.

Children by 2nd wife, Ann Deborah Holloway:

8. Emma James FORREST: b May 19, 1887, Messick, York County, Virginia; d May 19, 1892, Messick; d. s. p.

9. John Thomas ("Epps") FORREST: b January 11, 1889, Messick, York County, Virginia; m January 10, 1910, Sarah Elizabeth Watkins (b October 26, 1891, Messick, York County, Virginia; d October 27, 1969, Williamsburg, buried Western Cemetery, Messick, Virginia), the daughter of Robert Mead and Sarah Sylvester (Forrest) Watkins (*Marriage Record No.1, 1854-1928, York County*, page 51, line 708); d April 29, 1949, in Richmond, Virginia, buried in the Western Cemetery, Poquoson. See next F.1.1.8.9.

FT.1.1.8.1
LEMUEL MANSFIELD DUNCAN FORREST
And MISSOURI HALL WATKINS
Of Messick, Poquoson, York County

Lemuel Mansfield Duncan Forrest was born on December 9, 1858, in Messick, York County, Virginia.

Lemuel M. D. Forrest married in Messick, Virginia, on January 22, 1880, Missouri ("Lou") Hall Watkins (b October 26, 1858; d December 21, 1959, buried Western Cemetery), daughter of Henry and Sarah Anne (Linton) Watkins (*Marriage Record No. 1, 1854-1928, York County*, page 11, line 203).

In 1900, Lemuel M. Forrest and family are listed in the Poquoson Magisterial District, York County census, dwelling 326-334, as follows:

Forrest	Lemuel M.	head	Dec 1859	40
	Missouri H.	wife	Oct 1859	40
	Arenthia S.	daughter	May 1881	19
	Robert H.	son	Mar 1883	17
	Minnie E.	daughter	Nov 1885	14
	Elijah V.	son	Mar 1888	12
	Lemuel V.	son	May 1890	10
	John W.	son	Jul 1892	7
	Osborne	son	Dec 1893	6
	James B.	son	Apr 1897	3

In 1910, Lemuel M. Forrest and family are listed in the Poquoson, York County, Virginia census, dwelling 211-216, as follows:

Forrest	Lemuel M.	head	52	VA	m-30	
	Missouri H.	wife	52	VA	m-30	7-7
	Lemuel V.	son	19	VA		
	John W.	son	17	VA		
	Ausburn	son	15	VA		
	James B.	son	13	VA		
	Howard G.	son	9	VA		

Lemuel Forrest died on May 24, 1930, and is buried in the Western Cemetery, Poquoson. Mrs. Missouri Forrest outlived her husband by nearly 30 years; she was everybody's "Aunt Lou".

1. Arenthia Susan ("Sadie"/"Sudie") FORREST: b May, 1881, York County, Virginia; m April 16, 1901, William Albert Evans (b February 22, 1878; d March 22, 1945, buried

Western Cemetery), the son of William and Sarah Evans. See next FT.1.1.8.1.1.

2. Robert Henry FORREST: b March 13, 1884, York County, Virginia; m November 26, 1904, Bernice L. Evans (b August 1, 1886), the daughter of George D. and Jane Evans; d on June 18, 1950, and is buried in the Western Cemetery. See next FT.1.1.8.1.2.

3. Minnie E. FORREST: b November, 1885, York County, Virginia; m February 20, 1904, William Herbert Amory (b February 10, 1885, Virginia; d July 20, 1952, buried Western Cemetery), the son of John Franklin and Maria Amory. See next FT.1.1.8.1.3.

4. Elijah V. FORREST: b March 22, 1888, York County, Virginia; m on December 23, 1907, Mary Margaret Gibbs (b May 22, 1889; d May 3, 1966, buried Western Cemetery), the daughter of J. and A. Gibbs; d July 10, 1955, buried Western Cemetery. See next FT.1.1.8.1.4.

5. Lemuel Vaden FORREST: b May 25, 1890, York County, Virginia; m December 23, 1911, Lillie Beatrice Forrest (b May 25, 1890), the daughter of John Andrew and Alice (Rollins) Forrest; d November 5, 1943. See next FT.1.1.8.1.5.

6. John W. FORREST: b July 6, 1893, York County, Virginia; m November 30, 1912, Mary Viola Pauls, the daughter of John and Rosanna (Messick) Pauls. See next FT.1.1.8.1.6.

7. Osborne ("Ausburn") FORREST: b December 15, 1894, Messick, York County, Virginia; m September 8, 1916, Margaret ("Maggie") Indiana Pauls (b September 16, 1898; January 19, 1985), the daughter of John and Rosanna (Messick) Pauls; d on April 1, 1990, and is buried in the Parklawn Memorial Cemetery, Hampton, Virginia. See next FT.1.1.8.1.7.

8. James Blanchard FORREST: b April 10, 1898, York County, Virginia; m July 7, 1923, Mary Lillian Moore (b June 23, 1906; March 25, 1996), the daughter of John H. and Julia Beal Moore; d October 24, 1952. See next FT.1.1.8.1.8.

9. Howard Garland FORREST: b March 24, 1901, York County, Virginia; m 1st September 21, 1921, Eudora ("Nonie") Amory (b May 23, 1904; d August 10, 1947, buried in the Western Cemetery), the daughter of George W. and Bernie Amory; m 2nd December 22, 1959, Rita Moore Hunt; d May 23, 1971, buried Western Cemetery. See next FT.1.1.8.1.9.

FT.1.1.8.1.1
ARENTHIA SUSAN FORREST and WILLIAM ALBERT EVANS
Of Messick, York County, Virginia

Arenthia Susan ("Sadie"/"Sudie") Forrest was born in May, 1881, York County, Virginia.

Miss Arenthia Susan Forrest married on April 16, 1901, William Albert Evans (b February 22, 1878, York County; d March 22, 1945, buried Western Cemetery), the son of William and Sarah Evans (*Marriage Record No.1, York County*, page 56, line 15). They resided in Messick on the on the "Main Poquoson Road" (1910).

He was a merchant (1901) and a waterman.

In 1910, William A. Evans and family are listed in the York County, Virginia census, dwelling 208-213, as follows:

Evans	William A.	head	32	m-1 9
	Rentha S.	wife	29	m-1 5-3
	Eva J.	daughter	8	s
	Lemuel V.	son	6	s
	Erma H.	daughter	10/12	s

(*Colonial Cousins*, page 52; *Freeman Forebears*, page 51).

1. Eva Irene EVANS: b March 12, 1902, York County; m 1st Josiah (Joseph) Huggett (died in the November 7, 1924, bus-train accident); m 2nd John Thomas Page (b January 28, 1896; d January 3, 1955, buried Western Cemetery); resided in Messick; d June 14, 1971, buried Western Cemetery, Poquoson.

2. Lemuel Vaden EVANS: b 1904, York County; m in York County on February 21, 1925, Mary Evelyn Watkins, age 18, the daughter of H.W. and Shellie Watkins (*Marriage Record No.1, 1854-1928, York County*, page 98, line 4); resided in Messick.

3. Erma H. EVANS: b 1909, York County; m William Johnson of Fox Hill.

4. Osborne EVANS: m 1st Ester Graham; m 2nd Flossie Forrest, the daughter of Floyd and Naomi Forrest; resides in Florida.

FT.1.1.8.1.2
ROBERT HENRY FORREST and BERNICE L. EVANS
Of Messick, Poquoson, York County

Robert Henry Forrest was born on March 13, 1884, York County, Virginia.

Robert H. Forrest married on November 26, 1904, Bernice L. Evans (b August 1, 1886), the daughter of George D. and Jane Evans.

In 1910, Robert Forrest and family were listed in the Poquoson, York County census, dwelling 469-478, as follows:

Evans	George D.	head	57	VA	widow
Forrest	Robert	s-i-l	25	VA	m-1
	Bernie L.	daughter	22	VA	m-1 2-2
	Marvin	son	4	VA	
	Melvin	son	5/12	VA	

Robert H. Forrest died on June 18, 1950, and is buried in the Western Cemetery, Poquoson.

1. Marvin FORREST: b 1906, York County, Virginia; m abt 1926, Louise Guy.

    1. Barbara Ann FORREST:

2. Melvin FORREST: b 1910, York County, Virginia.

3. Margaret H. FORREST: m Melvin Holloway (b November 29, 1916; d January 17, 1966, buried Western Cemetery, Poquoson) See next FT.1.1.8.1.2.3.

FT.1.1.8.1.2.3
MARGARET H. FORREST and MELVIN HOLLOWAY

Margaret H. Forrest married Melvin Holloway (b November 29, 1916; d January 17, 1966, buried Western Cemetery, Poquoson).

1. Jackie HOLLOWAY: m Joyce Butler.

    1. Julie HOLLOWAY: m Mike Bryant.

    2. Marvin HOLLOWAY:

    3. Teresa HOLLOWAY:

2. Melvin Lee HOLLOWAY: m Susan Hancock.

    1. Tommy Lee HOLLOWAY:

    2. Robert Scott HOLLOWAY:

FT.1.1.8.1.3
MINNIE E. FORREST and WILLIAM HERBERT AMORY
Of Poquoson, York County, Virginia

Minnie E. Forrest was born in November, 1885, York County, Virginia.

Miss Minnie E. Forrest married on February 20, 1904, Herbert Amory (b February 10, 1885, Virginia; d July 20, 1952, buried Western

Cemetery, Poquoson), the son of John Franklin and Maria Amory.

In 1910, William H. Amory and family are listed in the Poquoson, York County, Virginia census, dwelling 190-195, as follows:

Amory	William H.	head	25	m-1 6
	Minnie E.	wife	24	2-2
	Helen F.	daughter	5	
	Evelyn L.	daughter	3	

They lived on "Poquoson Road ending at Amory's Wharf Back River".

1. Helen F. AMORY: b September 12, 1905, York County, Virginia; m Robert Stephen Holloway (b December 11, 1903, Messick; d October 24, 1995); d on December 26, 1937, and is buried in the Western Cemetery, Poquoson. See next FT.1.1.8.1.3.1.

2. Evelyn AMORY: b 1907, York County, Virginia; m Henry Stewart Clarke, Sr. See next FT.1.1.8.1.3.2.

3. Anna Charline AMORY: m Henry Stephen Ward (b January 17, 1911, York County, Virginia; d November 16, 2000), the son of Eddie Grover and Elizabeth (Joyner) Ward. See next FT.1.1.8.1.3.3.

FT.1.1.8.1.3.1a
HELEN F. AMORY and ROBERT STEPHEN HOLLOWAY
Of York County, Virginia

Helen F. Amory was born on September 12, 1905, York County, Virginia.

Miss Helen F. Amory married at Trinity Methodist Church, Poquoson, Virginia, Robert Stephen Holloway (b December 11, 1903, Messick, Poquoson, York County, Virginia).

Robert worked at the shipyard in Wilmington, North Carolina, as a leading assistant foreman, during World War II, and after the war he worked for N. A. C. A., later renamed the N. A. S. A. He was a shipfitter and steelworker.

Mrs. Helen F. (Amory) Holloway died on December 26, 1937, and is buried in the Western Cemetery, Poquoson.

    1. Gordon Duane HOLLOWAY: b January 10, 1931, Riverside Hospital, Newport News, Virginia; York County Circuit Court Judge; m in Milford, Delaware, December 29, 1951, Roma Patricia Grier (b January 2, 1932, Milford, Delaware), of Milford, Delaware. See next FT.1.1.8.1.3.1.1.

    2. Anna Marie HOLLOWAY: b June 21, 1935; d June 28, 1935, buried Weston Cemetery, Poquoson, Virginia.

FT.1.1.8.1.3.1b
ROBERT STEPHEN HOLLOWAY and EUNICE HUFF
Of York County, Virginia

Robert Stephen Holloway married 2nd Eunice Huff (b March 5, 1911; d January 24, 1988), of Henderson, North Carolina, and sister to Hilda Huff, wife of Sidney Holloway.

Robert S. Holloway died on October 24, 1995, and is buried at Parklawn Memorial Park, Hampton, Virginia.

FT.1.1.8.1.3.1.1
GORDON DUANE HOLLOWAY and ROMA PATRICIA GRIER
Of Williamsburg, Virginia

Gordon Duane Holloway was born January 10, 1931, in the Riverside Hospital, Newport News, Virginia, probably one of the earlier Poquoson folks born in a hospital. He served as Senior Class President and is a 1947 Poquoson High School graduate.

1951
G. DUANE HOLLOWAY
FIRST CLASSMAN, VIRGINIA MILITARY INSTITUTE

Gordon Duane Holloway received a Bachelor of Arts in History from the Virginia Military Institute (VMI), Lexington, Virginia.

Gordon Duane Holloway married in Milford, Delaware, December 29, 1951, Roma Patricia Grier (b January 24, 1932), of Milford, Delaware. G. Duane attended the Marshall-Wythe School of Law, College of William and Mary, graduating in 1955, with a B. C. L. He had a general law practice from 1955 until 1980. He served as a Substitute County Judge, York County, Virginia, from 1957 until 1959, and was Commonwealth's Attorney for York County from 1960 until 1971. He served from 1980 until 1994, as a Judge of the Ninth Judicial Circuit, and was Chief Judge for the period 1989-1991. He has been a Judge Designate, Ninth Judicial Circuit from 1995 until the present.

In 1964 and 1965, he was President of the Virginia Waterman's Association.

They reside in (2000) Williamsburg.

1. Steven Frank HOLLOWAY: b July 26, 1955, Mary Immaculate Hospital, Hampton, Virginia; m Patricia Joyner (b November 6, 1954), of Ivor, Virginia. See next FT.1.1.8.1.3.1.1.1.

2. John Early HOLLOWAY: b January 28, 1959, Mary Immaculate Hospital, Hampton, Virginia; m Andrea Burzyk (b September 12, 1961), of Plymouth, Massachusetts. See next FT.1.1.8.1.3.1.1.2.

3. William ("Bill") Grier HOLLOWAY: b June 21, 1964, Hampton General Hospital, Hampton, Virginia; m Kimberly Banks (June 21, 1973), of Richmond, Virginia.

4. James ("Jim") Stuart HOLLOWAY: b January 22, 1969, Hampton General Hospital, Hampton, Virginia; m Anna Gibson (b July 1, 1963), of Winston Salem, North Carolina.

1995
JUDGE G. DUANE HOLLOWAY

FT.1.1.8.1.3.1.1.1
STEVEN FRANK HOLLOWAY and PATRICIA JOYNER

Steven Frank Holloway was born on July 26, 1955, in the Mary Immaculate Hospital, Hampton, Virginia.

Steven Frank Holloway married Patricia Joyner (b November 6, 1954), of Ivor, Virginia.

1. Harrison Joyner HOLLOWAY: b May 26, 1985.

2. Gordon Grier HOLLOWAY: b November 3, 1986.

FT.1.1.8.1.3.1.1.2
JOHN EARLY HOLLOWAY and ANDREA BURZYK

John Early Holloway was born January 28, 1959, at Mary Immaculate Hospital, Hampton, Virginia.

John Early Holloway married Andrea Burzyk (b September 12, 1961), of Plymouth, Massachusetts.

1. Andrew McCabe HOLLOWAY (twin): b June 17, 1997.

2. Robert Forrest HOLLOWAY (twin): b June 17, 1997.

FT.1.1.8.1.3.2
EVELYN AMORY and HENRY STEWART CLARKE, SR.

Evelyn Amory was born in 1907, York County, Virginia.

Miss Evelyn Amory married Henry Stewart Clarke, Sr.

1. Henry Stewart CLARKE, Jr:

    1. Robert CLARKE:

    2. Nanette CLARKE:

FT.1.1.8.1.3.3
ANNA CHARLINE AMORY and HENRY STEPHEN WARD

Anna Charline Amory married Henry Stephen Ward (b January 17, 1911, Messick, Poquoson, York County, Virginia; d November 16, 2000), the son of Eddie Grover and Elizabeth (Joyner) Ward.

1. Jeannine WARD: m Charles Sibbers.

    1. Linda M. SIBBERS: m Kevin Bertram.

    2. Don Wesley SIBBERS:

    3. Lisa SIBBERS: m Todd Bowden.

2. Don William WARD: m Elizabeth Jackson.

    1. William Nathan WARD:

    2. Anna Elizabeth WARD:

3. Anna Marie WARD: m 1st Richard Holzer (deceased); m 2nd Gary McLain; resides Panama City, Florida.

    1. Paul Ward HOLZER:

    2. Adam C. MCLAIN.

FT.1.1.8.1.4
ELIJAH V. FORREST and MARY MARGARET GIBBS
Of Poquoson, York County

Elijah V. Forrest was born on March 22, 1888, York County, Virginia.
Elijah V. Forrest married on December 23, 1907, Mary Margaret Gibbs (b May 22, 1889; d May 3, 1966, buried Western Cemetery), the daughter of J. and A. Gibbs.
In 1910, Elijah V. Forrest and family are listed in the Poquoson Township, York County, Virginia census, dwelling 179-184, as follows:

Forrest Elijah V. head   21 VA m-1
           Mary M.   wife   20 VA m-1 0-0

Elijah Forrest died on July 10, 1955, and is buried in the Western Cemetery, Poquoson.

1. Hazel Inez FORREST: b October 18, 1912, York County, Virginia; m December, 1930, Elwood Martin (b March 28, 1912), the son of Jacob and Laura Martin. See next FT.1.1.8.1.4.1.

2. William Melvin FORREST: b July 26, 1914, York County, Virginia; m Marjorie; d February 25, 1962.

3. Julia FORREST: m Leon Taylor.

4. Elijah Sterling FORREST: b May 23, 1925, York County, Virginia; m September 28, 1946, Coretta Rollins (b July 4, 1927), the daughter of Thomas Jefferson and Agatha Ward Rollins. See next FT.1.1.8.1.4.4.

FT.1.1.8.1.4.1
HAZEL INEZ FORREST and JACOB ELWOOD MARTIN

Hazel Inez Forrest was born on October 18, 1912, York County, Virginia.
Miss Hazel Inez Forrest married on December, 1930, Elwood Martin (b March 28,

1912, York County, Virginia), the son of Jacob and Laura Martin (*Marriage Record No. 2, York County*, page 4, line 70).

Jacob Martin died on July 26, 1981, and is buried in the Parklawn Memorial, Hampton, Virginia.

1. Nan Carey MARTIN: b June 28, 1931; m Alan Eugene Evans.

2. Jacob Elwood ("Buster") MARTIN, Jr: b April 6, 1933; m in Richmond, Virginia, in 1953, Sandra Greenwood; resides at 36 Hudgins Road.

FT.1.1.8.1.4.4
ELIJAH STERLING FORREST and CORETTA ROLLINS

Elijah Sterling Forrest was born on May 23, 1925, York County, Virginia.

Elijah Sterling Forrest married September 28, 1946, Coretta Rollins (b July 4, 1927), the daughter of Thomas Jefferson and Agatha Ward Rollins.

1. Becky Sue FORREST: b June 23, 1950; m December 12, 1970, Harold Emory Moore (b August 25, 1949).

    1. James Sterling MOORE: b September 19, 1972.

    2. Justin Morton MOORE: b January 29, 1982.

    3. Starkey MOORE:

2. Robert ("Bobby") Sterling FORREST: b March 15, 1955; m June 29, 1974, Marsha Susan Wilson (b June 7, 1956).

    1. Karen Nicole FORREST: b January 9, 1980.

3. Regina Rollins FORREST: b May 13, 1958; m August 28, 1978, Richard Duane Backus (b May 17, 1957).

    1. Jonathan Duane BACKUS: b February 3, 1980.

4. Russell FORREST: b July 20, 1959; m December 22, 1979, Tammy Carol Jones.

FT.1.1.8.1.5
LEMUEL VADEN FORREST
And LILLIE BEATRICE FORREST
Of Poquoson, York County, Virginia

Lemuel Vaden Forrest was born on May 25, 1890, York County, Virginia.

Lemuel Vaden Forrest married on December 23, 1911, Lillie Beatrice Forrest (b May 25, 1890), the daughter of John Andrew and Alice (Rollins) Forrest.

Lemuel Forrest died on November 5, 1943, and is buried in the Western Cemetery, Poquoson.

(*Ancestry and Descendants of Peter B. Smith*, n. d., pages 42-43).

1. Wallace Fayette FORREST [Sr.]: b September 30, 1912; m June 13, 1942, Helen Inez Ward (b December 22, 1911).

    1. Wallace Fayette FORREST, Jr: b September 30, 1944; m Diane Elizabeth Nolte.

    2. Clinton Lemuel FORREST (Sr.): b April 12, 1948; m Doris Elaine Robinette.

        1. Clinton Lemuel FORREST, Jr: b June 16, 1968.

        2. Steven Wayne FORREST: b September 30, 1970.

FT.1.1.8.1.6
JOHN W. FORREST and MARY VIOLA PAULS
Of York County, Virginia

John W. Forrest was born on July 6, 1893, York County, Virginia.

John W. Forrest married on November 30, 1912, Mary Viola ("Ola") Pauls, the daughter of John and Rosanna (Messick) Pauls.

1. Edna Earle FORREST: unmarried.

2. John Lemuel FORREST: m Ethel Spence.

   1. Crissie Mae FORREST: m Jack Stone, Sr.

      1. Jackie STONE, Jr:

      2. Tarek STONE:

      3. Parker STONE:

   2. Lisa FORREST: m 1st John W. Holloway; m 2nd Robert W. Woods, Jr.

      1. John Wayne HOLLOWAY, Jr.

      2. Shannon HOLLOWAY:

      3. Kristin WOODS:

FT.1.1.8.1.7
OSBORNE FORREST and MARGARET INDIANA PAULS
Of Messick, Poquoson, York County, Virginia

Osborne ("Ausburn" in the 1910 census) Forrest was born on December 15, 1894, Messick, York County, Virginia.

Osborne Forrest married on September 8, 1916, Margaret ("Maggie") Indiana Pauls (b September 16, 1898; d January 19, 1985), the daughter of John and Rosanna (Messick) Pauls. Osborne was "an artist with a pocket knife.

Using the knife as his only tool, he constructs Jacob's Ladders in bottles and makes old-time brooms" (undated newspaper article).

Osborne Forrest died on April 1, 1990.

1. James Osborne FORREST, Jr: b June 21, 1918; m February 26, 1936, Mary Virginia Jarvis (b October 22, 1916; d October 6, 1999); d October 22, 1995, and is buried in the Parklawn Memorial Cemetery, Hampton, Virginia. See next FT.1.1.8.1.7.1.

FT.1.1.8.1.7.1
JAMES OSBORNE FORREST and MARY VIRGINIA JARVIS

James Osborne Forrest, Jr. was born on June 21, 1918, York County, Virginia. His mother, Maggie wanted a son named James and also wanted him named after her husband Osborne; thus James Osborne Forrest, Jr., was named, and nicknamed "June".

James Osborne Forrest, Jr., married Mary Virginia Jarvis (b October 22, 1916; d October 6, 1999).

James Osborne Forrest died on October 22, 1995, and is buried in the Parklawn Memorial Cemetery, Hampton, Virginia.

1. James Osborne FORREST, III: b April 15, 1938; d August 15, 1941.

2. Harry Calvin FORREST (Sr.): b December 7, 1945; m September 5, 1964, Vandelia ("Dee") Lee Forrest (b October 2, 1947). See next FT.1.1.8.7.1.2.

3. Mary Margaret FORREST: b November 23, 1947; d November 24, 1996.

FT.1.1.8.7.1.2
HARRY CALVIN FORREST and VANDELIA LEE FORREST

Harry Calvin Forrest, Sr., was born on December 7, 1945. Harry Calvin Forrest married

September 5, 1964, Vandelia ("Dee") Lee Forrest (b October 2, 1947), the daughter of William Hugh Forrest and Coretta Dawson Moore.

    1. Harry Calvin FORREST, Jr: b September 26, 1966; m October 14, 1995, Tina Ann Carswell (b September 19, 1974).

        1. Kenneth William FORREST: b October 15, 1996.

        2. Tyler James Calvin FORREST: b September 13, 2000.

    2. Kenneth Wayne FORREST: b May 24, 1968; d November 27, 1968.

    3. Andrea Lee FORREST: b August 14, 1971; m April 20, 1996, Jeffrey Allen Ambrose (b December 29, 1971).

        1. Evan Henry AMBROSE: b May 14, 2000.

    4. Kara Janine FORREST: b April 30, 1977.

FT.1.1.8.1.8
JAMES BLANCHARD FORREST and MARY LILLIAN MOORE
Of Poquoson and Hampton, Virginia

James Blanchard Forrest was born on April 10, 1898, York County, Virginia.

James Blanchard Forrest married on July 7, 1923, Mary Lillian Moore (b June 23, 1906; d March 25, 1996), the daughter of John H. and Julia Beal Moore.

James Forrest died on October 24, 1952, and is buried in the Oakland Cemetery, Hampton, Virginia.

    1. Julia Frances FORREST: b April 25, 1924; m September 11, 1944, James Albert Parron; d January 4, 1979.

1. Penelope Ann PARRON: b July 9, 1945.

2. James Blanchard PARRON: b February 18, 1949.

2. Imogene ("Emma Jean") Hall FORREST: b September 6, 1925; m April 7, 1947, Bradford Taylor; d January 21, 1996.

1. Donald Mark TAYLOR: b May 31, 1957.

2. Kent Van TAYLOR: b February 22, 1959.

3. Robert Blanchard FORREST: b February 7, 1929; m December 1, 1946, Mary Stevens.

1. Mary Linda FORREST: b July 8, 1948.

4. Gwendolyn Moore FORREST: b September 7, 1929; m 1st October 14, 1951, Duane Howard Ward (d May 5, 1981); m 2nd April 3, 1983, Robert Henry Callis (d June 2, 1998).

1. Michael Duane WARD: b August 1, 1952.

2. Richard Dennis WARD: b September 15, 1953.

3. Teresa Lynn WARD: b January 22, 1957; m August 16, 1997, Larry Haywood.

5. Marion Lillian FORREST: b May 12, 1931; m 1st June 7, 1952, Gene Mitchell Rollins (d November 29, 1975); m 2nd July 20, 1989, Charles A. Counts.

1. Jeffrey Brent ROLLINS: b August 15, 1953; m February 5, 1977, Karen West.

2. Robert Mitchell ROLLINS: b June 4, 1955.

3. William Gene ROLLINS: b November 11, 1958.
4. Kelly Eilene ROLLINS: b June 26, 1963.

6. Charlotte Elizabeth FORREST: b October 6, 1937; m July 13, 1955, Frank A. Spencer.

1. Thomas Edward SPENCER: b November 24, 1958.

7. Mary Lou FORREST: b July 27, 1939; m July 8, 1961, William Hamilton Wood.

FT.1.1.8.1.9a
HOWARD GARLAND FORREST and EUDORA AMORY
Of Poquoson, York County

Howard Garland Forrest (Sr.) was born on March 24, 1901, Poquoson, York County, Virginia.

Howard Garland Forrest married 1st at the Trinity Methodist Church, Messick, Poquoson, York County, Virginia, September 21, 1921, Eudora ("Nonie") Amory (b May 23, 1904; d August 10, 1947, buried in the Western Cemetery), the daughter of George W. Amory, Sr., and Bernie Lawson.

Howard was a seafood dealer in Poquoson.

Howard Garland Forrest died May 25, 1971, and is buried in the Weston/Western Cemetery, Poquoson.

1. Eudora ("Dorabelle") Belle FORREST: b October 15, 1922, Hampton, Virginia; m in Messick, Poquoson, Virginia, June 29, 1946, Richard Gordon Cox, Sr. (b October 9, 1917, Fredericksburg, Virginia; d February 2, 1990, buried Parklawn Cemetery, Hampton). See next FT.1.1.8.1.9.1.

2. Howard Garland FORREST, Jr: b October 30, 1927, Hampton, Virginia; m at the Methodist Parsonage in Norfolk, Virginia, December 26,

1948, Betty Milla Cox (b September 21, 1928, Hampton, Virginia), the daughter of Melvin and Ora (Topping) Cox. See next FT.1.1.8.1.9.2.

FT.1.1.8.1.9b
HOWARD GARLAND FORREST and RITA MOORE HUNT
Of Poquoson, York County

Howard Garland Forrest, Sr., married 2nd at the Trinity Methodist Church, Messick, Poquoson, York County, Virginia, December 22, 1959, Rita Moore Hunt (b July 30, 1904).

Howard Forrest died on May 23, 1971, and is buried in the Western Cemetery, Poquoson.

FT.1.1.8.1.9.1
EUDORA BELLE FORREST and RICHARD GORDON COX
Of Poquoson, Virginia

Eudora ("Dorabelle") Belle Forrest was born on October 15, 1922, Hampton, Virginia.

Miss Dorabelle Forrest married in Messick, Poquoson, Virginia, on June 29, 1946, Richard Gordon Cox (b October 9, 1917, Fredericksburg, Virginia; d February 2, 1990, buried Parklawn Cemetery, Hampton). Dorabelle met her future husband while she was attending Mary Washington College. She graduated in 1943 with a B.S. in Music Education. Richard Gordon Cox was a career U.S. Army and Air Force officer, retiring with the rank of Colonel in 1967. His military career included service in World War II, the Korean War, and Vietnam War.

Dorabelle was a public school music teacher for 4 ½ years and a director of the church choir for 22 years. Dorabelle resides (2000) in Poquoson, Virginia.

1. Richard Gordon COX, Jr: b May 8, 1947, Washington, D.C; serviced in the US Army in Vietnam.

2. Barbara Dee COX: b November 13, 1948, Washington, D.C; m 1st Gary Lee Carl; m 2nd Robert Lee Hodges, Jr.

1. Amory Anne CARL: b June 5, 1966, Hampton, Virginia; m 1st Dennis Rosso; m 2nd Craig Lozaw.

1. Alyssa Ashley LOZAW: b December 12, 1992.

2. Christopher Douglas LOZAW: b February 15, 1995.

2. Robert Lee HODGES, III: b Hampton, Virginia.

3. Van Forrest COX: b August 27, 1950, Albuquerque, New Mexico.

FT.1.1.8.1.9.2
HOWARD GARLAND FORREST, Jr.,
And BETTY MILLA COX
Of Poquoson and Newport News, Virginia

Howard Garland Forrest, Jr., was born on October 30, 1927, Hampton, Virginia. He was drafted for World War II.

Howard Garland Forrest married at the Methodist Parsonage in Norfolk, Virginia, on December 26, 1948, Betty Milla Cox (b September 21, 1928, Hampton, Virginia), the daughter of Melvin and Ora (Topping) Cox. Howard was a contracts analysis at the Newport News Shipbuilding and Dry Dock Company, Newport New Virginia. Howard and Betty resided most of their lives in Poquoson, only moving out to Newport News, Virginia, on September 1, 2000.

Betty was a teacher in the public school system, church pre-school and kindergarten.

1. Howard Garland FORREST (III): b September 24, 1952, Hampton, Virginia; m 1st

1976, Donna Tyndall; m 2nd 1984, Debbie Daniel Burcher.

    1. Corie Michele FORREST: b June 26, 1980.

    2. Nonie Elizabeth FORREST: b September 10, 1957, Hampton, Virginia; d October 5, 1957.

    3. Kenneth Melvin FORREST: b December 17, 1959, Hampton, Virginia; m 1985, Robyn Fox Merilic.

    1. Kelli Renea FORREST: b January 14, 1981.

FT.1.1.8.4
ROBERT LEE FORREST
And MELISSA VIRGINIA HOLLOWAY
Of Messick, Poquoson District, York County

Robert Lee (Bob Lee) Forrest was born on August 27, 1865, in Messick, Poquoson, York County, Virginia.

Robert Lee Forrest married in York County, Virginia, on January 22, 1885, Melissa Virginia Holloway (b April 16, 1865, Messick; d on June 26, 1946, Hampton, Virginia, buried Western Cemetery), daughter of Elias Rosser and Mary Susan (Amory) Holloway (*Marriage Record No. 1, 1854-1928. York County*, page 17, line 485).

In 1900, Robert L. Forrest and family are listed in the Poquoson Magisterial District, York County census, dwelling 357-365, as follows:

```
Forrest  Robert L.    head   Aug 1865 34 m-15
         Melissa H.   wife   Apr 1865 35 3-2
         Mary E. (sic) daug  Jan 1886 14 VA
         Ira B.       son    Jan 1888 12 VA
```

In 1910, he was a storekeeper, and his store, "R. L. Forrest and Son" was on Poquoson Avenue, just one house west of Messick Road. He lived on the "Main Poquoson Road leading to Amory's Wharf."

In 1910, Robert L. Forrest and family are listed in the Poquoson Magisterial District, York County census, dwelling 122-127, as follows:

Forrest	Robert L.	head	45	VA	m-25
	Malisa V.	wife	45	VA	3-2
	Ira B.	son	16	VA	

Robert Forrest died on December 8, 1940, and is buried in the Western Cemetery, Poquoson.

1. Mary ("Mamie") Susan FORREST: b February 12, 1886, Messick, Virginia; m in York County on April 25, 1907, James Sledd Quinn (b April 12, 1885; d November 11, 1967), the son of William F. Quinn and Derusha Amory (*Marriage Record No.1, 1854-1928, York County*, page 47, line 566); d December 17, 1954. See next FT.1.1.8.4.1.

2. Ira Bledsoe FORREST: b February 7, 1888, Messick, York County, Virginia; m January 19, 1913, Lola Florence Bradshaw (b May 21, 1891, buried Western Cemetery beside her husband), the daughter of John Lemuel Bradshaw and Rosanna Watkins; d February 14, 1959, buried Western Cemetery. See next FT.1.1.8.4.2.

3. Virginia ("Virgie") FORREST: b July 20, 1890, Messick, York County, Virginia: d infant, October 12, 1892, Messick, Virginia, buried Trinity Churchyard; d. s. p.

FT.1.1.8.4.1
MARY SUSAN FORREST and JAMES SLEDD QUINN

Mary Susan Forrest was born on February 12, 1886.

Miss Mary Susan Forrest married James Sledd Quinn (b April 12, 1885, York County, Virginia; d December 17, 1954).

Mrs. Mary Susan (Forrest) died on February 14, 1959.

1. Margaret Lee QUINN: b September 25, 1908; m Harry Linwood Carmines (b April 14, 1908; d December 27, 1943); d November 10, 1990. See next FT.1.1.8.4.1.1.

2. Beulah Forrest QUINN: m Chase H. Bush.

3. Rosalie Virginia QUINN: m Thomas Henry ("Jack") Isaacs. No children.

FT.1.1.8.4.1.1
MARGARET LEE QUINN and HARRY LINWOOD CARMINES
Of Hampton, Virginia

Margaret Lee Quinn was born on September 25, 1908.

Miss Margaret Lee Quinn married Harry Linwood Carmines (b April 14, 1908; d December 27, 1943). They resided in Hampton, Virginia, where he was the Chief of the Hampton Fire Department. He also worked in his father's men's clothing store, and the back door faced the fire department so whenever there was a fire - he was right there ready to go.

Harry Linwood Carmines died December 27, 1943. Harry went on the roof of the pharmacy next to the clothing store that was owned by his sister Virginia to change a light bulb. He fell and broke his leg, which was set expeditiously. However, the Doctor did not realize that his he had also broken a rib that had punctured his lung.

1. Robert Lee CARMINES: b July 30, 1939, in the "old" Dixie Hospital, Hampton, Virginia; m Betti Lou Matkins of Washington, North Carolina.

    1. Jeffrey CARMINES: b December 12, 1962.

    2. Lisa CARMINES: b April 4, 1964.

2. Virginia ("Sue") Lee CARMINES: b November 11, 1943, in the "old" Dixie Hospital, Hampton, Virginia; m in Elizabeth City, North Carolina, August 17, 1963, Richard Shirley Ellyson (b August 11, 1937, New Kent County, Virginia).

    1. Elizabeth Ellen ELLYSON: b April 1, 1964.

    2. Cheryl Lynn ELLYSON: b September 26, 1966.

    3. Lee Ann ELLYSON: b April 18, 1973.

FT.1.1.8.4.2
IRA BLEDSOE FORREST and LOLA FLORENCE BRADSHAW
Of Messick, York County

Ira Bledsoe Forrest was born on February 7, 1888, in Messick, York County, Virginia.

Ira Bledsoe Forrest married on January 19, 1913, Lola Florence Bradshaw (b May 21, 1891, buried Western Cemetery beside her husband), the daughter of John Lemuel Bradshaw and Rosanna Watkins (*Marriage Record No. 1, 1854-1928, York County*, page 55, line 877). Ira Forrest was the postmaster of Messick for over 30 years until the incorporation of Poquoson as a city eliminated the Messick Post Office.

Ira Bledsoe Forrest died on February 14, 1959, and is buried in the Western Cemetery.

1. Carrie Elaine FORREST: b October 9, 1914, Poquoson, York County, Virginia; d January 26, 1917, Poquoson, buried Western Cemetery, Poquoson, York County.

2. Carroll Thomas FORREST: b October 14, 1916, Poquoson, York County, Virginia; m October 23, 1943, Jessie Fay Forrest (b September 23, 1919, Messick, York County, Virginia; d July 13, 2000), the daughter of John Thomas ("Epps") and Sarah E. (Watkins) Forrest; d April 2, 1986, buried Western Cemetery, Poquoson. See next FT.1.1.8.4.2.2.

3. Harry Grey FORREST: b May 31, 1919, Poquoson, York County, Virginia; m at The Methodist parsonage on May 17, 1941, Lella Ellen ("Mae") Cook, the daughter of Clyde and Sara Powell Cook. See next FT.1.1.8.4.2.4.

FT.1.1.8.4.2.2
CARROLL THOMAS FORREST and JESSIE FAY FORREST
Of Messick, York County

Carroll Thomas Forrest was born on October 14, 1916, Poquoson, York County, Virginia.

Carroll Thomas Forrest married on October 23, 1943, Jessie Fay Forrest (b September 23, 1919, Messick, York County, Virginia; d July 13, 2000), the daughter of John Thomas ("Epps") and Sarah E. (Watkins) Forrest. Carroll Thomas Forrest was the first mayor of the City of Poquoson.

Jessie Forrest was very active in community affairs, and accumulated a very large and well-documented collection of Poquoson family history. She was the preeminent family historian for Poquoson. Jessie Fay was a member of the Daughters of the American Revolution (D.A.R.), and the Poquoson Historical Commission. She served as the Poquoson City Historian and also served for many years on the Poquoson Public Library board. She was a member of Trinity United Methodist Church, Poquoson, for 68 years.

JESSIE FAY

"Mrs. Forrest helped found Poquoson's current rescue squad and the Poquoson Historical Society. She was the first woman in Virginia to hold the rank of rescue squad captain. Her's was not an honorary title; she often responded to calls for assistance and taught first aid to other rescues and Boy Scouts" ... "She was a member of the Jamestown Society, the Colonial Dames of the Seventeenth Century, Charles Parish Chapter of the Daughters of the American Revolution, and the daughters of the War of 1812" (Obituary, "Poquoson Community Leader, Jessie Faye Forrest dies", July 15, 2000, Daily Press Newspaper, Newport News, Virginia).

Carroll Thomas Forrest died on April 2, 1986, Virginia.

Mrs. Jessie Fay Forrest died on July 13, 2000. A memorial service was held at Trinity United Methodist Church, Poquoson, lead by the Rev. Milford C. Rollins and the Rev. Bill Davidson.

1. Carroll Mark FORREST: b April 30, 1947; d September 24, 1979, and is buried in the Western Cemetery, Poquoson.

2. Elizabeth Ann FORREST: b 1952; resides (2000) in Dingmans Ferry, Pennsylvania, works in New York City as an artist and musician.

FT.1.1.8.4.2.3
HARRY GREY FORREST and LELLA ELLEN COOK
Of Messick, Poquoson, York County

Harry Grey ("Jimmy") Forrest was born on May 31, 1919, at 1360 Poquoson Avenue, Messick. He joined the Naval Reserve in 1939, and was called to active duty on April 2, 1941. He was given 48 hours to report, was sent to New York and then *sat on my tail for two months waiting for a ship.* Jimmy Forrest served in the Pacific Submarine Squadron on detached duty to Admiral Rockwell's staff in Australia. He was on active duty for a little over five years, and served a total of 26 years of Naval Reserve duty.

Harry Grey Forrest married at the Methodist parsonage on May 17, 1941, Lella Ellen ("Mae") Cook, the daughter of Clyde and Sarah Powell Cook.

After the war, he eventually became the Executive vice-president of the First National Bank of Poquoson. He was a member of the Poquoson Board of Supervisors from 1956 to 1975, serving until December 31, 1975. He was a two-term member of the Poquoson City Council serving from 1982 until 1994.

1. Elaine Grey FORREST: b February 10, 1948, Hampton, Virginia; m 1st Cary Tennis (died within 30 days after his marriage of cancer); m 2nd Daniel Vandervort.

    1. Catherine VANDERVORT: b January 30, 1970, Hampton, Virginia.

    2. Jennifer VANDERVORT: b August 4, 1973, Hampton, Virginia.

2. Melissa FORREST: October 21, 1952; m Gregory Gardy.

    1. Katelyn Elizabeth GARDY: b October 3, 1985.

FT.1.1.8.9
JOHN THOMAS FORREST and SARAH ELIZABETH WATKINS
Of Messick, Poquoson District, York County, Virginia

John Thomas ("Epps") Forrest was born on January 11, 1889, in Messick, York County, Virginia.

JOHN THOMAS FORREST

John Thomas Forrest married on January 10, 1910, Sarah Elizabeth Watkins (b October 26, 1891), Messick, York County, Virginia; d October 27, 1969, Williamsburg, buried Western Cemetery, Messick, Virginia), daughter of Mead Robert and Sarah Sylvester (Forrest) Watkins (*Marriage Record No. 1, 1854-1928, York County*, page 51, line 708).

In 1910, John Thomas Forrest and family are listed in the household of his father-in-law, Mead R. Watkins, in the York County census, dwelling 104-109.

John Forrest died on April 29, 1949, in Richmond, Virginia, and is buried in the Western Cemetery.

1. Robert Edgar FORREST: b February 28, 1912, Messick, York County, Virginia; m in Norfolk, Virginia, on June 17, 1933, Gladys Elizabeth Moore (b October 30, 1911, York County), daughter of Nancy (Wainwright) and Alexander Moore; d March 28, 1993. See next FT.1.1.8.9.1.

2. Sarah Anne FORREST: b 1916, Messick, York County, Virginia; d 1916, d. s. p.

3. Jessie Fay FORREST: b September 23, 1919, Messick, York County, Virginia; m October 23, 1943, Carroll Thomas Forrest (b October 14, 1916; d April 2, 1986), the son of Ira B. and Lola Bradshaw Forrest; d July 13, 2000. See next FT.1.1.8.4.2.2.

4. Ann Watkins FORREST (twin): b March 17, 1923, Messick, York County, Virginia; m in South Mills, North Carolina, in 1941, Lyman Dan Forrest, son of Virginia (Holloway) and Essie Forrest; d November 24, 1978, in Newport News, Virginia, buried Western Cemetery.

5. FORREST (twin): stillborn on March 17, 1923, Messick.

6. Thomas Wilfred FORREST: b March 2, 1928, Messick, York County, Virginia; m in Jeffs, York County, Virginia, on March 11, 1955, Rosa Dixon (b May 29, 1935, York County), the daughter of William Bain Dixon and Geraldine Madola Murphy. See next FT.1.1.8.9.6.

FT.1.1.8.9.1
ROBERT EDGAR FORREST and GLADYS ELIZABETH MOORE
Of York County, Virginia

Robert Edgar Forrest was born on February 28, 1912, Messick, York County, Virginia.

Robert Edgar Forrest married in Norfolk, Virginia, on June 17, 1933, Gladys Elizabeth Moore (b October 30, 1911, York County), daughter of Nancy (Wainwright) and Alexander Moore.

Robert Edgar Forrest died on March 28, 1993.

1. Janice Marie FORREST: b August 30, 1936, York County, Virginia; m November 6, 1954, Clyde Lawrence Edwards.

2. Ted Moore FORREST: b April 6, 1942, York County, Virginia; m June 12, 1964, Loretta ("April") Watson.

3. Tim Ray FORREST: b July 16, 1944.

FT.1.1.8.9.6
THOMAS WILFRED FORREST and ROSA DIXON
Of York County, Virginia

Thomas Wilfred Forrest was born on March 2, 1928, Messick, York County, Virginia.

Thomas Wilfred Forrest married in Jeffs, York County, Virginia, on March 11, 1955, Rosa Dixon (b May 29, 1935, York County), the daughter of William Bain and Geraldine Madola (Murphy) Dixon.

1. Thomas Dale FORREST: b December 30, 1955, York County, Virginia.

2. Barry Jay FORREST: b May 10, 1961, York County, Virginia.

FT.1.1.9
MARTHA ANN FORREST and WILLIAM PAGE
Of Messick, Poquoson, York County, Virginia

Martha Ann Forrest was born in 1839 (or 1838 according to the 1850 census) (1835-1840) York County, Virginia. She might be the Ann Forrest, age 12, who was enumerated with the George Page family on July 26, 1850 (1850 York County census, dwelling 21-21).

Miss Martha Ann Forrest married about 1856, William Page (b 1836, York County, Virginia), the son of William Page and Rachel Messick.

In 1860, William Page and family are listed in the Post Office Halfway House, York County, Virginia census, dwelling 88-88, as follows:

Page	William	head	24	VA	oysterman
	Martha Ann	wife	21	VA	
	Thomas	son	3		
Page	Nancy	NR	23		
Tailor	Virginia	NR	9		

In 1870, William Page and family are listed in the Poquoson Township, York County, Virginia census, dwelling 268-284, as follows:

Page	William	head	35	VA	farmer
	Martha A.	wife	30	VA	keep house
	Thomas C.	son	13	VA	
	William W.	son	9	VA	
	Lewis S.	son	7	VA	
	John D.	son	10/12	VA	

In 1880, Wm. Page and family are listed in the Poquoson District, York County, Virginia census, dwelling 133-133, as follows:

Page	Wm.	head	43	VA oysterman
	William	son	19	VA at home
	Skidmore	son	15	VA at home
	John	son	12	VA at home
	Monroe	son	8	VA at home

Children of William Page and his 1st wife, Martha Ann Forrest:

1. Thomas Curtis PAGE: b 1858, York County; baptized in Trinity Church in 1859; m in York County on June 27, 1878, Irene S. Hopkins, age 20 (b 1857), the daughter of James and Ann Hopkins; oysterman (1878).

2. William Wesley PAGE: b September 18, 1859 (March, 1862), York County, Virginia; m 1st 1895, Fannie; m 2nd 1908, Euphemia Anne Watkins (b April 25, 1880; d May 25, 1953, buried Western Cemetery), the daughter of Elias James and Disey Watkins, and sister to Sarah Virginia Watkins; d January 16, 1945, buried Western Cemetery beside his 2nd wife.

3. Lewis Skidmore PAGE: b March 6, 1864, York County, Virginia; m in York County on November 19, 1882, Ellen (Ella) L. Insley, age 18 (b November 29, 1861; d January 12, 1947, buried Western Cemetery), the daughter of Gilbert and Harriet Insley; d December 6, 1935, buried Western Cemetery.

4. John D. PAGE: b 1869, York County, Virginia; m in York County on August 23, 1890, Sarah Virginia Watkins, age 17, the daughter of Elias James and Disey Watkins; waterman (1890).

5. Monroe PAGE: b 1872, York County, Virginia.

FT.1.1.9b
WILLIAM PAGE and CATHERINE THOMAS
Of Messick, Poquoson, York County

William Page married 2nd on July 16, 1882, Catherine Thomas, age 20, the daughter of Harvey (sic) (*Marriage Record No.1, 1854-1928, York County*, page 25, line 36).

FT.1.1.11
ABRAHAM FORREST and SARAH ELIZABETH TOPPING
Of Messick, Poquoson District,
York County, Virginia

Abraham Forrest was born on December 7, 1842, in Messick, York County, Virginia.

Abraham Forrest married in Messick, York County, Virginia, on March 16, 1865, Sarah Elizabeth Topping (b November 17, 1845; d August 1, 1915, buried Western Cemetery), the daughter of John Topping and Martha Dixon.

He was a farmer (1870) and a sailor (1880).

In 1870, Abraham Forrest and family are listed in the Poquoson Township, York County, Virginia census, dwelling 269-286, as follows:

Forrest	Abraham	head	26	VA	farmer
	Sarah E.	wife	23	VA	keep house
	Anna L.	daughter	3	VA	
	Sarah S.	daughter	1	VA	

In 1880, A. Forrest and family are listed in the York County census, dwelling 132-132, as follows:

Forrest	A.	head	35	laborer
	Sarah	wife	32	keep house
	Annie	daughter	13	at home
	Sarah	daughter	10	at home
	Martha	daughter	8	at home
	Wm. T.	son	6	at home
	Mary	daughter	5	at home
	Irene	daughter	4	at home
	Robt Lee	son	1	at home

Abraham Forrest died in Messick, on February 11, 1894, and is buried Western Cemetery.

In 1900, Sarah Forrest [widow] and family are listed in the Poquoson Magisterial District, York County census, dwelling 409-417, as follows:

Forrest	Sarah	head	Nov 1847	52	wd.
	Irene S.	daughter	Nov 1876	23	s
	Robert L.	son	Jan 1879	21	s
	John C.	son	Aug 1884	15	s

In 1910, Sarah Forrest, widow, is listed in the household of her son Cleveland Forrest in the Poquoson Magisterial District, York County census, dwelling 102-107, as follows:

Forrest	Cleveland	head	25	VA m-1
	Jane	wife	18	VA m-1 0-0
	Sarah E.	mother	62	VA wd, 10-9

1. Annie Laura FORREST: b December 1, 1866, Messick, York County, Virginia; m December 10, 1887, John W. Rollins, son of Samuel and Matilda Rollins (*Marriage Record No. 1, 1854-1928, York County*, page 20, line 614); d Hampton, Virginia, on May 29, 1957, buried in the Western cemetery. See next FT.1.1.11.1.

2. Sarah Sylvester ("Toss") FORREST: b October 31, 1869, Messick, York County, Virginia; m October 24, 1886, Robert Mead Watkins, son of Henry and Sarah A. Watkins (*Marriage Record No. 1, 1854-1928, York County*, page 19, line 579); d August 14, 1957, buried Western Cemetery.

3. Martha Jane FORREST: b June 17, 1871, Messick, York County, Virginia; m February 26, 1893, William F. Quinn, son of Benjamin F. and Sarah Quinn (*Marriage Record No.1, 1854-1928, York County*, page 28, line 981); d October 31, 1953, Poquoson, Virginia.

4. William Thomas ("Tom Cherry") FORREST: b November 2, 1873, Messick, York County, Virginia; m December 26, 1899, Susanna Elizabeth Lawson, daughter of Elisha and Mary E. Lawson (*Marriage Record NO. 1, 1854-1928, York County*, page 36, line 68); d January 28, 1936. See next FT.1.1.11.4.

5. Mary Elizabeth FORREST: b March 23, 1874, Messick, York County, Virginia; m December 28, 1893, James B. Simpson (b December 24, 1871; d April 4, 1931, buried Western Cemetery, Poquoson), son of Henry and Susan Simpson (*Marriage Record No. 1, 1854-1928, York County*, page 29, line 1015); d March 29, 1962.

6. Irene Sevilla FORREST: b November 11, 1876, Messick, York County, Virginia; m December 25, 1902, Christopher Watkins (d October, 1937), the son of Littleton and Sarah Watkins (*Marriage Record No. 1, 1854-1928, York County*, page 41, line 284). Christopher Watkins and his only son, Basil, were lost at sea in October, 1937. Irene (Forrest) Watkins died January 10, 1956, Poquoson, Virginia.

    1. Basil WATKINS: d October, 1937, lost at sea.

7. Robert Lee ("Bob Spider") FORREST: b January 31, 1878, Messick, York County, Virginia; m June 19, 1908, Cotha C. Diggs (b May 28, 1886; d November, 1982), the daughter of Elkanah and Bunah Diggs of Mathews County, Virginia; d 1936, buried Western Cemetery, Poquoson. See next FT.1.1.11.7.

8. Missouri Frances FORREST: b September 11, 1880, Messick, York County, Virginia; m July 1, 1899, John Franklin Hunt, son of W. E. and Missouri Hunt (*Marriage Record No. 1, 1854-1928, York County*, page 35, line 48; d December 12, 1967.

9. John Healy FORREST: b August 2, 1882, Messick, York County, Virginia; d September 4, 1882, buried Western Cemetery, Poquoson.

10. John Cleveland FORREST: b August 27, 1884, Messick, York County, Virginia; m 1909, Jane Begor (b August 19, 1892), daughter of William Edward Begor and Sarah Theresa Page (another source says daughter of Solon Begor and Matilda Jane Bradshaw); d March 2, 1923.

FT.1.1.11.1a
EMMA J. FORREST and JOHN W. ROLLINS
Of Poquoson District, York County, Virginia

John W. Rollins was born on May 3, 1863. He was an oysterman (1881) and watermen (1887).

John W. Rollins married 1st on May 7, 1881, Emma J. Forrest (b April 23, 1861; d December 1, 1884, buried Western Cemetery), age 18, the daughter of Robert and Mary Forrest (*Marriage Record No.1, 1854-1928, York County*, page 23, line 24).

RS.1.1.11.1b
ANNIE LAURA FORREST and JOHN W. ROLLINS
Of Poquoson District, York County, Virginia

Annie Laura Forrest was born on December 1, 1866.

Miss Annie Laura Forrest, age 21, the daughter of Abraham and Sarah Forrest, married in York County on February 10, 1887, as his 2nd wife, John W. Rollins (*Marriage Record No.1, 1854-1928, York County*, page 32, line 13).

In 1900, John W. Rollins and family are listed in the Poquoson Magisterial District, York County, Virginia census, dwelling 360-368, as follows:

Rollins	John W.	head	May 1862	37	m-14
	Annie L.	wife	Dec 1866	33	5-4
	Mamie M.	daughter	Sep 1887	12	s
	Bessie G.	daughter	Dec 1881	11	s
	John A.	son	May 1894	6	s

	Henry C.	son		Sep 1896	3 s

In 1910, John W. Rollins and family are listed in the Poquoson, York County, Virginia census, dwelling 145-150, as follows:

Rollins	John W.	head	46	VA	m-2
	Annie L.	wife	44	VA	m-1 5-4
	John A.	son	16	VA	
	Henry C.	son	13	VA	
Forrest	John O.	s-i-l	23	VA	m-1
	Bessie	daughter	21	VA	m-1 1-1
	Helen	daughter	10/12	VA	

John W. Rollins died on September 21, 1949; buried Western Cemetery.

1. Mary ("Mamie") M. ROLLINS: b September, 1887, Virginia.

2. Bessie ROLLINS: b December, 1888, Virginia: m in 1909, Otis Forrest (b 1887, Virginia).

3. John A. ROLLINS: b May, 1894, Virginia; m Mary Elizabeth.

4. Henry C. ROLLINS: b September, 1896, Virginia; m Elizabeth.

FT.1.1.11.4
WILLIAM THOMAS FORREST
And SUSANNA ELIZABETH LAWSON
Of Poquoson, York County, Virginia

William Thomas ("Tom Cherry") Forrest was born on November 2, 1873, Messick, York County, Virginia.

William Thomas Forrest married on December 26, 1899, Susanna Elizabeth Lawson, daughter of Elisha and Mary E. Lawson (b October, 1875) (*Marriage Record No. 1, 1854-1928, York County*, page 36, line 68).

In 1900, William T. Forrest and family are listed in the Poquoson Magisterial District, York County, Virginia census, dwelling 384-392, as follows:

```
Forrest  William T.  head       Nov 1875  26   m-0
         Elizabeth   wife       Oct 1875  24   0-0
```

In 1910, William T. Forrest and family are listed in the Poquoson, York County, Virginia census, dwelling 160-163, as follows:

```
Forrest  William T.  head           35     VA   m-10
         Susan E.    wife           33     VA   3-3
         Ava A.      daughter        9     VA
         Harvey T.   son             3     VA
         Mary E.     daughter     11/12    VA
```

William Forrest died on January 28, 1936, and is buried in the Western Cemetery.

1. Ava Alline (Allene) FORREST: b September 23, 1900.

2. Harvey T. FORREST: b 1907, York County, Virginia; d April 28, 1997, buried in the Clark Cemetery, Hampton, Virginia.

3. Mary Elizabeth FORREST: b May 1, 1909, York County, Virginia; she was 11 months old when the 1910 census was taken; m abt 1929, Edward Barrows Saunders.

4. Melvin FORREST: b abt 1911.

FT.1.1.11.7
ROBERT LEE FORREST and COTHA C. DIGGS
Of Poquoson, York County, Virginia

Robert Lee ("Bob Spider") Forrest was born on January 31, 1878, Messick, Virginia.

Robert Lee Forrest married on June 19, 1907, Cotha C. Diggs (b May 24, 1886; d November, 1982), the daughter of Elkanah and Bunah Diggs of Mathews County, Virginia.

In 1910, Robert L. Forrest and family are listed in the York County, Virginia census, dwelling 103-108, as follows:

```
Forrest  Robert L.    head          30 VA m-1
         Cotha C.     wife          23 VA m-1 1-1
         Chrystal L.  daughter 1 3/12  VA
```

Robert Lee Forrest died in 1936, and is buried in the Western Cemetery, Poquoson.

1. Chrystal L. FORREST: b July 28, 1908; m Walter Haywood Forrest. See next FT.1.4.1.3.6.

2. Ruby E. FORREST: abt 1911; m Robert Watkins, the son of Morris and Josephine Watkins.

    1. Randall WATKINS:

3. Robert Elkanah FORREST: b November 26, 1911; m Anne Lewis (b August 4, 1918) of Hampton.

4. John Cleveland FORREST: b abt 1920.

CHAPTER THREE
THE ABRAHAM FORREST FAMILY
POQUOSON DISTRICT, YORK COUNTY, VIRGINIA

FT.1.3a
ABRAHAM FORREST and SUSAN CALLIS
Of Poquoson, York County, Virginia

Abraham Forrest was born on February 15, 1812 (1810-1815, Mathews County, Virginia; also stated as being born in 1825, according to the 1850 census). Agnes Holloway Carmines had stated that Abraham Forrest (b 1812) was a brother to Henry ("Long Henry") Forrest and Thomas Humphrey Forrest.

Abraham Forrest married 1st in York County on November 23, 1837, Susan Callis (Y. M. B., November 23, 1837). This marriage proven, since the witnesses were Thomas Forrest (presumed to be his brother) and Hinde Holloway, a person who knew his father Abraham Forrest. Susan (Callis) Forrest mostly likely died soon afterwards (between 1838 and 1841).

FT.1.3b
ABRAHAM FORREST and MARY EMILY
Of Poquoson, York County, Virginia

Abraham Forrest married 2nd about 1842, Mary Emily (b January 1, 1822; d January 31, 1866, buried Western Cemetery). They resided in Poquoson, Virginia, where he was an inland sailor (1860) and an oysterman (1850, 1870).

In 1850, Abraham Forrest and family are listed in the York County, Virginia census, page 345, dwelling 35-35, as follows:

Forrest	Abraham	head	25	Mathews Co oysterman
	Mary	wife	28	York County
	Matilda	daughter	7	York County
	Mary	daughter	5	York County
	Maria	daughter	2	York County
	H. J.	son	9/12	York County

In 1860, Abraham Forrest is listed as the head of household in the Post Office Halfway House, York County, Virginia census, dwelling 99-99, as follows:

Forrest	Abraham	head	45	sailor inland
	Mary	wife	36	
	Matilda	daughter	16	
	Mary E.	daughter	14	
	Sarah	daughter	12	
	Thomas	son	10	
	Virginia	daughter	7	
	Abraham	son	5	
	Eliza	daughter	3	
	Bunivista	daughter	7/12	

In 1870, Abraham Forrest and family are listed in the Poquoson Township, York County, Virginia census, dwelling 150-159, as follows:

Forrest	Abraham	head	53	VA	oysterman
	Mary E.	daughter	21	VA	keep house
	Sarah M.	daughter	19	VA	at home
	Thomas H.	son	18	VA	oysterman
	Virginia	daughter	16	VA	at home
	James A.	son	14	VA	at home
(sic)	Indianna	daughter	8	VA	
	Henry D.	son	4	VA	

Abraham Forrest died on December 4, 1873, age 61 years, 2 months, 8 days, cause of death dropsy, parents unknown, born York County, Virginia, farmer, unmarried (*York County Register of Deaths*, York County Clerk's Office, Yorktown, Virginia).

NOTE: Presumably the "unmarried" citation refers to his status as a widower at his death.

1. Matilda FORREST: b 1843, York County, Virginia; d. s. p.

2. Mary Emily FORREST: b March 30, 1846, York County, Virginia; m January 28, 1873, John

Early Holloway, Jr. (b July 20, 1848; d March 12, 1895), the son of John Early Holloway and Harriett Ryder; d March 12, 1883, buried in the Western Cemetery, Poquoson. See next FT.1.3.2.

3. Thomas Henry FORREST: b 1849, York County, Virginia; age 9 months on July 27, 1850, according to the 1850 census); oysterman (1870); d. s. p.

4. Sarah Maria FORREST: b January 6, 1850, York County, Virginia; m January 31, 1891, Edward Henry Bradshaw, the son of William and Mary Ann Ford Bradshaw; d May 29, 1925, buried in the Western Cemetery, Poquoson.

5. Virginia G. FORREST: b May 2, 1855, York County, Virginia; m 1870, John B. Rollins (b 1847; d 1929); d February 13, 1946. See next FT.1.3.5.

6. James A. ("Abraham") FORREST: b May 15, 1855, York County, Virginia; went to sea as a young man; unknown as to when or where he died. See next FT.1.3.6.

7. Elizabeth FORREST: b 1857, York County, Virginia; d abt 1863.

8. Anne FORREST: b 1858, York County, Virginia; d abt 1863.

9. Bunevista ("Bunah") FORREST: b May 8, 1860, York County, Virginia; 7 months old when the census was taken; d October 11, 1862, buried Western Cemetery, Poquoson.

10. Indiana FORREST: b April 11, 1865, York County, Virginia; m February 19, 1881, Sidney D. Watkins (b April 1, 1858; d November 19, 1938, buried Western Cemetery), the son of Littleton and S. E. Watkins; d September 14, 1881 (sic), buried Western Cemetery. The year of death for Indiana, 1881, is listed in the *Cemeteries of Poquoson*, Volume, but the date is

obvious wrong as children are listed as being born to Indiana and Sidney as late as 1897. See next FT.1.3.10.

11. Henry D. FORREST: b February, 1867, York County, Virginia; m 1st January 6, 1887, Bunevista Quinn (this is the same Bunevista Quinn who married William Thomas "Toad" Forrest twice!); m 2nd August 6, 1898, Mary (E.) Irella Lawson (b May, 1874, York County). (1900 York County census, dwelling 352-360). See next FT.1.3.11.

12. Dorothy Susan FORREST: b York County, Virginia; m James Henry Simpson (b 1842; d 1931).

FT.1.3.2
MARY EMILY FORREST and JOHN EARLY HOLLOWAY
Of Messick, York County, Virginia

Mary Emily Forrest was born on March 30, 1846, York County, Virginia.

Miss Mary Emily Forrest married on January 28, 1873, John Early Holloway, Jr. (b July 20, 1848; d March 12, 1895), the son of John Early Holloway and Harriett Ryder. Witnesses were Elias Holloway (his half-brother) and Abraham Forrest (bride's father). John Early Holloway was a farmer and Watermen of Messick.

Mrs. Mary Emily (Forrest) Holloway died on March 12, 1883, and is buried in the Western Cemetery, Poquoson

John Early Holloway died on August 10, 1895, York County, and is buried in the Trinity Church Cemetery, Poquoson.

(*Colonial Cousins*, 1940, page 62, *Poquoson Watermen*, 1989, page 96).

1. Robert ("Bob Early") Abram HOLLOWAY: b March 16, 1875, York County, Virginia; m 1st at Trinity Church on December 25, 1879; d February 29, 1920, buried Western Cemetery, Poquoson); m 2nd on July 19, 1930, Ella Insley,

the daughter of James and Mary Insley; resided in Messick, Poquoson District, York County; d December 21, 1938, buried Western Cemetery.

2. Steven HOLLOWAY: b December, 1877, York County, Virginia; m in 1898, Annie B. ("Annabelle") Holloway, the daughter of John and Ellen Martin.

3. Agnes V. HOLLOWAY: b June 9, 1874, York County, Virginia; m C. T. Watkins; d July 20, 1895.

4. Pinkey HOLLOWAY: b February 1, 1880, York County, Virginia; d February 12, 1880, age 11 days old.

5. Mary M. HOLLOWAY: b March 13, 1883, York County, Virginia; d March 18, 1883, age 5 days old.

FT.1.3.5
VIRGINIA G. FORREST and JOHN BAILEY ROLLINS
Of Messick, Poquoson, York County, Virginia

Virginia G. Forrest was born on May 2, 1855, York County, Virginia.

Miss Virginia G. Forrest married in 1870, John B. Rollins (b September 27, 1847; d 1929), the son of Samuel Rollins and Mary L. Banks (according to Death Certificate 192668).

He was a farmer and had married 1st about 1865, Anstrus Lawson (b 1845). In 1870 and 1880, he was a farmer. They lived next door to (the present) 1474 Poquoson Avenue.

In 1870, John Rollins and family are listed in the Post Office Williamsburg. Poquoson District, York County, Virginia census, page 21, dwelling 153-162, as follows:

Rollins	John	22	m	farmer	VA
	Anstrus	25	f	keeping house	VA
	Elisha	4	m	at home	VA
	Mary E.	1	f	at home	VA

John B. Rollins married 2nd in 1875, Virginia G. Forrest (sometimes noted as Virginia F., since she was a Forrest) (b May 2, 1855; d February 13, 1946).

In 1880, John B. Rollins and family are listed in the Poquoson District, York County census, dwelling 135-135, as follows:

Rollins	John B.	head	33	VA	farmer
	Virginia	wife	22	VA	keep house
	Lishe	son	15	VA	at home
	Mary E.	daughter	12	VA	at home
	Clara B.	daughter	9	VA	at home
	Ellen O.	daughter	5	VA	at home
	R. Elmore	son	3	VA	at home
	Gabrila	daughter	1	VA	at home

John B. Rollins died on June 13, 1929. Both he and his 2nd wife, Virginia G. Forrest, are buried in the Western Cemetery on Poquoson Avenue, Poquoson, Virginia.

Children of John Rollins and his 1st wife, Anstrus Lawson:

1. Elisha ("Lishe") Mitchell ROLLINS: b 1865, York County, Virginia; d 1892 in Maryland.

2. Mary Elizabeth ROLLINS: b 1868, York County, Virginia; m Henry Ross; d 1962.

3. Clara B. ROLLINS: b 1871, Virginia.

Children of John Rollins and his 2nd wife, Virginia G. Forrest:

4. Ellen O. ROLLINS: b 1875, York County, Virginia.

5. Roman Elmore (R. Elnin) ROLLINS: b October, 1878, York County, Virginia; waterman; m in York County on April 27, 1904, Vara

Dryden, age 23, the daughter of James Dryden and Celestia Hopkins (*York County Marriage Book, No. 62*, page 16). They lived on what is currently Hudgins Road on the right hand side; d June 14, 1963.

   6. Gabrila ROLLINS: b 1879, York County, Virginia; d before 1900.

   7. Rhoda ROLLINS: b June, 1882, York County, Virginia; m Al Ketchum; d February 23, 1931.

   8. John Bailey ROLLINS: b September, 1884, York County, Virginia; m Emily Jarvis (d 1958); d 1967.

   9. Clara Belle ROLLINS: b May, 1886, York County, Virginia; m Hunter Todd; d 1967.

   10. Milford Buren ROLLINS: b September 18, 1889, York County, Virginia; m December 16, 1916, Maggie Quinn, the daughter of Thomas and Adlena (Forrest) Quinn; d 1979.

   11. Roland Royall ROLLINS: b September 3, 1892, York County, Virginia; m Emma Mathilda Bradshaw (b March 18, 1892; d April, 1976), the daughter of John Thaddus Bradshaw and Susan Wainwright; d August, 1982.

   12. Elisha Mitchell ROLLINS: b January, 1895, York County, Virginia; bp at Trinity on October 6, 1895 (*Trinity*, page 11); m Hazel Smith (d 1965) of Mathews County, Virginia; d 1978.

THE FORREST FAMILY   145

Letter from James A. Forrest to John Holloway
(for his sister Mrs. Mary Holloway)
Envelope from Amsterdam (Holland) dated
November 12, 1881

From James A. Forrest to John E. Holloway
(for his sister Mrs. Mary Holloway
Envelope Port of Monrovia (Liberia) off
West of Africa
Dated July 18, 1882

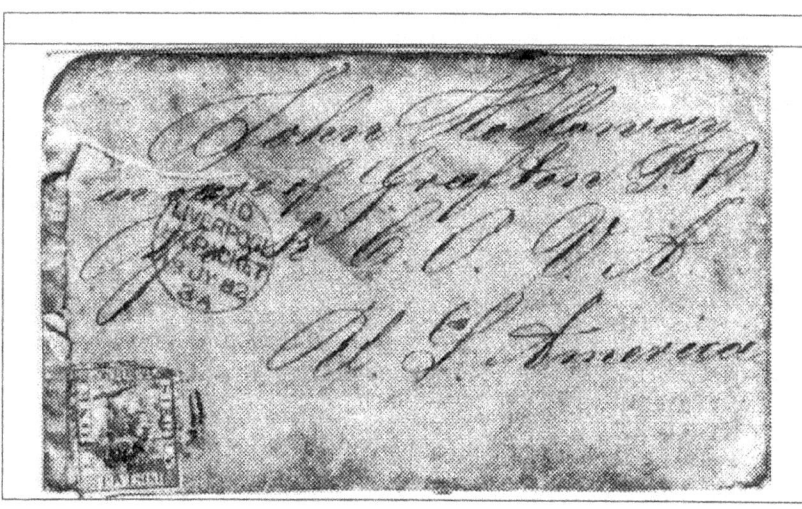

FT.1.3.6
JAMES A. FORREST
Of Poquoson, York County, Virginia

James A. ("Abraham") Forrest was born on May 15, 1855, York County, Virginia. He went to sea as a young man. In 1882, he was a sailor on the *U.S.S. Portsmouth*. James wrote many letters home from the foreign ports he was in which told of his travels all over the world.

It is unknown when or where he died.

FT.1.3.10
INDIANA FORREST and SIDNEY D. WATKINS
Of Poquoson, York County, Virginia

Indiana Forrest was born April 11, 1865, York County, Virginia.

Miss Indiana Forrest married February 19, 1881, Sidney D. Watkins (b April 1, 1858; d November 19, 1938, buried Western Cemetery), the son of Littleton and S. E. Watkins.

In 1910, Sidney D. Watkins and family are listed in the Poquoson, York County, Virginia census, dwelling 133-138, as follows:

Watkins	Sidney D.	head	51	m-27
	India	wife	48	10-3
	Elsie E.	daughter	10	
	Spencer	son	20	m-1
	Grace E.	d-i-l	18	1-1
	Nolan	gson	1/12	

Mrs. Indiana (Forrest) Watkins died September 14, 1881 (sic), and is buried in the Western Cemetery, Poquoson. The 1881 year of death for Indiana is listed in the *Cemeteries of Poquoson*, Volume, but the date is obvious wrong as children are listed as being born to Indiana and Sidney as late as 1897.

1. Henry W. WATKINS: b 1881; d 1881, buried Western Cemetery, Poquoson.

2. Sidney V. WATKINS: b 1890; d 1899, buried Western Cemetery, Poquoson.

3. Spencer WATKINS: b 1890, Virginia; m Grace E. (b 1892, Virginia).

    1. Nolan WATKINS: b 1910, York County, Virginia.

4. Tommie C. WATKINS: b 1891; d 1892, buried Western Cemetery, Poquoson.

5. Tommie L. WATKINS: b 1893; d 1894, buried Western Cemetery, Poquoson.

6. Nolian WATKINS: b 1897; d 1921, buried Western Cemetery, Poquoson.

7. Elsie E. WATKINS: b 1900, Virginia.

FT.1.3.11a
HENRY D. FORREST and BUENA VISTA QUINN
Of Poquoson, York County

Henry D. Forrest was born on February, 1867, York County, Virginia.

Henry D. Forrest married 1st on January 6, 1887, Bunevista Quinn (this is the same Buena Vista Quinn who married William Thomas Forrest twice!). Henry D. Forrest and Bunevista were divorced before 1899. No children.

FT.1.3.11b
HENRY D. FORREST and MARY IRELLA LAWSON
Of Poquoson, York County

Henry D. Forrest married 2nd on August 6, 1898, Mary (E.) Irella Lawson (b May, 1874, York County, Virginia).

In 1900 Henry D. Forrest and family are listed in the Poquoson Magisterial District, York County census, dwelling 352-360, as follows:

```
Forrest  Henry D.   head    Feb 1867  33   VA
         Mary E.    wife    May 1874  26   0-0
```

In 1910, Henry D. Forrest and family are listed in the Poquoson Township, York County, Virginia census, dwelling 174-179, as follows:

```
Forrest  Henry D.   head    42   VA m-2
         Mary E.    wife    35   VA m-1 0-0
```

CHAPTER FOUR
THE HENRY HARRY FORREST FAMILY
POQUOSON DISTRICT,
YORK COUNTY, VIRGINIA

FT.1.4
HENRY HARRY FORREST and MARY ROGERS SIMPSON
Of Poquoson, York County, Virginia

Henry Harry ("Long Henry") Forrest was born in September 22, 1818, in Mathews County, Virginia. Joe Frank Bunting stated that Thomas Humphrey Forrest was a half brother of Henry Forrest.

Henry Harry Forrest married about 1840, Mary (Polly) Rogers Simpson (b 1819 according to her tombstone or variously 1824, in Accomac County, Virginia; d September 1, 1904, age 85 years, Poquoson, York County, Virginia, buried Western Cemetery).

Henry Forrest was an oysterman (1850, 1870).

In 1850, Henry Forrest and family are listed in the York County, Virginia census, dwelling 18-18, as follows:

Forrest	Henry	31	Mathews oysterman
	Polly	28	Accomack
	James T.	9	York County
	William I.	6	York County
	Henry C.	3	York County

In 1860, Henry Forrest and family are listed in the Post Office Halfway House, York County, Virginia census, dwelling 120-120, as follows:

Forrest	Henry	head	40	sailor inland
	Polly	wife	40	
	James	son	17	sailor inland
	William	son	14	
	Cornelius	son	12	
	Mary	daughter	9	
	Virginia	daughter	6	
	Sarah	daughter	3	

              Robert   son   4/12

In 1870, Henry Forrest and family are listed in the Poquoson Township, York County, Virginia census, dwelling 138-145, as follows:

Forrest Henry   head   50   oysterman
         Polly   wife   46   keep house
         Sarah   daughter   14   at home
         Robert   son   10
         Elizabeth   daughter   7

"LONG HENRY"

In 1880, Henry Forrest and family are listed in the Poquoson District, York County, Virginia, census, dwelling 234-234, as follows:

Forrest Henry   Head   63   laborer
         Polley   wife   60   keep house
         Robt.   son   19   at home

Maria   daughter 15   at home

Henry Forrest died on August 18, 1897, and is buried in the Western Cemetery, Poquoson, Virginia.

In 1900, Polly Forrest was the head of a Poquoson Magisterial District, York County, Virginia census, dwelling 459-461, as follows:

Forrest Polly   head   Oct 1826 73   VA
        wd.   8 children 6 living (sic)

    1. James Thomas FORREST: b October 8, 1841, York County, Virginia; m in Elizabeth City County (Hampton) at St. John's Parish Church, on August 10, 1865, Lavinia Martin, the daughter of W.M. and Mary Jane Martin; d January 6, 1895, buried Western Cemetery. See next FT.1.4.1.

    2. William I. FORREST: b October 15, 1845, York County, Virginia; m January 9, 1869, Sarah Frances Watkins (September 28, 1849; d November 6, 1917, buried Tabernacle Churchyard), the daughter of Henry and Sarah Ann Linton Watkins; d May 30, 1911, buried Tabernacle Churchyard. See next FT.1.4.2.

    3. Henry Cornelius ("Eelie") FORREST: b September 8, 1847, York County, Virginia; m January 13, 1870, Virginia Emeline Hopkins (b January 12, 1852; d January 14, 1941, buried Western Cemetery); d December 8, 1919, buried Western cemetery. See next FT.1.4.3.

    4. Mary ("Polly") FORREST: b 1851, York County, Virginia.

    5. Virginia Viana FORREST: b May 8, 1853; m at St. John's Church, Hampton, Virginia, on April 16, 1870/1867, Joseph Bunting (b October 12, 1849; d January 14, 1923, buried Western Cemetery); d March 4, 1935, buried Western Cemetery.

6. Sarah Fimiah FORREST: b July 21, 1856; m July 8, 1876, Josiah Maxwell Huggett (b February 8, 1854; d October 13, 1939, buried Western Cemetery), the son of John Bonaparte and Sarah Margaret (Forrest) Huggett; d February 8, 1939. See next FT.1.4.6.

7. Robert Dolby FORREST: b March 16, 1860; m June 4, 1881, Ruhemma ("Duck") Rollins (b April, 1861; d 1932, buried Western Cemetery) (*Marriage Record No. 1, 1854-1928, York County*, page 13, line 191); d May 15, 1918, buried Western Cemetery. See next FT.1.4.7.

8. Elizabeth S: b August 10, 1862; m April 2, 1882, John H. Bradshaw (b September 10, 1860; d December 31, 1947, buried Western Cemetery) (*Marriage Record No. 1, 1854-1928, York County*, page 14, line 337); d September 1, 1950.

9. Maria FORREST: b 1865; living 1880 census. Possibly died young, as no further information.

10. L. E. FORREST: b October 15, 1877; d May 24, 1904, buried Western Cemetery.

FT.1.4.1
JAMES THOMAS FORREST and LAVINA MARTIN
Of Poquoson, York County, Virginia

James Thomas Forrest was born on October 8, 1841, in York County, Virginia.

James Thomas Forrest married 1st in St. John's Parish Church, Elizabeth City County (Hampton), on August 10, 1865, Lavina Martin (b February 10, 1852), the daughter of William M. and Mary Jane (Messick) Martin. Most likely their marriage was recorded at Ft. Monroe on August 10, 1865, as Lavinia Morgan (sic) and Thos. Forrest.

JAMES THOMAS FORREST
(Courtesy Barbara Whitlow)

In 1870, James T. Forrest and family are listed in the Poquoson Township, York County, Virginia census, dwelling 135-142, as follows:

```
Forrest  James T.     head       28  oysterman
         Lavina       wife       18  keep house
         William H.   son         4
         Mary J.      daughter    1
```

In 1880, Jas. Forrest and family are listed in the Poquoson District, York County, Virginia, census, dwelling 236-236, as follows:

```
Forrest  Jas.         Head       37  sailor
         Livina       wife       28  keep house
```

W. H.	son	14	at home
Mary	daughter	10	at home
Thos. S.	son	7	at home
John	son	5	at home
Roxanna	daughter	3	at home
Livina	daughter	1	at home

James Thomas Forrest died on January 6, 1895, and is buried in the Western Cemetery, Poquoson.

Mrs. Lavinia (Martin) Forrest married 2nd in 1899, to William H. Evans (b July, 1853); she took her four youngest daughters into the William Evans household.

In 1900, William H. Evans and family are listed in the Poquoson Magisterial District, York County, Virginia census, dwelling 450-458, as follows:

Evans	William H.	head	Jul 1853	46	m-1
	Lavenia A.	wife	Feb 1853	47	m-1
		13 children 11 living			
	Allen S.	son	Jul 1881	18	VA
	Cissella G.	daughter	Apr 1885	16	VA
Forrest	Cassie	stepdau	Dec 1883	16	VA
	Hersie	stepdau	Jul 1884	15	VA
	Maud	stepdau	Jun 1889	10	VA
	Gracie	stepdau	Oct 1891	8	VA
	Sarah M.	stepdau	Feb 1893	7	VA

Mrs. Lavina (Martin, Forrest) Evans died on December 2, 1906, and is buried in the Western Cemetery, Poquoson, York County, Virginia.

(Family Bible Record).

1. William Henry ("Buddy") FORREST: b August 2, 1866, York County, Virginia (Bible Record); m March 15, 1890, Maggie J. Quinn; d November 3, 1924, buried Western Cemetery. See next FT.1.4.1.1.

2. Mary Jane FORREST: b January 28, 1869/1867, York County, Virginia (Bible

Record); m August 18, 1888, John H. Ward; d October 10, 1929, buried Western Cemetery.

3. Thomas Lee FORREST: b December 28, 1871, York County, Virginia; m October 5, 1890, Fannie Lee Evans (b December 23, 1867); d March 30, 1958, buried Western Cemetery (Bible Record). See next FT.1.4.1.3.

4. John Samuel FORREST: b March 5, 1873, York County, Virginia (Bible Record); m January 8, 1898, Martha Imogene Chesser (d December 5, 1880; d June 3, 1971, buried Western Cemetery, Poquoson); d February 3, 1938, buried Western Cemetery. See next FT.1.4.1.4.

5. Roxanna Elizabeth FORREST: b September 15, 1877, York County, Virginia; m in York County on February 20, 1897, William D. Martin, the son of David and Julaney (Holloway) Martin; d March 17, 1945, buried Western Cemetery. See next FT.1.4.1.5.

6. Lavinia ("Van") Anne FORREST: b February 14, 1879, York County, Virginia (Bible Record); m in York County, on November 11, 1899, Elijah Franklin ("Frank") Firth (b April 5, 1878), the son of George Washington and Charlotte Temple (Insley) Firth; d July 6, 1966. See next FT.1.4.1.6.

7. Sarah Matilda FORREST: b February 27, 1881, York County, Virginia (Bible record); m October 5, 1901, James Thomas Firman; d 1964.

8. Savannah J. FORREST: b October 18, 1883, York County, Virginia; d March, 1884.

9. Savannah D. FORREST: b March 31, 1885, York County, Virginia; d March 29, 1887 (Bible record and tombstone).

10. Cassie Etta FORREST: b December 4, 1885, York County, Virginia (Bible Record); m October 18, 1902, Seth L. Ward; d 1968.

11. Hursena ("Hersie") James FORREST: b July 26, 1886, York County, Virginia (Bible Record); m January 23, 1904, Lennie Watkins, the son of Robert L. and Rachel Watkins; d December 12, 1904, buried Western Cemetery.

12. Grace ("Gracie") Virginia FORREST: b 1888, York County, Virginia; m March 27, 1909, Spencer Watkins.

13. Murdie Maud FORREST: b June 26, 1889, York County, Virginia; m September 7, 1909, Ollie Carmines, the son of W. T. and M. J. Carmines.

14. Sarah M. FORREST: b October, 1891, York County, Virginia.

FT.1.4.1.1
WILLIAM HENRY FORREST and MAGGIE J. QUINN
Of Poquoson, York County, Virginia

William Henry Forrest was born on August 2, 1866, Virginia (Bible Record).
William Henry Forrest married in March 15, 1890, Maggie J. Quinn.
In 1900, William H. Forrest and family are listed in the Poquoson Magisterial District, York County census, dwelling 332-340, as follows:

Forrest	William H.	head		Aug 1866	33	m-10
	Maggie J.	wife		May 1872	28	m-10
		4 children 2 living				
	Eskridge J.	son		Apr 1894	6	VA
	Sarah L.	daughter		Feb 1897	3	VA

In 1910, William H. Forrest and family are listed in the Poquoson, York County, Virginia census, dwelling 91-96, as follows:

| Forrest | William | head | 40 | VA | m-20 |
| | Maggie J. | wife | 38 | VA | 10-5 |

Essie J.	son	17	VA
Shellie B.	daughter	7	VA
Ersie J.	son	4	VA
Thelma J.	daughter	2	VA
Bertha M.	daughter	4/12	VA

In 1920, William Forrest and family are listed in the Poquoson Township, York County, Virginia census, dwelling 113-115, as follows:

Forrest	William	head	52	VA
	Maggie J.	wife	47	VA
	Shelie B.	daughter	17	VA
	Hersie J.	son	13	VA
	Thelma	daughter	11	VA
	Bertha M.	daughter	9	VA

William Forrest died on November 3, 1924, and is buried in the Western Cemetery.

1. Estridge ("Essie") James FORREST: b August 27, 1893, York County, Virginia; m August 29, 1914, Virginia Ann Holloway (b May, 1895, York County, Virginia), the daughter of John William and Savannah Holloway; d November 3, 1924, in the tragic bus accident. See next FT.1.4.1.1.1.

2. Sarah L. FORREST: February, 1897, York County, Virginia.

3. Shellie B. FORREST: b July 4, 1902, York County, Virginia; unmarried; d September 28, 1965.

4. Ersie ("Hurst") FORREST (twin): b 1905, York County, Virginia; m abt 1914, William Raymond Holloway (b 1914), the son of Albert James Holloway and Emily Jane Insley.

5. Thelma Wilma FORREST (twin): b 1905, York County, Virginia; m Robert Insley.

6. Bertha Maud FORREST: b January 10, 1910, Poquoson, York County, Virginia; m Lemuel

J. Insley; d March 6, 2000, age 90, Poquoson, Virginia (Bertha M. F. Insley Obituary).

    1. Lemuel J. INSLEY, Jr:

    7. Raymond B. FORREST: b November 19, 1916, York County, Virginia; d 1918, age 15 months, buried Western Cemetery.

FT.1.4.1.1.1
ESTRIDGE JAMES FORREST
And VIRGINIA ANN HOLLOWAY
Of Poquoson, York County, Virginia

    Estridge ("Essie") James Forrest was born on April 27, 1893, York County, Virginia.

    Essie James Forrest married on August 29, 1914, Virginia Ann Holloway (b May, 1895, York County, Virginia), the daughter of John William and Savannah Holloway.

    In 1920, Essie Forrest and family are listed in the Poquoson Township, York County, Virginia census, dwelling 112-114, as follows:

```
Forrest  Essie        head    24        VA
         Virginia A.  wife    24        VA
         Essie C.     son     1 11/12   VA
```

    Essie James Forrest died on November 3, 1924, in the tragic bus-train accident in Hampton.

    1. Essie C. FORREST: b 1918, York County, Virginia; m Ellender Holloway.

    2. Lyman Dan FORREST: b February 11, 1920; m 1940, Ann Watkins Forrest; d February 3, 1969, buried in the Western Cemetery, Poquoson.

    1. Ronald Dan FORREST: b January 20, 1942; d February 23, 1991, buried Western Cemetery, Poquoson.

    2. William Thomas FORREST:

FT.1.4.1.3
THOMAS LEE FORREST and FANNIE LEE EVANS
Of Poquoson, York County, Virginia

Thomas Lee Forrest was born on December 28, 1871, York County, Virginia.

Thomas Lee Forrest married on October 5, 1890, Fannie Lee Evans (b December 23, 1867).

In 1900, Thomas L. Forrest and family are listed in the Poquoson Magisterial District, York County census, dwelling 330-338, as follows:

```
Forrest  Thomas L.    head       Dec 1872  27    VA
         Fannie L.    wife       Dec 1867  32    VA
                      4 children 4 living
         Thomas C.    son        Jul 1891  8     VA
         Lavinia E.   daughter   Dec 1893  6     VA
         William J.   son        Jul 1897  2     VA
         Christine    daughter   Apr 1900  1/12  VA
```

In 1910, Thomas L. Forrest and family are listed in the Poquoson Township, York County, Virginia census, dwelling 176-181, as follows:

```
Forrest  Thomas L.    head              39   VA m-1
         Fannie L.    wife              40   VA m-1
                      6 children 6 living
         Thomas C.    son               18   VA
         Elizabeth    daughter          16   VA
         William J.   son               12   VA
         Christine    daughter          8    VA
         Raymond      son               6    VA
         Haywood E.   son               2    VA
```

Thomas Forrest died on March 30, 1958, and is buried in the Western Cemetery (Bible Record).

1. **Thomas Cornelius FORREST**: b July 26, 1891, York County, Virginia; m 1st July 13, 1912, Sadie V. Carmines (b October 15, 1887; d October 16, 1935, buried Western Cemetery); m

2nd Sylvia Dawson; d May 19, 1967, buried Western Cemetery, Poquoson.

  1. Hettie Leone FORREST: b September 7, 1913, York County, Virginia; m Warren Smith Forrest, Sr. (b March 1, 1908; d January 17, 1992).

  2. Lavinia Elizabeth FORREST: b December 16, 1893, York County, Virginia; m in Poquoson, on May 31, 1914, William James Insley (b October 5, 1891; d February 18, 1971, buried Western Cemetery), the son of Littleton J. and Virginia Insley; d March 8, 1948. See next FT.1.4.1.3.2.

  3. William Jennings FORREST: b July 12, 1897, York County, Virginia; m July 13, 1921, Lula Bell, the daughter of John and Rosie Bell.

    1. Mason FORREST:

  4. Christine Evans FORREST: b April 10, 1900, York County, Virginia; m April 11, 1925, Robert Mead Watkins, Jr.

  5. Raymond E. FORREST: b August 9, 1903, York County, Virginia; d December 17, 1919, buried Western Cemetery.

  6. Walter Haywood FORREST: b September 4, 1907, York County, Virginia; m Crystal Forrest, the daughter of Robert and Cotha Forrest. See next FT.1.4.1.3.6.

FT.1.4.1.3.2a
LAVINIA ELIZABETH FORREST
And WILLIAM JAMES INSLEY
Of Messick, Poquoson District, York County

Lavinia Elizabeth Forrest was born on December 16, 1893, York County, Virginia.

Miss Lavinia Elizabeth Forrest married in Poquoson, on May 31, 1914, William James Insley

THE FORREST FAMILY

(b October 5, 1891; d February 18, 1971, buried Western Cemetery), the son of Littleton J. and Virginia Insley (*Marriage Record No. 1, 1854-1928, York County*, page 79, line 20).

Mrs. Lavina Elizabeth (Forrest) Insley died on March 8, 1948, and is buried in the Western Cemetery, Poquoson.

1. Ethelyn INSLEY: m James Tracey; m 2nd Everett Ashburn. See next FT.1.4.1.3.2.1.

2. Garnett INSLEY: b 1916, Poquoson, Virginia; m 1st Harry Sager; m 2nd Harry Elam Holloway, the son of Hinde Holloway; d November 27, 2000, age 84, Poquoson, Virginia. See next FT.1.4.1.3.2.2.

3. Raymond INSLEY: m Roxie Lee Watkins.

William James Insley married 2nd Mollie (Forrest) Freeman, the widow of William Freeman, and the daughter of John Andrew and Alice (Rollins) Forrest.
(*Colonial Cousins*, page 59).

FT.1.4.1.3.2.1a
ETHELYN INSLEY and JAMES TRACEY

Miss Ethelyn Insley married 1st James Tracey.

1. Gerald TRACEY:

FT.1.4.1.3.2.1b
Mrs. ETHELYN INSLEY TRACEY and EVERETT ASHBURN

Mrs. Ethelyn (Insley) Tracey married 2nd Everett Ashburn.

2. Judy ASHBURN:

3. Joyce ASHBURN:

FT.1.4.1.3.2.2a
GARNETT INSLEY and HARRY SAGER

Garnett Insley was born in 1916, Poquoson, Virginia. She graduated from the Riverside Hospital School of Nursing, and retired from the Hampton Veterans, Hospital, Hampton, Virginia.

Miss Garnett Insley married 1st Harry Sager.

1. Elizabeth Obed SAGER; m 1st Murray T. Rowe; m 2nd Dennis W. Mager.

2. Mary Louise ("Bunny") SAGER: b April 9, 1944; m November 27, 1965, Eugene Thomas Forester, Jr., of Farmville, Virginia (deceased)

FT.1.4.1.3.2.2b
Mrs. GARNETT (INSLEY) SAGER
And HARRY ELAM HOLLOWAY

Mrs. Garnett (Insley) Sager married 2nd Harry Elam Holloway, the son of Hinde Holloway. She has resided, since 1991, at Imperial Plaza, Richmond, Virginia.

Mrs. Garnett (Insley Sager) Holloway died November 27, 2000, age 84, Poquoson, Virginia.

FT.1.4.1.3.6
WALTER HAYWOOD FORREST and CRYSTAL FORREST

Walter Haywood Forrest was born on September 4, 1907, York County, Virginia.

Walter Haywood Forrest married Crystal Forrest, the daughter of Robert and Cotha (Diggs) Forrest.

1. Janet Muriel FORREST: b May 22, 1930.

2. Jessie Miller FORREST: b August 30, 1931.

3. Bethany Estelle FORREST: b May 8, 1933.

4. Walter Leon FORREST: b November 28, 1934.

5. Robert Lee FORREST: b October 27, 1936.

6. Lois Anne FORREST: b May 23, 1938.

FT.1.4.1.4
JOHN SAMUEL FORREST and MARTHA IMOGENE CHESSER
Of Poquoson, York County, Virginia

John Samuel Forrest was born on March 5, 1875, York County, Virginia.

John Samuel Forrest married January 8, 1898, Martha Imogene Chesser (b December 5, 1880, York County, Virginia; d June 3, 1971, buried Western Cemetery, Poquoson, Virginia), the daughter of James and Elizabeth Chesser.

In 1900, John Sam'l Forrest and family are listed in the Poquoson Magisterial District, York County, Virginia census, dwelling 434-442, as follows:

Forrest	John Sam'l	head	Mar 1875 VA m-3
	Martha J.	wife	Dec 1880 VA 1-1
	James T.	son	Jan 1899 VA

In 1910, John S. Forrest and family are listed in the Poquoson Township, York County, Virginia census, dwelling 94-99, as follows:

Forrest	John S.	head	35	VA m-13
	Martha J.	wife	28	VA 5-5
	James T.	son	11	VA
	Bessie V.	daughter	9	VA
	Lavenia E.	daughter	6	VA
	John W.	son	3	VA
	Herman T.	son	10/12	VA

In 1920, John S. Forrest and family are listed in the Poquoson Township, York County, Virginia census, dwelling 123-125, as follows:

Forrest	John S.	head	44	VA
	Martha	wife	39	VA
	James T.	son	21	VA
	Lavenia E.	daughter	16	VA
	John	son	13	VA
	Herman T.	son	11	VA
	Nellie H.	daughter	6	VA
	Bertram E.	son	2 7/12	VA
Page	Bessie	daughter	19	VA

MRS. MARTHA IMOGENE (CHESSER) FORREST
(Courtesy Barbara Whitlow)

John Samuel Forrest died while working in his boat on the James River on February 3, 1938, and is buried in the Western Cemetery, Poquoson.

1. James Thomas FORREST: b January, 1899, York County, Virginia; m 1st March 26, 1921, Laura Rollins, the daughter of W. S. and Lavenia Rollins; 2nd Nina Peterson of Norfolk; d

January, 1973, buried Forest Lawn Cemetery, Norfolk, Virginia. See next FT.1.4.1.4.1.

    2. Bessie Viola FORREST: b January 7, 1901, York County, Virginia; m October 25, 1919, Victor Garland Page (b August 2, 1900; d January 6, 1951, buried Western Cemetery), the son of H. E. and Harriett Page; d August 20, 1983, buried Western Cemetery beside her husband. See next FT.1.4.1.4.2.

    3. Lavenia Elizabeth ("Wynie") FORREST: b November 8, 1903, York County, Virginia; m July 20, 1922, John Henry ("Buck") Forrest (b October 6, 1900; d July 3, 1981, buried Parklawn Cemetery, Hampton, Virginia); d November 24, 1976, buried Parklawn Cemetery beside her husband. See next under her husband's listing FT.1.1.7.3.6.

    4. John William FORREST: b August 28, 1907, York County, Virginia; m December 12, 1925, Birdie Golden Holloway, the daughter of Robert and Sarah Holloway. See next FT.1.4.1.4.4.

    5. Herman Taylor FORREST: b June 22, 1909, York County, Virginia; m June 16, 1937, Eva Irene Watkins, the daughter of Robert Mead Watkins and Sarah Sylvester (Toss) Forrest. See next FT.1.4.1.4.5.

    6. Eleanor ("Nell"/"Nellie") Hartness FORREST: b November 2, 1913, York County, Virginia; m in Fox Hill, Hampton, Virginia, on January 16, 1936, Thomas Hudgins (b January 22, 1910; d March 13, 1962). See next FT.1.4.1.4.6.

    7. Bertram ("Bert") Ellsworth FORREST: b April 2, 1917, Poquoson, York County, Virginia; m Florence Rideout; d December 31, 1999, Poquoson, Virginia (Bertram A. E. Forrest Obituary). See next FT.1.4.1.4.7.

FT.1.4.1.4.1
JAMES THOMAS FORREST and LAURA ROLLINS

James Thomas Forrest, was born January, 1899, York County, Virginia.

James Thomas Forrest married 1st on March 26, 1921, Laura Rollins, the daughter of W. S. and Lavenia Rollins.

JAMES THOMAS FORREST
(Courtesy Barbara Whitlow)

James Thomas Forrest married 2nd Nina Peterson of Norfolk.

James Thomas Forrest died in January, 1973, and is buried in the Forest Lawn Cemetery, Norfolk, Virginia

1. Thomas Edwin FORREST:

1. Caroline FORREST:

FT.1.4.1.4.2
BESSIE VIOLA FORREST and VICTOR GARLAND PAGE

Bessie Viola Forrest was born on January 7, 1901, York County, Virginia.

Miss Bessie Viola Forrest married on October 25, 1919, Victor Garland Page (b August 2, 1900; d January 6, 1951, buried Western Cemetery), the son of H. E. and Harriett Page.

Mrs. Bessie Viola (Forrest Page died August 20, 1983, and is buried in the Western Cemetery beside her husband.

1. John Fay PAGE (twin): b September 5, 1920; m February 15, 1941, Josephine Simpson Ward (b June 24, 1920; d May 27, 1976), the daughter of Andrew K. Ward and Ida J. Pauls; d April 12, 1986. See next FT.1.4.1.4.2.1.

2. Henry Gray PAGE (twin): b September 5, 1920; d approximately March, 1921 (6 months old).

3. Henry Gordon PAGE: b April 14, 1929; m April 29, 19--, Matilda Elizabeth Graham (b March 18, 1927) of Poquoson, Virginia. See next FT.1.4.1.4.2.3.

FT.1.4.1.4.2.1
JOHN FAY PAGE and JOSEPHINE SIMPSON WARD

John Fay Page (twin) was born on September 5, 1920.

John Fay Page married on February 15, 1941, Josephine Simpson Ward (b June 24, 1920;

d May 27, 1976), the daughter of Andrew K. Ward and Ida J. Pauls.

John Fay Page died on April 12, 1986.

1. Jean Gray PAGE: b January 12, 1942; m January 28, 1961, Dallas C. Gibbons (b March 6, 1939), the son of Benjamin G. Gibbons and Bernice Bonniwell of Hampton, Virginia.

    1. John Garland GIBBONS: b July 4, 1962; m November 24, 1984, Kelly M. Manning, the daughter of Mr. And Mrs. Cecil Manning of Hampton, Virginia.

    2. Thomas Page GIBBONS: b June 19, 1965.

2. Victor Fay PAGE: b December 31, 1950; m April 13, 1968, Pamela Kay Brown (b February 25, 1951), the daughter of R.C. Brown and Emma F. Rogers of Wilmington, North Carolina.

    1. Stephanie Ann PAGE: b December 11, 1981.

3. Jill Ann PAGE: b September 22, 1953; m June 1, 1974, Vincent (NMN) Figuenick, the son of Anthony Figuenick and Nellie Opal Sizemore of West Haven, Connecticut.

    1. Vincent Anthony FIGUENICK: b May 21, 1982.

    2. Elizabeth Anne FIGUENICK: b March 19, 1984.

FT.1.4.1.4.2.3
HENRY GORDON PAGE and MATILDA ELIZBAETH GRAHAM

Henry Gordon Page was born on April 14, 1929.

Henry Gordon Page married on April 29, 194-, Matilda Elizabeth Graham (b March 18, 1927) of Poquoson, Virginia.

1. Margaret Ann PAGE: b March 2, 1948; m 1st James Miskell; m 2nd Tony Current; m 3rd William Kennedy; m 4th Coates.

    1. Christina Ann KENNEDY: b January 21, 1977.

    2. Shane Gordon KENNEDY: died at 4 months of age of crib death.

2. Dennis Gordon PAGE: b April 26, 1956; m 1st Marilyn Rondeau; m 2nd Kimberly A. Moore.

    1. Eric Gordon PAGE: (son of Dennis Page and Marilyn Rondeau.

FT.1.4.1.4.4
JOHN WILLIAM FORREST and BIRDIE HOLLOWAY

John William Forrest was born on August 28, 1907, York County, Virginia.

John William Forrest married on December 12, 1925, Birdie Golden Holloway, the daughter of Robert and Sarah Holloway. He worked as an inspector in the Newport News Shipbuilding and Dry Company, Newport News, Virginia.

1. Eleanor Dale FORREST: b January 30, 1927, Messick, Poquoson, York County, Virginia; m May 11, 1946, Henderson Forrest. See next FT.1.4.1.4.4.1.

2. William ("Bill") Warren FORREST: b December 22, 1929, Messick, Poquoson, York County, Virginia; attended Messick Road School,

Poquoson; m December 30, 1950, Harriet Lane Page (b July 18, 1930); Bill is in marine engineering. See next FT.1.4.1.4.4.2.

3. Rose Doloris FORREST: b March 16, 1936, Messick, Poquoson, York County, Virginia; m September 18, 1954, Carlton Page Forrest (b October 4, 1934), the son of Raymond S. and Margaret Hogg Forrest; d November 12, 2000. See next FT.1.4.1.4.4.3.

FT.1.4.1.4.4.1
ELEANOR DALE FORREST and HENDERSON FORREST

Eleanor Dale Forrest was born on January 30, 1929, Messick, Poquoson, York County, Virginia.

Miss Eleanor Dale Forrest married May 11, 1946, Henderson Forrest.

1. Myrna Gail FORREST: b May 21, 1947; m January 5, 1967, Franklin Wechsler.

    1. Terri Lynn WECHSLER: b August 31, 1968.

    2. Bethany Michelle WECHSLER: b January 10, 1972.

    3. Jason Franklin WECHSLER: b December 19, 1973.

FT.1.4.1.4.4.2
WILLIAM WARREN FORREST and HARRIET LANE PAGE
Of Poquoson, Virginia

William ("Bill") Warren Forrest was born on December 22, 1929, Messick, Poquoson, York County, Virginia. He attended Messick Road School, Poquoson.

William Warren Forrest married on December 30, 1950, Miss Harriet Lane Page (b July 18, 1930). Bill is in marine engineering.

1. Martha Ann FORREST: b August 11, 1958, Dixie Hospital, Hampton, Virginia; m February 14, 1987, Peter John Watson (b November 14, 1945).

    1. Ian Trevor WATSON: b August 18, 1988.

2. William Bryan FORREST: b March 28, 1962, Dixie Hospital, Hampton, Virginia; m October 1, 1994, Laura Rigger.

    1. Dyland Riley FORREST: b November 23, 1999.

FT.1.4.1.4.4.3
ROSE DOLORIS FORREST and CARLTON PAGE FORREST

Rose Doloris Forrest was born on March 16, 1936, Messick, Poquoson, York County, Virginia.

Miss Rose Doloris Forrest married on September 18, 1954, Carlton Page Forrest (b October 4, 1934), the son of Raymond S. and Margaret Hogg Forrest.

Mrs. Rose Doloris (Forrest) Forrest died on November 12, 2000.

1. Gregory FORREST: b February 7, 1959.

2. Kimberley ("Kim") Page FORREST: b August 30, 1966.

FT.1.4.1.4.5
HERMAN TAYLOR FORREST and EVA IRENE WATKINS

Herman Taylor Forrest was born on June 22, 1909, York County, Virginia.

Herman Taylor Forrest married on June 16, 1937, Eva Irene Watkins, the daughter of Robert Mead Watkins and Sarah Sylvester ("Toss") Forrest.

1. Florence Fae FORREST: b November 6, 1938; m June 16, 1961, Amos Jefferson Mungo (b May 19, 1935). See next FT.1.4.1.4.5.1.

2. Bettie Taylor FORREST: b June 6, 1941; m 1st James Walker; m 2nd Terry Sharp. See next FT.1.4.1.4.5.2.

FT.1.4.1.4.5.1
FLORENCE FAE FORREST and AMOS JEFFERSON MUNGO

Florence Fae Forrest was born on November 6, 1938.

Miss Florence Fae Forrest married June 16, 1961, Amos Jefferson Mungo (b May 19, 1935).

1. Scott Jefferson MUNGO: b May 14, 1962.

2. Eric Thomas MUNGO: b March 5, 1964.

   1. Erin Carol MUNGO: b August 29, 1989.

3. Steven Keith MUNGO: b February 22, 1971.

FT.1.4.1.4.5.2a
BETTIE TAYLOR FORREST and JAMES WALKER

Bettie Taylor Forrest was born on June 6, 1941.

Miss Bettie Taylor Forrest married 1st James Walker.

1. James Taylor WALKER: b August 29, 1963.

    1. Ashley Loren WALKER: b November 18, 1988.

    2. Taylor Anne WALKER: b May 30, 1990.

    3. Logan Alayna WALKER: b September 28, 1994.

    4. James Cole WALKER: b November 29, 1996.

2. Shannon Luv WALKER: b September 22, 1974.

FT.1.4.1.4.5.2b
BETTIE TAYLOR (FORREST) WALKER and TERRY SHARP

Mrs. Bettie James (Forrest) Walker married 2nd Terry Sharp.

FT.1.4.1.4.6
ELEANOR HARTNESS FORREST and THOMAS HUDGINS

Eleanor ("Nell") Hartness Forrest was born on November 2, 1913, York County, Virginia.

Miss Eleanor H. Forrest married in Fox Hill, Hampton, Virginia, on January 16, 1936, Thomas Hudgins (b January 22, 1910; d March 13, 1962). He was a produce manager at Langley and also worked at the A & P and Wells Grocery in Buckroe, Virginia.

MRS. ELEANOR HARTNESS (FORREST) HUDGINS
(Courtesy Barbara Whitlow)

1. Thomas Clifton HUDGINS, Jr: b May 5, 1938; m Dorothy Meryle Forrest (b May 31, 1938).

1. Diane Lynne HUDGINS: b December 26, 1958; m February 4, 1980, Robert Taylor Holloway, Jr.

    1. Robert Taylor HOLLOWAY, III:

2. Barbara Jane HUDGINS: b October 3, 1942, Hampton, Virginia; m at Trinity Methodist Church, Poquoson, Virginia, June 17, 1961, Paul Anthony Whitlow (b September 27, 1940, Jarratt, Virginia). See next FT.1.4.1.4.6.2.

FT.1.4.1.4.6.2
BARBARA JANE HUDGINS and PAUL ANTHONY WHITLOW
Of Poquoson, Virginia

Barbara Jane Hudgins was born on October 3, 1942, in the "old" Dixie Hospital, Hampton, Virginia.

Miss Barbara Jane Hudgins married at Trinity Methodist Church, Poquoson, Virginia, on June 17, 1961, Paul Anthony Whitlow (b September 27, 1940, Jarratt, Virginia), the son of Elizabeth and Paul L. Whitlow.

1. Paul Anthony WHITLOW, Jr: b March 8, 1962, Dixie Hospital, Hampton, Virginia; m September 6, 1986, Patricia Parise, the daughter of Ralph and Tina Parise. See next FT.1.4.1.4.6.2.1.

2. Kimberly Anne WHITLOW: b October 6, 1964, Riverside Hospital, Newport News, Virginia; m 1st Charles Michael Merchant; m 2nd January 16, 1998, Edward Charles Herb, Jr. See next FT.1.4.1.4.6.2.2.

3. Natalie Lynne WHITLOW; b March 22, 1968, Riverside Hospital, Newport News, Virginia; m July 22, 1989, Richard Thomas Cannella. See next FT.1.4.1.4.6.2.3.

FT.1.4.1.4.6.2.1
PAUL ANTHONY WHITLOW, JR., and PATRICIA PARISE

Paul Anthony Whitlow, Jr., was born on March 8, 1962.

Paul Anthony Whitlow, Jr., married on September 6, 1986, Patricia Parise, the daughter of Ralph and Tina Parise of Aliquippa, Pennsylvania.

1. Meagan Elizabeth WHITLOW: b March 27, 1989.

2. Lauren Marie WHITLOW: b June 16, 1991.

3. Victoria Lynne WHITLOW: b May 5, 1994.

4. Toni-Anne WHITLOW: b November 22, 1997.

FT.1.4.1.4.6.2.2a
KIMBERLY ANNE WHITLOW
And CHARLES MICHAEL MERCHANT

Kimberly Anne Whitlow was born October 6, 1964.

Miss Kimberly Anne Whitlow married 1st Charles Michael Merchant

1. Michael Anthony MERCHANT: b February 27, 1987.

FT.1.4.1.4.6.2.2b
Mrs. KIMBERLY ANNE (WHITLOW) MERCHANT
And EDWARD CHARLES HERB, Jr.

Mrs. Kimberly Anne (Whitlow) Merchant married 2nd January 16, 1998, Edward Charles Herb, Jr.

2. William Preston Daniel HERB: b May 31, 1999.

FT.1.4.1.4.6.2.3
NATALIE LYNNE WHITLOW
And RICHARD THOMAS CANNELLA

Natalie Lynne Whitlow was born on March 22, 1968.

Miss Natalie Lynne Whitlow married July 22, 1989, Richard Thomas Cannella.

1. Richard Thomas CANNELLA, II: b February 15, 1996.

2. Travis Ryan CANNELLA: b October 20, 1997.

FT.1.4.1.4.7
BERTRAM ELLSWORTH FORREST and FLORENCE RIDEOUT
Of Poquoson, York County, Virginia

Bertram ("Bert") Ellsworth Forrest was born on April 2, 1917, Poquoson, Virginia.

Bertram Ellsworth Forrest married Florence Rideout. He was a waterman and retired as a pipefitter and welder for Local 540. He was a member of Masonic Lodge AF & AM No. 49, 32nd Degree Scottish Rite and a former Knights of Pithias Lodge No. 161.

Bertram Ellsworth Forrest died on December 31, 1999, Poquoson, Virginia (Bertram E. Forrest Obituary).

1. David Warren FORREST: m Joan Meadows. See next FT.1.4.1.4.7.1.

2. John Samuel FORREST: b September 13, 1953. See next FT.1.4.1.4.7.2.

FT.1.4.1.4.7.1
DAVID WARREN FORREST and JOAN MEADOWS

David Warren Forrest married Joan Meadows.

1. David Warren FORREST, II: b August 16, 1966; m February 15, 1989, Lisa Kay Crawford (b October 21, 1969).

    1. Savannah Leigh FORREST: b August 30, 1989.

    2. David James FORREST: b December 19, 1991.

2. Marty Louise FORREST: b April 6, 1969; m Gregory James Anderson.

    1. Cooper Forrest ANDERSON: b November 18, 1998.

    2. Blake Gordon ANDERSON: b March 7, 2000.

FT.1.4.1.4.7.2
JOHN SAMUEL FORREST

John Samuel Forrest was born on September 13, 1953.
John Samuel Forrest has the following child:

1. John Samuel FORREST, II: b November 24, 1973; m August 1, 1992, Christina Widener (b February 2, 1974).

    1. Taylor Nicole FORREST: b December 15, 1995.

    2. Madison McKenzie FORREST: b June 6, 1998.

FT.1.4.1.5
ROXANNA ELIZABETH FORREST and WILLIAM D. MARTIN
Of York County, Virginia

Roxanna Elizabeth Forrest was born on September 15, 1877, York County, Virginia.

Miss Roxanna Elizabeth Forrest married in York County on February 20, 1897, William D. Martin, the son of David and Julaney (Holloway) Martin (b March 24, 1875, at Messick Point, Poquoson District, York County, Virginia) (*Marriage Record No. 1, 1854-1928, York County*, page 49, line 9).

They lived on Messick Road close to Bell Lane.

The 1900 Poquoson Magisterial District, York County, Virginia, census, dwelling 466-474, taken June 27, 1900, lists William Martin, age 23, married 3 years, and family as follows:

```
Martin   William      Head     Mar 1877  23
         Rosanna E    wife     Sep 1876  23
         John L.      son      Jul 1898  1
         Julania      mother   Aug 1831  68, Wd
```

On July 16, 1903, W. D. Martin, born March 24, 1875, waterman, registered to vote in the Poquoson Precinct of York County, Virginia (*Voters Registration Book, Poquoson Precinct, York County, Virginia*).

The 1910 Poquoson District, York County, Virginia, census, dwelling 92-97, lists William D. Martin, and family as follows:

```
Martin   William D    head       33   M-1 13   VA
         Rosanna      wife       33   M-1 13   VA
         John L.      son        11            VA
         William C    son         9            VA
         Laura B      daughter    3            VA
```

The 1920 York County, census, dwelling 116-118, lists William Martin, age 42, and family as follows:

Martin	William	head	42
	Roxanna E	wife	43
	Laura B	daughter	13
	Thomas D	son	5

Mrs. Roxanna Elizabeth (Forrest) Martin died on March 17, 1945, and is buried in the Western Cemetery, Poquoson, Virginia.

(*Colonial Cousins*, page 50; *Trinity*, page 9).

1. John Linwood MARTIN: b July, 1898, York County, Virginia; m in Newport News on July 4, 1917, Elsie Watkins (b 1898), the daughter of S. O. and Indiana Watkins (*Marriage Record No. 1, 1854-1928, York County*, page 92, line 24); resided in Messick, Virginia.

2. William Colbert MARTIN: b 1901, York County, Virginia; bp 1902 at Trinity Church (*Trinity*, page 46); m Ethel; buried Western Cemetery.

3. Laura Beatrice MARTIN: b 1907, York County, Virginia; m at Jeffs, Poquoson, on April 4, 1925, Harvey Taylor Moore, the son of T. J. and Rhoda L. Moore (*Marriage Record No. 1, 1854-1928, York County*, page 98, line 19); resided on the corner of Bell Lane and Messick Road; her father lived next door.

4. Thomas D. MARTIN: b 1915, York County, Virginia; m Carrie Moore, the daughter of Alex Moore and Nancy Wainwright; resided Messick, Virginia; living (1986) in Florida.

FT.1.4.1.6
LAVINIA ANNE FORREST
And ELIJAH FRANK FIRTH
Of Messick, Poquoson, York County

Lavinia ("Van") Anne Forrest was born on February 14, 1879, York County, Virginia (Bible Record).

Miss Lavinia Forrest married in York County, on November 11, 1899, Elijah Frank Firth (b April 5, 1878, York County, Virginia, Virginia; d August 20, 1950, buried Western Cemetery), the son of George Washington and Charlotte Temple (Insley) Firth.

They lived on the "Back Road from Messick Point to main Poquoson Road" (1910) (now Ridge Road).

In 1910, Elijah F. Firth and family are listed in the Poquoson, York County, Virginia census, dwelling 74-77, as follows:

Firth	Elijah F.	head	32	m-1 10
	Lavinia A.	wife	29	m-1 10
5-3				
	Beulah	daughter	10	s
	Cora L.	daughter	7	s
	Charlotte T.	daughter	1 4/12	s

Mrs. Lavinia (Forrest) Firth died on July 6, 1966.

(*Colonial Cousins*, page 78).

1. Beluah FIRTH: b September 2, 1900, Messick; m July 18, 1920, John Bunyan Forrest, Sr. (d 1963, age 74, buried Parklawn Cemetery); resides 122 Forrest Road, Poquoson, Virginia. See next FT.1.1.6.4.4.

2. Cora Lee FIRTH: b January 1, 1903, York County, Virginia; m at Yorktown on November 29, 1928, Ira Smith, age 27, farmer, the son of Isaac Smith and Mary E. Hunt (*Marriage Record No. 1, 1854-1928, York County*, page 105, line 52); resided Poquoson.

3. Charlotte Temple FIRTH: b December 21, 1908; m Reverend Clinton Trayham Topping (b September, 1902, York County, Virginia).

4. Carolyn Forrest FIRTH: b August 6, 1918, York County, Virginia; unmarried (1988).

FT.1.4.2
WILLIAM I. FORREST and SARAH FRANCES WATKINS
Of Poquoson, York County, Virginia

William I. Forrest was born on October 15, 1845, Virginia.

William I. Forrest married January 9, 1868, Sarah Frances Watkins (b September 28, 1849; d November 6, 1917, buried Tabernacle Churchyard), the daughter of Henry and Sarah Ann Watkins. He was a oysterman (1870) and a sailor (1880).

In 1870, Wm. I. Forrest and family are listed in the Poquoson Township, York County, Virginia census, dwelling 139-147, as follows:

Forrest	Wm. I.	head	24	oysterman
	Sarah	wife	20	keep house
	Mary C.	daughter	1	

In 1880, Wm. I. Forrest and family are listed in the Poquoson District, York County, Virginia, census, dwelling 232-232, as follows:

Forrest	Wm. I.	Head	35	sailor
	Sarah	wife	32	keeping house
	Mary C.	daughter	11	at home
	J. H.	son	10	at home
	Wm.	son	6	at home
	Sarah	daughter	4	at home
	M. J.	daughter	1	at home

In 1900, William I. Forrest and family are listed in the Poquoson Magisterial District, York County census, dwelling 307-314, as follows:

Forrest	William I.	head	Oct 1845	54	m-33
	Sarah F.	wife	Sep 1849	50	9-6
	Mary C.	daughter	Nov 1869	30	VA
	Robert M.	son	Feb 1881	19	VA
	Larry P.	son	Dec 1882	17	VA
	Claytor C.	son	Oct 1885	14	VA
	Bertha	daughter	Feb 1889	11	VA

In 1910, William I. Forrest and family are listed in the Poquoson Township, York County, Virginia census, dwelling 239-244, as follows:

Forrest	William I.	head	64	VA m-1	
	Sarah F.	wife	60	VA m-1	9-6
	Bertha	daughter	21	VA	

William I. Forrest died on May 30, 1911, and is buried in the Tabernacle United Methodist Churchyard, Poquoson, Virginia.

1. Mary Celestia ("Lessie") FORREST: b November 12, 1868, York County, Virginia; m September 10, 1907, Alonzo Topping, the son of Bennett and Missie Topping; no issue; d July 18, 1946, buried Tabernacle United Methodist Churchyard Cemetery.

2. John Henry FORREST: b March 4, 1871, York County, Virginia; m December 25, 1897, Mary Elizabeth Callis (b May 8, 1873; d October 28, 1938), the daughter of D.G. and Martha E. Callis; d October 2, 1930, buried Tabernacle United Methodist Churchyard. See next FT.1.4.2.2.

2. William Thomas FORREST: b April 26, 1873, York County, Virginia; unmarried; d October 11, 1889, buried in the Trinity United Methodist Church Cemetery.

3. Sarah F. FORREST: b March 14, 1876, York County, Virginia; d September 28, 1889, buried in the Trinity Church United Methodist Cemetery, Poquoson.

4. Missouri Jane FORREST: b February 14, 1879, York County, Virginia; d October 1, 1889, buried in the Trinity United Methodist Church Cemetery.

5. Robert Mead FORREST: b February, 1881, York County, Virginia; m Lillian Dean; a shoe Merchant of Norfolk, Virginia; resided Raleigh Avenue, Norfolk. See next FT.1.4.2.5.

6. Leroy ("Larry") P. FORREST: b December, 1882, York County, Virginia: m November 28, 1903, Mary Vergie Forrest (b September, 1886), the daughter of Frank and Emma Forrest; d 1970, and is buried in Parklawn Memorial Cemetery, Hampton. See next FT.1.4.2.6.

8. Claytor C. FORREST: b October, 1885, York County, Virginia; m October 27, 1906, Virginia Bell Insley, the daughter of Littleton and Virginia Chenault Insley. See next FT.1.4.2.8.

9. Bertha FORREST: b February 21, 1891, York County, Virginia; m January 1, 1911, Edward Freeman, the son of J. W. and Hester Freeman; resided Jeffs, Poquoson, Virginia; d February 18, 1948.

FT.1.4.2.2
JOHN HENRY FORREST and MARY ELIZABETH CALLIS
Of Poquoson, York County, Virginia

John Henry Forrest was born on March 4, 1871, York County, Virginia.

John Henry Forrest married on December 25, 1897, Mary Elizabeth Callis (b May 8, 1873; d October 28, 1938), the daughter of Daniel G. and Martha Eliza Callis.

In 1910, John H. Forrest and family are listed in the Poquoson Magisterial District, York County, Virginia census, dwelling 455-463, as follows:

Forrest	John H.	head	Mar 1871	29
	Mary E.	wife	May 1873	27 VA
		m-2, 1 child 1 living		
	Asa	son	Dec 1899	5/12

In 1910, John H. Forrest and family are listed in the Poquoson Township, York County, Virginia census, dwelling 241-246, as follows:

Forrest	John H.	head	38	VA m-1
	Mary E.	wife	37	VA m-1 2-2
	Asa	son	10	VA
	William T.	son	2	VA

He was a substantial citizen and a prominent Methodist laymen of Jeffs, Poquoson.

John Henry Forrest died on October 2, 1930, and is buried in the Tabernacle Church Cemetery, Poquoson, Virginia.

1. Asa FORREST: b December, 1899, York County, Virginia, Virginia, according to 1910 York County census, born February 2, 1900, according to his tombstone; m Catherine Harvey; d August 20, 1940, buried Western Cemetery, Poquoson, Virginia.

2. William Taylor FORREST: b 1908, York County, Virginia; resided Fox Hill, Hampton.

FT.1.4.2.5
ROBERT MEAD FORREST and LILLIAN DEAN
Of Norfolk, Virginia

Robert Mead Forrest was born on February, 1881, York County, Virginia.

Robert Mead Forrest married Lillian Dean. He was a shoe Merchant of Norfolk, Virginia, and resided on Raleigh Avenue, Norfolk.

1. John Wilkins FORREST: m Adeline Hitt.

   1. John Wilkins FORREST, Jr:

2. Robert Mead FORREST:

FT.1.4.2.6
LEROY P. FORREST and MARY VERGIE FORREST
Of Poquoson, York County, Virginia

Leroy ("Larry") P. Forrest was born in December, 1882, York County, Virginia.

Leroy P. Forrest married on November 28, 1903, Mary Vergie Forrest (b September, 1886), the daughter of Frank and Emma Forrest.

In 1910, Leroy P. Forrest and family are listed in the Poquoson Township, York County, Virginia census, dwelling 271-278, as follows:

```
Forrest  Leroy P.   head   25  VA  m-1
         Mary V.    wife   23  VA  m-1 1-1
         David T.   son     4  VA
```

Leroy P. Forrest died in 1970, and is buried in the Parklawn Memorial Cemetery, Hampton, Virginia.

1. David T. FORREST: b 1906, York County, Virginia; m Hazel Eppes.

    1. Billie Dove FORREST:

    2. David J. FORREST:

2. William FORREST:

FT.1.4.2.8
CLAYTOR C. FORREST and VIRGINIA BELL INSLEY
Of Poquoson, York County, Virginia

Claytor C. Forrest was born on October, 1885, York County, Virginia.

Claytor C. Forrest married on October 27, 1906, Virginia ("Jennie") Bell Insley, the daughter of Littleton and Virginia Chenault Insley.

In 1910, Claytor C. Forrest and family are listed in the Poquoson Township, York County, Virginia census, dwelling 240-245, as follows:

```
Forrest  Claytor C. head    23   VA m-1
         Virginia B. wife   23   VA m-1 1-1
         William J. son      2   VA
```

Later, they moved to Hampton, Virginia.

1. William John FORREST: b 1908, York County, Virginia.

2. Doris FORREST: m Judson Black; residence Hampton, Virginia

3. Sarah FORREST:

4. Mildred FORREST:

FT.1.4.3
HENRY CORNELIUS FORREST
And VIRGINIA EMELINE HOPKINS
Of Poquoson, York County, Virginia

Henry Cornelius ("Eelie") Forrest was born on September 8, 1847, in York County, Virginia.

Henry Cornelius Forrest married on January 13, 1870, Virginia Emeline Hopkins (b January 12, 1852; d January 14, 1941, buried Western Cemetery). He was an oysterman (1870).

In 1870, Henry C. Forrest and family are listed in the Poquoson Township, York County, Virginia census, dwelling 139-146, as follows:

Forrest	Henry C.	head	22	oysterman
	Virginia	wife	19	keep house

In 1880, Cornelius Forrest and family are listed in the Poquoson District, York County, Virginia, census, dwelling 233-233, as follows:

Forrest	Cornelius	Head	30	sailor
	Virginia	wife	30	keeping house
	Annie	daughter	10	at home
	James H.	son	6	at home
	Maria	daughter	4	at home
	Samuel	son	3	at home
	Robert S.	son	10/12	at home

In 1900 Henry Cornelius Forrest and family are listed in the Poquoson Magisterial District, York County, Virginia census, dwelling 316-324, as follows:

Forrest	Henry Cornelius,	head	Sep 1849	50	VA
	Virginia E.	wife	Jun 1852	48	VA
	10 children 8 living				
	Lemuel	son	Oct 1878	21	VA
	Robert L.	son	Jan 1881	19	VA
	William W.	son	May 1882	18	VA
	Stewart M.	son	Sep 1884	15	VA
	Andrew C.	son	Jul 1887	12	VA
	Annie J.	daughter	Mar 1890	10	VA
	Virgie E.	daughter	Apr 1893	7	VA

In 1910, Henry C. Forrest and family are listed in the Poquoson Township, York County, Virginia census, dwelling 233-238, as follows:

Forrest	Henry C.	head	60	VA m-1
	Virginia	wife	58	VA m-1
	10 children-7 living			
	Stewart M.	son	23	VA
	Andrew C.	son	20	VA
	Annie J.	daughter	19	VA
	Virgie E.	daughter	17	VA

Henry Forrest died on December 8, 1919, and is buried in the Western Cemetery, Poquoson.

1. Annie FORREST: b 1870, York County, Virginia.

2. James H. FORREST: b 1874, York County, Virginia; d January 12, 1889.

3. Dorothy Maria FORREST: b April 14, 1875, York County, Virginia; m November 14, 1896, Albert McHenry Firth (February 12, 1873; d September 25, 1951), the son of George Firth; d June 25, 1946. See next FT.1.4.3.3.

4. Lemuel FORREST: b October 14, 1878, York County, Virginia; d May 24, 1941, buried Western Cemetery, Poquoson.

5. Robert L. FORREST: b January, 1881, York County, Virginia.

6. William W. FORREST: May, 1882, York County, Virginia; m in 1908, Ruth V. (b 1890); d abt 1955. See next FT.1.4.3.6.

7. Stewart M. FORREST: b September, 1884, York County, Virginia; d abt 1925.

8. Andrew C. FORREST: b July 3, 1887, York County, Virginia; m August 16, 1913, Maggie L. Riggins (b June 15, 1898; d December 15, 1958),

the daughter of Alex and Mattie Riggins; d May 13, 1948. See next FT.1.4.3.8.

9. Annie J. FORREST: b March, 1890, York County, Virginia; m Charles I. Dyson.

10. Vergie E. FORREST: b April, 1893, York County, Virginia; m Earl S. Holloway, the son of Smith Holloway and Rosanna Wilson; d 1980, buried Parklawn Memorial Park, Hampton, Virginia.

11. Alice B. HOPKINS FORREST (adopted): b 1896, York County, Virginia.

FT.1.4.3.3
DOROTHY MARIA FORREST and ALBERT MCHENRY FIRTH
Of Messick, Poquoson, York County

Dorothy Maria Forrest was born on April 14, 1875, York County, Virginia.
Miss Dorothy Maria Forrest married on November 14, 1896, Albert McHenry Firth (February 12, 1873; d September 25, 1951), the son of George Firth (*Marriage Record No.1, 1854-1928, York County*, page 48, line 43).
In 1900, Albert M. Firth and family are listed in the Poquoson Magisterial District, York County, Virginia census, dwelling 315-323, as follows:

Firth	Albert M.	head	Feb 1870	30	m-4
	Dorothy M.	wife	Apr 1875	25	1-1
	Eura A.	daughter	Sep 1897	2	

In 1910, Albert M. Firth and family are listed in the York County, Virginia census, dwelling 234-239, as follows:

Firth	Albert M.	head	38	m-1 13	
	Dorothy M.	wife	35	m-1 13	5-5
	Ura A.	daughter	12		
	Mattie L.	daughter	9		
	Virginia	daughter	6		

            Virgie B.   daughter   4
            John L.   son   1 8/12

Mrs. Dorothea M. (Forrest) Firth died on June 25, 1946.

Albert McHenry died on September 26, 1951, and is buried in a private plot in the Western Cemetery, Poquoson, Virginia.

1. Eura ("Ura") A. FIRTH: b September, 1897, York County, Virginia; m in Messick on January 6, 1915, Lance M. Bradshaw, age 24, the son of John T. and Susan Y. Bradshaw (*Marriage Record No. 1, 1854-1928, York County*, page 80, line 1).

2. Mattie Lee FIRTH: b 1901, York County, Virginia; between March 28, and April 20, 1920, a marriage license was taken out by Gerald J. Patesel, age 23, born Marshall County, Indiana, the son of Richard and Lucy Patesel, and Mattie Lee Firth, age 19 (however there is no record of the marriage being performed, *Marriage Record No. 1, 1854-1928*, York County, page 90, line 24); m on February 7, 1927 (also recorded as August 11, 1928), Lemuel Lynwood Bradshaw, age 29, waterman, the son of John Lemuel and Rosanna Bradshaw (*Marriage Record No.1, 1854-1928, York County*, page 102, line 7, and page 104, line 22).

3. Virginia T. FIRTH: b 1904, York County, Virginia; m Allen Loper.

4. Virgie Belle FIRTH: b 1906, York County, Virginia.

5. John Lemuel FIRTH: b 1908, York County, Virginia; bp September 29, 1909, at Trinity (Trinity , page 48); m Murdie Carmines, the daughter of Hope and Bertha Carmines.

6. Alvin FIRTH: m Catherine.

FT.1.4.3.6
WILLIAM W. FORREST and RUTH V.
Of Poquoson, York County, Virginia

William W. Forrest was born in May, 1882, York County, Virginia.

William W. Forrest married in 1908, Ruth V. (b 1890).

In 1910, William W. Forrest and family are listed in the York County, Virginia census, dwelling 237-242, as follows:

```
Forrest  William W.  head   28      m-1 2      VA
         Ruth V.     wife   20      m-1 2 1-1  VA
         Mildred     dau    1 6/12  s          VA
```

1. Mildred FORREST: b 1910, York County, Virginia.

FT.1.4.3.8
ANDREW C. FORREST and MAGGIE L. RIGGINS

Andrew C. Forrest was born on July 3, 1887, York County, Virginia.

Andrew C. Forrest married on August 16, 1913, Maggie L. Riggins (b June 15, 1898; d December 15, 1958), the daughter of Alex and Mattie Riggins.

Andrew C. Forrest died on May 13, 1948, and is buried in the Western Cemetery, Poquoson.

1. Howell Sinclair FORREST: b September 11, 1914; d July 1, 1988, in Roanoke, Virginia, buried in Parklawn Memorial Cemetery, Hampton, Virginia

2. Leo Carl FORREST (Sr.): b March 22, 1926; m September 22, 1945, Mary Virginia Carmines (d January 4, 2001), the daughter of Ollie James and Annie Sedelia Ward Carmines; d July 17, 1976. See next FT.1.4.3.8.2.

FT.1.4.3.8.2
LEO CARL FORREST and MARY VIRGINIA CARMINES

Leo Carl Forrest (Sr.) was born on March 22, 1926.

Leo Carl Forrest married September 22, 1945, Mary Virginia Carmines (d January 4, 2001), the daughter of Ollie James and Annie Sedelia Ward Carmines.

Leo Carl Forrest died July 17, 1976.

1. Jennifer Carol FORREST: b March 18, 1951; m 1st May 18, 1971, James Ambrose Epps, Jr; m 2nd 1975, Randal Joe Ament.

2. Theresa Delia FORREST: b June 22, 1954; m April 8, 1977, David Ashby Smith (b June 17, 1950).

    1. Misty Lee SMITH: b July 12, 1978.

    2. Ashby Marie SMITH: b September 4, 1984.

3. Leo Carl FORREST, Jr: b April 28, 1958. Occupation: Mech. Engineer.

4. Sonya Lee FORREST: b May 15, 1964; m March 8, 1984, Michael Eugene Wells, Jr. (b March 24, 1964).

    1. Michael Eugene WELLS, Jr: b May 27, 1987.

    2. Steffi Joyce WELLS: b May 24, 1990.

    3. Dayton Thomas WELLS: b March 29, 1995.

FT.1.4.6
SARAH FIAMAH FORREST and JOSIAH MAXWELL HUGGETT
Of Poquoson District, York County

Sarah Fimiah Forrest was born on July 21, 1856.

Miss Sarah Fimiah Forrest married on July 8, 1876, Josiah Maxwell Huggett (b February 8, 1854, York County; d October 13, 1939, buried Western Cemetery), the son of John Bonaparte and Sarah Margaret (Forrest) Huggett.

In 1880, Josiah Huggett and family are listed in the York County census, dwelling 235-235, as follows:

Huggett	Josiah	head	23	sailor
	Sarah	wife	21	keeping house
	Ed. F.	son	4	at home
	John H.	son	1	at home

In 1900, Josiah M. Huggett and family are listed in the York County census, dwelling 378-386, as follows:

Huggett	Josiah M.	head	Feb 1854	46	m-22
	Sarah E.	wife	Jul 1855	44	9-9
	Edward F.	son	Jul 1876	23	s
	John H.	son	Jan 1879	21	s
	Maggie J.	daughter	Nov 1881	18	s
	Polly	daughter	Sep 1884	15	s
	William T.	son	Apr 1887	13	s
	Annie	daughter	Feb 1890	10	s
	Sarah M.	daughter	Jun 1893	6	s
	Josiah	son	Aug 1894	5	s
	Robt. L.	son	Jan 1898	2	s

Mrs. Sarah Fimiah (Forrest) Huggett died on February 8, 1939.

Josiah M. Huggett died on October 13, 1939, and is buried in the Western Cemetery.

1. Edward Franklin HUGGETT: b July 30, 1876, York County, Virginia; m in York County on April 27, 1901, Ester E. Insley, age 20, the daughter of Josiah and Alice J. Insley

(*Marriage Record No. 1, 1854-1928, York County*, page 57, line 43); d April 1, 1961, buried Western Cemetery.

2. John H. HUGGETT: b January 27, 1879, York County, Virginia; m in York County on December 21, 1904, Ida M. Powell, age 22, the daughter of R.B. and Sarah L. Powell (*Marriage Record No.1, 1854-1928, York County*, page 63, line 51); boatman (1904); d April 17, 1926, buried Western Cemetery.

3. Mary Jane HUGGETT: b November 21, 1882, York County, Virginia; m in York County on October 13, 1900, John Willis Insley; November 5, 1964, York County, Virginia.

4. Polly HUGGETT: b September 1, 1884, York County, Virginia; m J. Thomas Jordon.

5. William T. HUGGETT: b April 24, 1887, York County, Virginia; served 318 Infantry Division World War I: d February 3, 1961, buried Western Cemetery.

6. Bethany Ann ("Annie") HUGGETT: b February, 1890, York County, Virginia; m Andrew Ira Forrest.

7. Sarah ("Sadie") Margaret HUGGETT: b June 18, 1893, York County, Virginia; unmarried; d March 31, 1981, Messick, York County, Virginia.

8. Josiah (Joseph) M. HUGGETT (Jr.): b August 15, 1894, York County, Virginia; m Eva Evans (b March 12, 1902), the daughter of W. Albert and Sudie Evans; d November 7, 1924, in the Hampton bus-train accident, buried Western Cemetery.

9. Robert Lee HUGGETT: b January 29, 1898, York County, Virginia; d January 20, 1994, Poquoson, Virginia.

FT.1.4.7
ROBERT DOLBY FORREST and RUHEMMA ROLLINS
Of Poquoson, York County, Virginia

Robert Dolby Forrest was born on March 16, 1861, York County, Virginia.

Robert Dolby Forrest married on June 4, 1881, Ruhemma ("Duck") Rollins (b April, 1861, York County, Virginia; d 1932, buried Western Cemetery) (*Marriage Record No. 1, 1854-1928, York County*, page 13, line 292).

In 1900, Robert D. Forrest and family are listed in the Poquoson Magisterial District, York County, Virginia census, dwelling 396-404, as follows:

Forrest	Robert D.	head	Mar 1861	39	m-18
	Rhuhummer	wife	Apr 1861	39	1-1
	William O.	son	Mar 1887	13	VA

In 1910, Robert D. Forrest and family are listed in the Poquoson, York County, Virginia census, dwelling 94-99, as follows:

Forrest	Robert D.	head	50	m-28
[sic]	Rushunmer	wife	56	1-1

Robert Forrest died on May 15, 1918, and is buried in the Western Cemetery.

1. William Otis FORREST: b March, 1887, York County, Virginia; m on July 6, 1907, Bessie Rollins (b 1889), the daughter of John D. Rollins. William Otis Forrest is a grandson of Henry Harry Forrest. See next FT.1.4.7.1.

FT.1.4.7.1
WILLIAM OTIS FORREST and BESSIE ROLLINS
Of Poquoson, York, County, Virginia

William Otis Forrest was born in 1887, York County, Virginia.

William Otis Forrest married on July 6, 1907 Bessie Rollins (b 1889), the daughter of John D. Rollins.

William Otis Forrest is a grandson of Henry Harry Forrest.

In 1910, William O. Forrest and family are listed in the household of his father-in-law, John W. Rollins, in the Poquoson, York County, Virginia census, dwelling 145-150, as follows:

Rollins	John W.	head	46	VA	m-2
	Annie L.	wife	44	VA	m-1 5-4
	John A.	son	16	VA	
	Henry C.	son	13	VA	
Forrest	William O.	s-i-l	23	VA	m-1
	Bessie	daughter	21	VA	m-1 1-1
	Helen	gddaug	10/12	VA	

1. Helen FORREST: b 1909, York County, Virginia.

CHAPTER FIVE
THE HENRY NATHANIEL FORREST FAMILY
POQUOSON DISTRICT,
YORK COUNTY, VIRGINIA

FT.2
HENRY NATHANIEL FORREST and MARTHA ANN ROLLINS
Of Poquoson, York County, Virginia

Henry Nathaniel ("Short Henry") Forrest (Sr.) was born in 1814 (1820), in York County (according to the 1850 census), in Baltimore, Maryland (according to his enlistment in the Confederate Army).

Henry Nathaniel Forrest married about 1844, Martha (Mary A.) Rollins (b April 9, 1826; d 1902, buried Western Cemetery), the daughter of Samuel and Elizabeth (Wilson) Rollins. Henry Forrest had various occupations: fisherman (1850), inland sailor (1860), farmer (1870).

In 1850, Henry Forrest and family are listed in the York County, Virginia census, page 345B, dwelling 41-41, as follows:

Forrest	Henry	head	30	York County fisherman
	Martha A.	wife	25	York County
	Rebecca	daughter	5	York County
	Wm.	son	2	York County
	Henry	son	1	York County

In 1860, Henry Forrest and family are listed in the Post Office Halfway House, York County, Virginia census, dwelling 92-92, as follows:

Forrest	Henry	head	44	sailor inland
	Martha	wife	34	
	Rebecca	daughter	15	
	Henry	son	10	
	Cifson	son	8	
	Ann Eliza	daughter	7/12	
Rollins	Major	NR	46	sailor inland

Henry Nathaniel Forrest, age 44, enlisted on June 3, 1861, at Williamsburg. He was the oldest soldier in the 32nd Virginia Infantry Regiment. His occupation on the muster rolls is listed as sailor. He was described at the time as 5'10", dark complexion, dark hair, dark eyes. Henry was present on all muster rolls except absent on furlough on August 31, 1861; absent detailed to the ordnance department, January 2, 1862; absent sick February 11-21, 1863, until absence without leave (AWOL) on September 23, 1863. He was listed as deserted on October 13, 1863. He took the Oath of Allegiance to the Federal Government on October 13, 1863, and released to his home in York County, Virginia. He was described at this time as 48 (sic) years old, 5'-6". Dark complexion, black hair, blue eyes, occupation sailor (source: *32nd Virginia Infantry*, Jes Hansen).

In 1870, Henry N. Forest and family are listed in the Poquoson Township, York County, Virginia census, dwelling 123-130, as follows:

Forest	Henry N.	head	56	MD	farmer
	Martha A.	wife	43	VA	keep house
	Henry N.	son	21	VA	oysterman
	Cyphrum	son	18	VA	oysterman
	John F.	son	13	VA	at home
	Ann E.	daughter	10	VA	at home
	Isaac H.	son	5	VA	
	Samuel	son	2	VA	

Henry Nathaniel Forrest was an inland sailor and spent much of his time on the Chesapeake Bay, and out at sea. It is family tradition that, as he was returning from a trip there was an smallpox epidemic on his ship, so he decided to continue on to Baltimore. He is reputed to have died before 1880, of this epidemic, at Sparrow's Point, Baltimore, Maryland.

This Forrest family is not known to be part of the Abraham Forrest family of Mathews

County, Virginia, and later of Poquoson, York County, Virginia.

In 1880, [Mrs.] Martha Forrest and family are listed in the Poquoson District, York County, Virginia, census, dwelling 92-92, as follows:

Forrest	Martha	head	54	keeping house
	Isaac	son	15	at home
	Sam'l	son	12	at home
Mirgin [sic]	Eliza	daughter	20	at home
(Martin)	George	s-i-l	19	at home

1. Rebecca Susan FORREST: b October 20, 1845, York County, Virginia; m abt 1863, Steven Wesley Ward (b February 10, 1840; d August 10, 1891), son of Seth Ward and Sarah Watkins; d May 8, 1913.

2. William FORREST: b 1848, York County, Virginia; possibly died before 1860.

3. Henry Nathaniel FORREST (II): b 1850, York County, Virginia; m in the Methodist Church on December 25, 1872, Virginia Holloway (b 1849), the daughter of Wilton Holloway. See next FT.2.3.

4. James Sife ("Cyphrum/Cipon") FORREST: b November 16, 1851, York County, Virginia; m on December 23, 1871, Mary Jane Amory (b June 9, 1855; d December 3, 1930, buried Western cemetery), the daughter of Thomas C. and Jane Martin Amory; d October 16, 1936, buried Western Cemetery. See next FT.2.4.

5. John Franklin FORREST: b November 29, 1857, York County, Virginia; m February 3, 1877, Ruth F. Davis (b November 2, 1856; d February 19, 1928), the daughter of John E. and Sarah A. Davis; d February 24, 1923, buried Western Cemetery. See next FT.2.5

6. Ann Elizabeth FORREST: b February, 1859 (7 months old when the census was taken), York

County, Virginia; m 1st in York County on June 25, 1880, George W. Martin (b 1861; d abt 1899), the son of David and Julaney Martin; m 2nd July 4, 1898, William E. Hopkins, the son of James Archie and Ann (Messick) Hopkins. See next FT.2.6.

7. Isaac H. FORREST: b 1865, York County, Virginia; m 1st abt 1885, Emma; m 2nd December 3, 1919, Mary Elizabeth Thomas (b 1881, York County, Virginia). See next FT.2.7.

8. Samuel FORREST: b January 12, 1868, York County, Virginia; m 1891, Gertrude Dryden (b March 7, 1875; d December 9, 1955), the daughter of Wesley Dryden; d January 15, 1951, buried Western Cemetery, Poquoson. See next FT.2.8.

FT.2.3
HENRY NATHANIEL FORREST and VIRGINIA HOLLOWAY
Of Poquoson, York County, Virginia

Henry Nathaniel Forrest (II) was born in 1850, York County, Virginia.

Henry Nathaniel Forrest married in the Methodist Church on December 25, 1872, Virginia Holloway (b 1849), the daughter of Wilton Holloway.

In 1880, Henry Forrest and family are listed in the Poquoson District, York County, Virginia census, dwelling 122-122, as follows:

Forrest	Henry	head	30	waterman
	Virginia	wife	30	keep house
	Harriet	daughter	1	at home
Bunting	Wirt	NR	16	

1. Harriet FORREST: b 1879, York County, Virginia.

FT.2.4
JAMES SIFE FORREST and MARY JANE AMORY
Of Poquoson, York County, Virginia

James Sife ("Cyphrum/Cipon") Forrest was born on November 16, 1851, York County, Virginia. He was known variously as Ciphron (1860), Cyphrum (1870), James S. L. (1900, 1910).

He was a sailor (1880).

James Sife Forrest married in Poquoson at the home of Robert Forrest on December 23, 1871, Mary Jane Amory (b June 9, 1855; d December 3, 1930, buried Western Cemetery). They lived in Poquoson, Virginia.

In 1880, James Forrest and family are listed in the Poquoson District, York County, Virginia census, dwelling 123-123, as follows:

Forrest	James	head	27	sailor
	Mary	wife	25	keeping house
	Eliza	daughter	8	at home
	H. T.	son	5	at home
	Geo. W.	son	3	at home
	Jane	daughter	4/12	at home

In 1900, James S. L. Forrest and family are listed in the Poquoson Magisterial District, York County, Virginia census, dwelling 349-351, as follows:

Forrest	James S.	head	Nov 1848	51	VA
	Mary J.	wife	June 1855	45	VA
	6 children 6 living				
	George W. S., son		Mar 1878	22	VA
	William K. son		Dec 1881	18	VA
	Alfred S. son		Jul 1890	9	VA

In 1910, James S. Forrest and family are listed in the Poquoson Township, York County, Virginia census, dwelling 183-188, as follows:

Forrest	James S.	head	56	VA	m-1	
	Mary J.	wife	56	VA	m-1	6-6
	Alfred S.	son	19	VA		

        George S.   son   33   VA m-1
        Nettie   d-i-l   27   VA m-1 0-0

James Sife Forrest died on October 16, 1936, and is buried in the Western Cemetery, Poquoson.

1. Izora ("Eliza") FORREST: b December 3, 1872, York County, Virginia; m December 20, 1892, James Littleton Firth (b October 27, 1863; d November 19, 1951), the son of George and Charlotte Firth; d December 20, 1962, buried Western Cemetery.

   1. Naomi FIRTH: b October 10, 1895, York County, Virginia; d October 13, 1899, York County, Virginia, buried Western Cemetery, Poquoson.

2. Henry Thomas FORREST: b March 10, 1875, York County, Virginia; m March 4, 1899, Carrie R. Freeman (b March 10, 1875; d December 20, 1954, buried Western Cemetery), the daughter of Carroll and Emma S. Freeman. See next FT.2.4.2.

3. George S. FORREST: b March 16, 1877, York County, Virginia; m February 20, 1910, Nettie Smith (b abt 1877), the daughter of Isaac and Mary E. Smith; d September 21, 1943, and is buried in the Smith Cemetery, #2, Poquoson, Virginia. See next FT.2.4.3.

4. Malvina Jane FORREST: b February, 1878, York County, Virginia; m 1st abt 1898, Percevial Adams; m 2nd Whitaker.

5. William King FORREST: b December 1, 1882, York County, Virginia; m January 3, 1903, Esther Smith (b December 9, 1884; d October 27, 1959), daughter of C. W. and Elizabeth Smith; d September 19, 1962, buried in the Smith Cemetery. See next FT.2.4.5.

6. Alfred S. FORREST: b July, 1890, York County, Virginia; never married.

FT.2.4.2
HENRY THOMAS FORREST and CARRIE R. FREEMAN
Of Poquoson, York County, Virginia

Henry Thomas Forrest was born on March 10, 1875, York County, Virginia.

Henry Thomas Forrest married on March 4, 1899, Carrie R. Freeman (b March 10, 1875; d December 20, 1954, buried Western Cemetery), the daughter of Carroll and Emma S. Freeman.

In 1910, Henry T. Forrest and family are listed in the Poquoson, York County, Virginia census, dwelling 107-163, as follows:

Forrest	Henry T.	head	34	VA	m-1
	Carrie	wife	28	VA	m-1 2-2
	Mary M.	daughter	10	VA	
	Henry M.	son	11	VA	

1. Henry Milton FORREST: b July 14, 1899, York County, Virginia; m April 30, 1927, Nellie Geneva Forrest (b April 30, 1906), the daughter of John Andrew Forrest (I) and Alice Geneva Rollins; d August 13, 1977. See next FT.2.4.2.1.

2. Mary M. FORREST: b 1900, York County, Virginia.

FT.2.4.2.1
HENRY MILTON FORREST and NELLIE GENEVA FORREST

Henry Milton Forrest was born on July 14, 1899, York County, Virginia.

Henry Milton Forrest married on April 30, 1927, Nellie Geneva Forrest (b April 30, 1906), the daughter of John Andrew Forrest (I) and Alice Geneva Rollins.

Henry Milton Forrest died on August 13, 1977.

1. Carrie Elaine FORREST: b July 22, 1928; m William Melvin Rollins, Sr. (b December 11, 1927), the son of William Thomas and Mary C. (Evans) Rollins. See next FT.2.4.2.1.1.

2. Henry Milton FORREST, Jr: b January 24, 1931; m August 29, 1953, Muriel Dean Insley (b August 30, 1934). See next FT.2.4.2.1.2.

3. Alice Nell FORREST: b August 17, 1941; m August 8, 1959, Albert Nelson Firth, Sr. (b July 17, 1941). See next FT.2.4.2.1.3.

FT.2.4.2.1.1
CARRIE ELAINE FORREST
And WILLIAM MELVIN ROLLINS

Carrie Elaine Forrest was born on July 22, 1928.

Miss Carrie Elaine Forrest married William Melvin Rollins, Sr. (b December 11, 1927), the son of William Thomas and Mary C. (Evans) Rollins.

1. William Melvin ROLLINS, Jr: b November 30, 1947; m August 27, 1966, Nancy Ellen Lawson (b February 25, 1947). See next FT.2.4.2.1.1.1.

2. David Forrest ROLLINS: b April 29, 1949; m July 31, 1971, Sharlene Ann Sikara (b July 28, 1954). See next FT.2.4.2.1.1.2.

3. Susan Kathryn ROLLINS: b January 5, 1952; m August 8, 1970, Harry Keith Tucker, Sr. (b February 8, 1950). See next FT.2.4.2.1.1.2.

4. Thomas Milton ROLLINS: b October 27, 1957.

5. Lawrie Leigh ROLLINS: b June 5, 1959; m June 6, 1980, Wayne Edward Silver, Jr.

6. Betty Marie ROLLINS: b February 8, 1968.

FT.2.4.2.1.1.1
WILLIAM MELVIN ROLLINS, JR.
And NANCY ELLEN LAWSON

William Melvin ROLLINS, Jr: b November 30, 1947.

William Melvin Rollins married August 27, 1966, Nancy Ellen Lawson (b February 25, 1947).

1. Bethany Elaine ROLLINS: b April 2, 1968.

2. Bonnie Ellen ROLLINS: b May 22, 1970.

3. Joseph Lee ROLLINS: b October 13, 1971.

4. Holly Jane ROLLINS: b May 13, 1973.

FT.2.4.2.1.1.2
DAVID FORREST ROLLINS and SHARLENE ANN SIKARA

David Forrest Rollins was born on April 29, 1949.

David Forrest Rollins married July 31, 1971, Sharlene Ann Sikara (b July 28, 1954).

1. Daniel James ROLLINS: b April 3, 1973.

2. David Nicholas ROLLINS: b April 23, 1978.

FT.2.4.2.1.1.2
SUSAN KATHRYN ROLLINS and HARRY KEITH TUCKER

Susan Kathryn Rollins was born on January 5, 1952.

Susan Kathryn Rollins married August 8, 1970, Harry Keith Tucker, Sr. (b February 8, 1950).

1. Elizabeth Kate TUCKER: b July 20, 1971.

2. Harry Keith TUCKER, Jr: b February 25, 1974.

3. James Milton TUCKER: b July 16, 1979.

FT.2.4.2.1.2
HENRY MILTON FORREST and MURIEL DEAN INSLEY

Henry Milton Forrest, Jr., was born on January 24, 1931.

Henry Milton Forrest, Jr., married on August 29, 1953, Muriel Dean Insley (b August 30, 1934).

1. Julie Lynn FORREST: b December 23, 1957; m Joseph John Haczewski (b April 3, 1956).

    1. Jennifer Renne HACZEWSKI: b July 19, 1979.

FT.2.4.2.1.3
ALICE NELL FORREST and ALBERT NELSON FIRTH

Alice Nell Forrest was born on August 17, 1941.

Miss Alice Nell Forrest married on August 8, 1959, Albert Nelson Firth, Sr. (b July 17, 1941).

1. Albert Nelson FIRTH, Jr: b July 4, 1962.

2. Michael Lynn FIRTH: b February 3, 1965.

3. Andrea Dee FIRTH: b January 25, 1968.

FT.2.4.3
GEORGE S. FORREST, Sr., and NETTIE SMITH
Of Poquoson, York County, Virginia

George S. Forrest, Sr., was born on March 16, 1877, York County, Virginia.

George S. Forrest married on February 20, 1910, Nettie Smith (b abt 1877), the daughter of Isaac and Mary E. Smith.

George S. Forrest, Sr., died September 21, 1943, and is buried in the Smith Cemetery, #2, Poquoson, Virginia.

1. Aldrich ("Shim") FORREST: b July 4, 1911; m Margaret Freeman.

2. George S. FORREST, Jr: b April 21, 1917; m May 3, 1941, Lucille Hunt.

   1. Sandra H. FORREST: b February, 1942; m Donald Lawson.

   2. Nancy F. FORREST: b 1947; m Donald W. Hirschberg.

FT.2.4.5
WILLIAM KING FORREST and ESTHER SMITH
Of Messick, Poquoson, York County, Virginia

William King Forrest was born on December 1, 1882, York County, Virginia.

William King Forrest married on January 3, 1903, Esther Smith (b December 9, 1884; d October 27, 1959), daughter of C. W. and Elizabeth Smith.

In 1910, William K. Forrest and family are listed in the Poquoson Township, York County, Virginia census, dwelling 184-189, as follows:

Forrest	William K.	head	27	VA
	Esther	wife	27	VA
	Betty V.	daughter	5	VA

William King Forrest died on September 10, 1962, buried in the Smith Cemetery, #2, Poquoson, Virginia.

1. Betty Violet FORREST: b January 22, 1905, York County, Virginia; attended Poquoson High School and Mary Washington College in Fredericksburg, taught school for two years before her marriage; m on June 23, 1925, Alton M. White; d August 8, 2000, Poquoson, Virginia.

    1. Wallie Gene WHITE: m Charlene.

    2. Esther Marie WHITE: m Proctor.

2. W. K. FORREST: m Elizabeth.

FT.2.5
JOHN FRANKLIN FORREST and RUTH F. DAVIS
Of Poquoson, York County, Virginia

John Franklin Forrest was born on November 29, 1857.

John Franklin Forrest married at Fish Neck in the home of Sarah A. Davis on February 3, 1877, Ruth F. Davis (b November 2, 1856; d February 19, 1928), the daughter of John E. and Sarah A. Davis. Witnesses to the marriage were John Hopkins and Lucy Charles.

In 1880, J. F. Forrest and family are listed in the Poquoson District, York County, Virginia census, dwelling 134-134, as follows:

Forrest	J. F.	head	21	sailor
	Ruth	wife	20	keep house
	Blanch	daughter	1	at home

John Forrest died on February 24, 1923, and is buried in the Western Cemetery beside his wife.

In 1910, Frank Forrest and family are listed in the York County census, dwelling 171-176, as follows:

Forrest	Frank	head	51	m-32	
	Ruth F.	wife	53	m-32	5-4
	Reginal	son	17		

1. Blanche M. FORREST: b January 30, 1879, York County, Virginia; m November 12, 1898, Elisha T. Lawson, the son of Isaac and Irella Lawson; d November 3, 1963.

2. John H. ("John Buckram") FORREST: b August, 1882, York County, Virginia; m December 24, 1903, Hattie Bradshaw (b 1885), the daughter of John and Susan Bradshaw. See next FT.2.5.2.

3. Cora A. FORREST: b November, 1886, York County, Virginia; m December 2, 1905, Samuel

Carmines, the son of John P. and Elizabeth ("Lizzie") (Rollins) Carmines.

4. Reginald FORREST: b August, 1892, York County, Virginia; m March 20, 1915, Grace Matilda Carmines (b August 30, 1893; d January 28, 1978), the daughter of John P. and Elizabeth ("Lizzie") (Rollins) Carmines. See next FT.2.5.4.

FT.2.5.2
JOHN H. FORREST and HATTIE BRADSHAW
Of Poquoson, York County

John H. ("John Buckram") Forrest was born on August, 1882, York County, Virginia.
John H. Forrest married on December 24, 1903, Hattie Bradshaw (b 1885), the daughter of John and Susan Bradshaw.
In 1910, John H. Forrest and family are listed in the Poquoson, York County, Virginia census, dwelling 162-167, as follows:

Forrest	John H.	head	31	VA m-1
	Hattie	wife	25	VA m-1 1-1
	Hilda V.	daughter	3	VA

1. Hilda V. FORREST: b 1907, York County, Virginia.

FT.2.5.4
REGINALD FORREST and GRACE MATILDA CARMINES
Of Poquoson, York County, Virginia

Reginald Forrest was born in August, 1892, York County, Virginia.
Reginald Forrest married on March 20, 1915, Grace Matilda Carmines (b August 30, 1893; d January 28, 1978), the daughter of John P. and Elizabeth ("Lizzie") Carmines.

1. Lillian Ronelda FORREST: b May 26, 1916; m 1st April 30, 1956, Joseph Montgomery (b

December 25, 1916; d April 30, 1956); m 2nd after 1956, Woodrow Johnson.

 1. Susanna Forrest MONTGOMERY: b August 22, 1937; m Charlton Wyant Mann.

  1. Leslie Suzanne MANN: b November 26, 1960.

  2. Charlotte Ronelda MANN: b October 12, 1962.

 2. Reginald F. FORREST: b July 26, 1922; d April 3, 1928, buried Western Cemetery.

 3. Gracie Mae FORREST: b January 4, 1927; m April 17, 1948, Edwin Thomas Kruszewski (b December 23, 1920).

  1. Reginald Thomas KRUSZEWSKI: b March 1, 1952; m August 30, 1977, Patricia Heberling.

   1. Leah Jean KRUSZEWSKI: b September 26, 1982.

   2. Michael Joseph KRUSZEWSKI: b September 10, 1957.

 4. Kenneth Ernell FORREST, Sr: b August 3, 1933; m March 4, 1961, Barbara Smith (b February 12, 1935).

  1. Kenneth Ernell FORREST, Jr: b July 14, 1964.

FT.2.6a
ANN ELIZABETH FORREST and GEORGE W. MARTIN
Of Poquoson, York County, Virginia

Ann Elizabeth Forrest was born in February, 1859 (7 months old when the census was taken), York County, Virginia.

Miss Ann Elizabeth Forrest married 1st in York County on June 25, 1880, George W. Martin (b 1861, Poquoson District, York County, Virginia; d before 1898), the son of David and Julaney Martin (*Marriage Record No. 1, 1854-1928, York County*, page 22, line 64).

George Martin was member of Trinity Methodist Church in the 1890s. He withdrew his membership from Trinity in 1899 (*Trinity*, page 26).

> NOTE: This entry may be referring to his son, or possibly referring to his removal from the active Trinity rolls after his death.

Evidently, George W. Martin died before 1898.

1. Henry D. MARTIN: b December 25, 1881, York County, Virginia; m in York County on May 24, 1902, Goldie Evans, the daughter of W. H. and Catherine B. Evans (*Marriage Record No. 1, 1854-1928, York County*, page 58, line 19); after Henry's death, Goldie Evans Martin married her brother in law, Charles F. Martin, whom she outlived; and then married her husband's uncle, John ("Jack") Robert Martin. Henry D. Martin died about 1910.

2. George ("Butcher") W. MARTIN: b October, 1882, York County, Virginia; m in York County on March 27, 1902, Annie E. Pauls, the daughter of William Pauls and Rena Hopkins (*Marriage Record No. 1, 1854-1928, York County*, page 58, line 12); they removed with all their family to Town's Creek near Oyster, in

Northampton County, on the ocean side of the Eastern Shore.

3. John ("Jack") MARTIN: b November, 1884, York County, Virginia; d October 21, 1946; buried in the Western Cemetery, Poquoson Avenue, Poquoson.

4. Charles Frederick (Frederick H.) MARTIN: b November, 1886 (May 15, 1888), York County, Virginia; m in 1907, Lona Jane Bradshaw (b March 24, 1890; d February 27, 1953); in 1910 enumerated as Frederick C. Martin. Resided on Messick Road, just before where "Penny" Martin and "Mellie" Martin lived opposite each other.

5. Samuel C. MARTIN: b September, 1888, York County, Virginia; in 1910, his sister-in-law, Goldie Martin, and her two children were living with him; m after 1910 his widowed sister in law, Goldie Evans Martin; d before June 22, 1911.

6. Isaac ("Ike") MARTIN: b 1889, York County, Virginia; m abt 1911 Maud Carpenter; operated a seafood business in Messick, Poquoson, Virginia; d accidentally when he was electrocuted by an electric fan.

7. Martha J. ("Baby Sis") MARTIN: b September, 1891, York County, Virginia; m in York County on May 29, 1909, Crosby Forrest, the son of R. J. and Eliza Forrest (*Marriage Record No. 1, 1854-1928, York County*, page 71, line 22).

FT.2.6b
ANN ELIZABETH (FORREST) MARTIN
And WILLIAM E. HOPKINS
Of Poquoson, York County, Virginia

Mrs. Ann (Forrest) Martin, widow, married 2nd in York County on July 4, 1898, William E. Hopkins (*Marriage Record No. 1, 1854-1928, York County*, page 51, line 33) , the son of James Archie and Ann (Messick) Hopkins.

The 1900 Poquoson Magisterial District, York County, Virginia, census, dwelling 463-473, taken June 27, 1900, lists William E. Hopkins, age 41, married 2 years, and family as follows:

Hopkins	William E	Head	Nov 1858	41
	Annie	wife	Feb 1859	41
Martin	Henry D	S. Step	Dec 1881	18
	George W	S. Step	Oct 1882	17
	John I	S. Step	Nov 1884	15
	Charles F	S. Step	Oct 1886	13
	Samuel C	S. Step	Sep 1888	11
	Martha J	D. Step	Sep 1891	8

(*Colonial Cousins*, page 50).

FT.2.7a
ISAAC H. FORREST and EMMA
Of Poquoson, York County, Virginia

Isaac H. Forrest was born in 1865, York County, Virginia.

Isaac H. Forrest married about 1885, 1st Emma.

FT.2.7b
ISAAC H. FORREST and MARY ELIZABETH THOMAS
Of Poquoson, York County, Virginia

Isaac H. Forrest married 2nd on December 3, 1919, Mary Elizabeth Thomas (b 1881, Virginia), the daughter of Wise and Elizabeth Thomas (see *York County Will Book 14*, page 245, 247).

In 1920, Isaac H. Forrest and family are listed in the Poquoson, York County, Virginia census, dwelling 20-20, as follows:

```
Forrest  Isaac H.    head    55   VA
         Elizabeth   wife    39   VA
```

FT.2.8
SAMUEL FORREST and GERTRUDE DRYDEN
Of Poquoson, York County, Virginia

Samuel Forrest was born on January 12, 1868 (1867 in the 1900 census), York County, Virginia.

Samuel Forrest married in 1891, Gertrude Dryden (b March 7, 1875; d December 9, 1955, buried Western Cemetery), the daughter of Wesley Dryden. She was called "Lulu E." in the 1900 York County census, although no one in Messick remembers her by this name.

In 1900, Samuel Forrest and family are listed in the Poquoson Magisterial District, York County census, dwelling 320-328, as follows:

Forrest	Samuel	head	Jun 1867	33	VA
	Lula	wife	Mar 1875	25	2-2
	William	son	Feb 1892	8	VA
	Everett	son	Sep 1898	1	VA
	Martha A.	Mother	Apr 1826	72	wd.

In 1910, Samuel Forrest and family are listed in the Poquoson, York County, Virginia census, dwelling 169-174, as follows:

Forrest	Samuel	head	41	VA	m-19	
	Gertie	wife	35	VA	m-19	3-3
	William H.	son	18	VA		
	Everett	son	11	VA		
	Dennis	son	8	VA		

Samuel Forrest died on January 31, 1951, and is buried in the Western Cemetery, Poquoson.

1. William Hope FORREST: b February 5, 1892, York County, Virginia; m abt 1919, Lettie Jane Messick (b December 22, 1899; d December 1, 1958, buried Western Cemetery). See next FT.2.8.1.

2. Everett FORREST: b September 1, 1898, York County, Virginia; m August 1, 1936, Sarah Moore (b September 13, 1910, York County, Virginia), the daughter of Harry Freeman Moore and Bettie P. Woodson. See next FT.2.8.2.

3. Dennis FORREST: b January 28, 1902, York County, Virginia; m abt 1922, Lovey C. (b August 26, 1903); d December 14, 1982, Mathews County, Virginia, and is buried in the Christ Church Cemetery, Mathews County, Virginia.

    1. Samuel FORREST: b abt 1936.

4. Vivian FORREST: m "Bud" Barnette.

FT.2.8.1
WILLIAM HOPE FORREST and LETTIE JANE MESSICK
Of Poquoson, York County, Virginia

William Hope Forrest was born on February 5, 1892, York County, Virginia.

William Hope Forrest married about 1919, Lettie Jane Messick (b December 22, 1899; d December 1, 1958, buried Western Cemetery).

In 1920, William H. Forrest and family are listed in the Poquoson Township, York County, Virginia census, dwelling 129-131, as follows:

Forrest	William H.	head	27	VA
	Lettie J.	wife	21	VA
	Gertrude	daughter	4	VA
	Leman T.	son	4/12	VA

William Hope Forrest died on December 3, 1966, and is buried in the Western Cemetery, Poquoson, Virginia.

1. Gertrude FORREST: b 1916, York County, Virginia.

2. Leman T. FORREST: b 1920, York County, Virginia.

3. John Messick FORREST: b October 31, 1942, York County; m April 21, 1962, Shirley Mae Ward (b September 21, 1943, York County), the daughter of Calvin Knight Ward and Sarah Melissa Darnell.

    1. John Messick FORREST (Jr): b July 28, 1963, York County, Virginia.

FT.2.8.2
EVERETT FORREST and SARAH MOORE
Of York County, Virginia

Everett Forrest was born on September 1, 1898, York County.

Everett Forrest married on August 1, 1936, Sarah Moore (b September 13, 1910, York County, Virginia), the daughter of Harry Freeman Moore and Bettie P. Woodson.

1. Bette P. Woodson FORREST: b January 11, 1940, York County, Virginia.

2. Vivian Marcella FORREST: b March 27, 1946, York County, Virginia; m September 11, 1964, Thomas Davis Hogge.

3. Nannie Moore FORREST: b February 25, 1957, York County, Virginia.

CHAPTER SIX
THE THOMAS HUMPHREY FORREST FAMILY OF POQUOSON, YORK COUNTY, VIRGINIA

FT.3a
THOMAS HUMPHREY FORREST and JOYCE MARTIN
Of Poquoson, York County, Virginia

Thomas ("Tom Tit") Humphrey Forrest was born on January 6, 1835, Virginia.

> NOTE: Thomas H. Forrest was born January, 1837, according to the 1900 York County census. According to the 1900 census, his father was born in Virginia, and his mother was born in Virginia. According to the 1910 census, his father was born in Virginia, and his mother was born in Maryland.

Thomas Humphrey Forrest married 1st about 1860, Joyce ("Jicy") Martin (b 1847; d before 1870).

Children of Thomas H. Forrest and his 1st wife, Joyce Martin:

1. John Crevasser ("Pat") FORREST: b 1861, York County, Virginia; m 1st September 7, 1886, Sarah W. Hopkins (b December 11, 1864; d June 5, 1892); m 2nd June 15, 1897, Martha Emma Powell (1863; d 1972, buried Trinity Cemetery, Poquoson); d 1926, buried Western Cemetery. See next FT.3.1.

2. Joyce ("Joicy"/"Jesse") Anne FORREST: b January, 1864, York County, Virginia; m July 2, 1884, Robert T. Holloway, the son of E. R. and Mary (Amory) Holloway. See next FT.3.2.

FT.3b
THOMAS HUMPHREY FORREST and MARY E. DEAL
Of Poquoson, York County, Virginia

Thomas ("Tom Tit") Humphrey Forrest married 2nd in 1870, Mary E. Deal (b May 11, 1848; d March 3, 1924).

In 1870, Thomas Forrest and family are listed in the Poquoson Township, York County, Virginia census, dwelling 157-166, as follows:

Forrest	Thomas	head	35	VA	farmer
	Mary E.	wife	23	VA	keep house
	John C.	son	8	VA	
	Joicey A	daughter	4	VA	
Amory	Arrilla	NR	19	VA	at home

In 1880, T. H. Forrest and family are listed in the Poquoson District, York County, Virginia, census, dwelling 229-229, as follows:

Forrest	T. H.	head	42	sailor
	Mary	wife	31	keeping house
	Jesse	daughter	14	at home
	Rebecca	daughter	4	at home
	Lee	son	1	at home

In the 1900 and 1910 census records, Thomas Forrest had been the father of 11 children by his 2nd wife, of which only 4 were still living.

In 1900, Thomas H. Forrest and family are listed in the Poquoson Magisterial District, York County, Virginia census, dwelling 386-394, as follows:

Forrest	Thomas H.	head	Jan 1837	63	m-30
	Mary E.	wife	May 1848	52	11-4
	Ethebert L.	son	May 1880	20	VA
	Andrew I.	son	Feb 1888	12	VA

In 1910, Thomas H. Forrest and family are listed in the Poquoson, York County, Virginia census, dwelling 226-231, as follows:

Forrest	Thomas H.	head	76	VA	m-2	m-45
	Mary E.	wife	68	VA	m-1	11-4
	Andrew J.	son	22	VA	m-1	
	Annie	d-i-l	21	VA	m-1	0-0

Thomas H. Forrest died on January 31, 1913, and is buried in the Trinity Cemetery, Poquoson.

Children of Thomas H. Forrest and his 2nd wife, Mary E. Deal:

3. Rebecca FORREST: b 1876, York County, Virginia; m July 4, 1896, Oscar E. Robins.

4. Ethelbert Lee FORREST: b March, 1880, York County, Virginia; m 1908, Nannie C. West (b 1887; d 1967); d 1958, buried Providence Cemetery, Gloucester.

1. Lillian C. FORREST: b September 15, 1908; m June 14, 1934, Jefferson Lee Quinn, II (b 1895; d December, 1963), the son of Jefferson Lee Quinn, I and Martha E. Cox. (1910 York County census).

2. Maggie FORREST: b 1916; m Mr. Gray; d 1994, buried in Providence Cemetery, Gloucester, Virginia.

5. Andrew I. FORREST: b February 4, 1888, York County, Virginia; m July 10, 1909, Annie Huggett; d May 29, 1959, buried Western Cemetery, Poquoson.

FT.3.1a
JOHN CREVASSER FORREST and SARAH W. HOPKINS
Of Poquoson, York County, Virginia

John Crevasser ("Pat") Forrest was born in November, 1860, York County, Virginia.

John Crevassar Forrest married 1st September 7, 1886, Sarah W. Hopkins (b December 11, 1864; d June 5, 1892), the daughter of James Archie and Ann Messick Hopkins.

Children of John C. Forrest and his 1st wife, Sarah E. Hopkins:

1. Ethel J. FORREST: b July, 1887, York County, Virginia; m June 9, 1908, Edward Lennie Watkins, the son of Robert L. and Rachel A. Watkins.

2. Joyce ("Joicy") L. FORREST: b April, 1890, York County, Virginia; m April 23, 1910, William A. Graham (b October 9, 1888; d May 27, 1944), the son of W. B. and Margaret Weston Graham.

    1. John B. GRAHAM:

FT.3.1b
JOHN CREVASSER FORREST
And MARTHA EMMA POWELL
Of Poquoson, York County, Virginia

John Crevassar ("Pat") Forrest married 2nd June 15, 1897, Martha Emma Powell (b 1863; d 1972, buried Trinity Cemetery), the daughter of Jack and Peggy Weston Powell.

In 1900, John C. Forrest and family are listed in the Poquoson Magisterial District, York County, Virginia census, dwelling 339-347, as follows:

Forrest						
	John C.	head	Nov 1860	39		VA
	Martha E.	wife	Apr 1878	22	1-1	
	Ethel J.	daughter	Jul 1887	12		VA
	Jicy L.	daughter	Apr 1890	10		VA

	Viola	daughter	Mar 1898	2	VA
Parks	John O.	nephew	Aug 1891	8	VA

In 1910, John C. Forrest and family are listed in the Poquoson Township, York County, Virginia census, dwelling 196-201, as follows:

Forrest	John C.	head	47	VA m-2
	Martha E.	wife	31	VA m-1
	3 children 3 living			
	Viola	daughter	12	VA
	Ernest L.	son	9	VA
	Nettie E.	daughter	5	VA

John C. Forrest died in 1926, and is buried in the Western Cemetery, Poquoson, Virginia.

Children of John C. Forrest and his 2nd wife, Martha Emma Powell:

3. Viola FORREST: b March, 1898, York County, Virginia; m December 25, 1915, R. E. Haywood.

4. Earnest Linwood FORREST (Sr.): b September 27, 1900, York County, Virginia; m in Messick, York County, Virginia, on December 24, 1921, Sudie Viola Insley (b July 9, 1901, York County; d June 4, 1994, Poquoson, and is buried in the Western Cemetery, Messick, Poquoson, Virginia); d December 29, 1962, buried Western Cemetery. See next FT.3.1.4.

5. Nettie Ellis FORREST: b 1905, York County, Virginia; m abt 1925, Edwin Holloway, the son of R. W. and Sadie W. Holloway.

FT.3.1.4
EARNEST LINWOOD FORREST and SUDIE VIOLA INSLEY

Earnest Linwood Forrest, Sr., was born on September 27, 1900.

Earnest Linwood Forrest married in Messick, York County, Virginia, on December 24, 1921, Sudie Viola Insley (b July 9, 1901, York County; d June 4, 1994, Poquoson, and is buried in the Western Cemetery, Messick, Poquoson, Virginia).

Earnest Linwood Forrest died on December 29, 1962, buried Western Cemetery.

1. Earnest Linwood FORREST: (Jr.): b February 6, 1923; m Edna L. Carmines (b December 7, 1924; d June, 1993). See next FT.3.1.4.1.

2. (Peter) Harold FORREST: b January 28, 1925; m Vera Lee (b August 7, 1920).

3. Vergie Griggs FORREST: b October 11, 1927; m James Wilbur Firth; d April 29, 1992.

4. Betty Sue FORREST: b June 6, 1930; m Herbert Wright (b June 6, 1930). See next FT.3.1.4.4.

5. John Thomas FORREST: b June 10, 1938; m on January 21, 1961, Janice Gail Burke (b December 1, 1939). See next FT.3.1.4.5.

6. (Baby Boy) FORREST: b September 25, 1948; d September 25, 1948.

7. Carroll Fay FORREST: b January 19, 1941; m Judy Reed Forrest (b February 20, 1944). See next FT.3.1.4.7.

FT.3.1.4.1
EARNEST LINWOOD FORREST and EDNA L. CARMINES

Earnest Linwood Forrest (Jr.) was born on February 6, 1923.

Earnest Linwood Forrest married Edna L. Carmines (b December 7, 1924; d June, 1993).

1. Edna June FORREST: m Mark McClelland (deceased).

    1. Heather MCCLELLAND: b April, 1977

FT.3.1.4.4
BETTY SUE FORREST and HERBERT WRIGHT

Betty Sue Forrest was born on June 6, 1930.

Miss Betty Sue Forrest married Herbert Wright (b June 6, 1930).

1. Wanda Jane WRIGHT: b April 28, 1958.

2. Herbert WRIGHT, Jr: b October 24, 1959; m in September, 1986, Andrea Roberts.

    1. Drew WRIGHT: b July 9, 1990.

    2. Tiffany WRIGHT: b July 3, 1987.

    3. Amanda WRIGHT: b July 9, 1990.

3. Cathy ("Sissy") Viola WRIGHT: b July 30, 1962; m on April 29, 1989, Glenn Everett (b November 3, 1964).

    1. Donald Glenn EVERETT, III: b September 19, 1991.

4. James ("Jimmy") WRIGHT: b November 7, 1964.

FT.3.1.4.5
JOHN THOMAS FORREST and JANICE GAIL BURKE

John Thomas Forrest was born on June 10, 1938.

John Thomas Forrest married on January 21, 1961, Janice Gail Burke (b December 1, 1939).

1. John Thomas FORREST, Jr: b December 27, 1961.

2. Tina Marie FORREST: b December 1, 1968; m James Case.

    1. Amanda CASE:

3. William FORREST:

4. Frances FORREST:

FT.3.1.4.7
CARROLL FAY FORREST and JUDY REED FORREST

Carroll Fay Forrest was born on January 19, 1941.

Carroll Fay Forrest married Judy Reed Forrest (b February 20, 1944).

1. Robert ("Robbie") FORREST:

    1. Joshua FORREST:

    2. Angela FORREST:

FT.3.2
JOYCE ANN FORREST and ROBERT T. HOLLOWAY
Of Poquoson, York County, Virginia

Joyce ("Joicy"/"Jesse") Anne Forrest was born in January, 1864, York County, Virginia.

Miss Joyce Anne Forrest married on July 2, 1884, Robert T. Holloway (b March, 1861, York County, Virginia), the son of E. R. and Mary (Amory) Holloway (*Marriage Record No. 1, 1854-1928*, York County, page 28, line 18).

In 1900, Robert T. Holloway and family are listed in the York County census, dwelling 440-448, as follows:

Holloway	Robert T.	head	Mar 1861	39	m-17
	Jicy A.	wife	Jan 1864	36	9-7
	Nancy A.	daughter	Mar 1885	15	s
	Arthur	son	Apr 1889	11	s
	Robert M.	son	Mar 1891	9	s
	Annie	daughter	Dec 1892	7	s
	Eva	daughter	Nov 1894	5	s
	Jennie	daughter	Mar 1897	3	s
	Hugh G.	son	Oct 1899	7/12	s

Robert T. Holloway died August 1, 1929, and is buried in the Warwick Memorial Methodist Churchyard, Warwick County, Virginia (Forrest, 1994, page 85).

Colonial Cousins, 1940, page 57; *Poquoson Waterman*, 1989, page 97).

1. Nancy Ada HOLLOWAY: b March, 1885, York County, Virginia; m Preston Freeman; resided Menchville, Warwick County, Virginia.

2. Arthur HOLLOWAY: b April, 1889, York County, Virginia.

3. Robert M. HOLLOWAY (Jr.): b March, 1891, York County, Virginia; resided Menchville, Warwick County, Virginia.

4. Victoria Annie HOLLOWAY: b December, 1892, York County, Virginia; bp July 4, 1896, at Trinity Church ("Trinity", page 14).

5. Eva J. HOLLOWAY: b November, 1894, York County, Virginia; bp at Trinity Church on July 4, 1896 ("Trinity", page 14).

6. Jennie HOLLOWAY: b March, 1896, York County, Virginia; bp at Trinity Church on July 4, 1896 ("Trinity", page 14); m Floyd Holloway.

7. Hugh G. HOLLOWAY: b October, 1899, York County, Virginia.

BIBLIOGRAPHY

Bradshaw, Ura Ann, and Watkins, Vincent, *York County: Volume One, 1000 Marriages 1628-1900*, Privately printed, 1957.

Carmines, Franklin Taylor, *Poquoson's War Between the States 1861-1865*, 2nd edition, Revised, Poquoson Historical Commission, 1992, 58 pages.

Confederate Military History, A Library of Confederate States History, in Twelve Volumes, written by Distinguished Men of the South, and edited by Gen. Clement A. Evans of Georgia, 1899, Confederate Publishing Company. "Chapter VIII: Operations about Norfolk and Yorktown - Battle of Big Bethel - Burning of Hampton", pages 122-151.

Forrest, Jessie Fay, *No! No! A Thousand Times No! or Why the Village of Poquoson, Virginia Became Incorporated after Three Hundred and Nineteen Years*, 2nd edition, Revised, Poquoson Historical Commission, 1993, 10 pages, plus 16 unnumbered pages of photographs.

Forrest, Jessie Fay, edited by Mero, James H., *Cemeteries of City of Poquoson, Virginia, and Some Cemeteries of York County, Virginia*, published by Hugh S. Watson, Jr., Genealogical Society, Hampton, Virginia, no date, 144 pages.

Hansford, Thelma, *York County History, Geography and Government*, typescript, no date, York County Public Library.

The History of Tabernacle Methodist Church, Poquoson, Virginia

The History of Trinity United Methodist Church, Poquoson, Virginia 1882-1992, Privately Published by a Committee of Trinity United Methodist Church, 1982, 78 pages.

Holloway, James T., "Holloway Family History", 36 typescript pages of an unpublished manuscript, courtesy of James T. Holloway, September 21, 1998.

Hopkins, Garland Evans, *Colonial Cousins, being the history, genealogy, heraldry, homes and traditions of the Holloway and related families originating in the original shire of Charles River, now York County, Virginia*, Privately published, 1940.

Hopkins, Garland Evans, *York County Source Book, York County Historical Monograph No. 4*, Privately published, Winchester, Virginia, 1942.

Hopkins, Walter Lee, *Hopkins of Virginia and Related Families*, J. W. Ferguson and Sons, Printers, Richmond, Virginia, 1931. Chapter XVI: "Hopkins of York County, Virginia," pages 241-245.

Ironmonger, Elizabeth Hogg, *Thomas James, Clerk of Kingston Parish 1783-1796, Ancestry and Descendants 1653-1961*, 1961.

Jensen, Les, *32nd Virginia Infantry*, 1990, H. E. Howard, Inc., 216 pages.

Martin, Dr. Fred William, Sr., and Willett, Albert J., *The Martin Family of the Poquoson District, of York County, Virginia, with additional notes on Portsmouth, Virginia, and Grafton District, York County, Virginia*, Heritage Books, Inc., Bowie, Maryland, 1994, 317 pages.

Miller, Francis Trevelyan, *The Photographic History of the Civil War*, 10 Volumes, Thomas Yoseloff, "Part III, The Struggle For Richmond - Yorktown: Up the Peninsula", pages 252-276, and "Part I, The Rise of Lee - Antietam - The Invasion of the North", pages 58-78.

Official Records of the Union and Confederate Navies in the War of the Rebellion, in multiple Series, House of Representatives, Government Printing Office, Washington, D. C.

Series I, Vol. 6, 1897: "Boat Expedition up Back River, Virginia, July 24, 1861," pages 34-35; "Headquarters Forces from Cockletown, Halfway House, Va., July 25, 1861," pages 35-36; "Report of Acting Master Studley, U.S. Navy, commanding U.S.S. Young River, regarding batteries on the York and Poquosin Rivers, and the crossing by small boats of the York River," pages 484-485.

Series I, Vol. 9, 1899: "Report of Lieutenant-Commander Babcock, U.S. Navy, transmitting report regarding capture of canoe with two Confederate soldiers, February 25, 1863," page 504.

Parham, John T., "Thirty-Second at Sharpsburg, Graphic Story of Work Done on One of the Bloodiest of Fields - Forty-five Per Cent. Loss. - Shot at From Behind a Stone Fence - Samples of Personal Courage," as quoted in the "Southern Historical Society Papers," Vol. 34, pages 250-253.

Poquoson Historical Commission, Pamphlet and Newsletters,

Watkins, Vincent, "Brief History of Poquoson", 1st Annual Poquoson Seafood Festival, Poquoson Historical Commission, 1984, 14 pages.

"Poquoson (Bull Island) Heritage", Newsletter, beginning, Vol. 86-1, July 4, 1986, and current to Vol. 93-8, August 21, 1993.

Watkins, Thomas Vincent, *A History of Poquoson Virginia in Three Parts (1631-1860)*, 1988.
"Part One (1631-1660) The First Settlers", 75 pages.
"Part Two (1660-1789) The Colonial Period", 69 pages.
"Part Three (1789-1860) The New Invasion", 95 pages.

White, Robert Ellerson, *Ancestry and Descendants of Peter B. Smith and his wife Catherine G. Smith, Including Family Names: Armistead, Butler, Carmines, Davis, Diggs, Forrest, Foster, Gayle, Hudgins, Moore, Presson, Rollins, Tatterson, Wainwright, White, Wood, and many others 1734-1984*.

Willett, Albert J., *Poquoson Watermen, A Guide to Messick District, Poquoson Virginia Families of Martin, Holloway, Forrest, Topping, Messick, Rollins, Carmines, Insley, Firth, Evans, Hopkins, Page, Pauls, Ferguson, Forman, Huggett, Linton, Thomas, Gilbert*, Southern Historical Press, Easley, South Carolina, 1988, 392 pages.

Willett, Albert J., and Martin, Dr. Fred William, Sr., *The Martin Family of the Poquoson District, of York County, Virginia, with additional notes on Portsmouth, Virginia, and Grafton District, York County, Virginia*, Heritage Books, Inc., Bowie, Maryland, 1994, 317 pages.

Walter Lee Hopkins, *Hopkins of Virginia and Related Families*, J. W. Ferguson and Sons, Richmond, Virginia, 1931, chapter XVI, "Hopkins of York County, Virginia", pages 241-245.

Copies of Bible Records, as located in the Poquoson Library.

York County Original Records as found at the York County Courthouse, Yorktown, Virginia, examples such as:

Marriage Record No. 1, 1856-1928, York County, York County Courthouse, Yorktown, Virginia.

York County Court Records, 1631-1800, 23 Volumes of Wills, Deeds, Orders, etc., York County Courthouse, Yorktown, Virginia.

Most census records have been extracted from original census records found at various libraries, courthouses, and the Virginia State Archives; some were extracted from published census records and a full citation of these follows:

1810 York County, Virginia, census

1820 York County, Virginia, census

1830 York County, Virginia, census, transcribed by June Banks Evans, Bryn Ffyliaid Publications, 1989.

1840 York County, Virginia, census, transcribed by June Banks Evans, Bryn Ffyliaid Publications, 1988.

1850 U. S. Census, Elizabeth City County, Virginia, John F. Schunk, editor, S-K Publications, 1990.

1850 U. S. Census, Warwick County, Virginia, John F. Schunk, editor, S-K Publications, 1989.

York County, Virginia, 1850 Census, John F. Schunk, editor, S-K Publications, 1986.

1850 Slave Schedule, Poquoson District, York County, Virginia

1860 Slave Schedule, Poquoson District, York County, Virginia

1860 "Free Inhabitants in the County of *York*, in the State of *Virginia* enumerated by me on the ____ day of *June* 1860. Post Office *Halfway House*.

1870 "Inhabitants in *Poquoson Township*, in the County of *York*, State of *Virginia*, enumerated by me on the ____ day of *October*, 1870" Post Office: *Williamsburg*".

1880 "Inhabitants in *Poquoson District*, in the County of *York*, State of *Virginia*, enumerated by me on the ____ of June, 1880."

1900, Twelfth Census of the United States, Poquoson Magisterial District, York County, Virginia, June, 1900

1910, Thirteenth Census of the United States, Poquoson District, York County, Virginia

1920, Fourteenth Census of the United States, Poquoson District, York County, Virginia

ACKNOWLEDGEMENTS

The editor of this volume makes no claim to originally in all research that is presented. The present volume would not be possible without the direct contribution of many researchers some known, many unknown, who have preserved and recorded Poquoson genealogy and shared the very significant efforts of their research. I wish to acknowledge a few who have made significant contributions to recording that history and who have either directly or indirectly helped to make this volume possible. Yet, this list does not do justice to the many others who have helped to preserve, record and pass on the history of those families who have toiled to earn a living from the marshes and the sea and who passed on worthwhile virtues and values to be treasured from one generation to generation.

Phyllis Atkinson, 14 Brown's Neck Road, Poquoson, Virginia, for her contributions to Poquoson history and in particular data on the Holloway, Rawlins, and Baptist families.

Donald Carmines, Mesa, Arizona, for his help on the Carmines family.

Garland Evans Hopkins for publishing his work on Poquoson genealogy, *Colonial Cousins.*

Mrs. Jessie Fay Forrest (1919-2000), of Poquoson, Virginia, for her lifelong interest in Poquoson history. Without her continual help, support, friendship and advice, neither the earlier volume *Poquoson Watermen*, 1988, *The Martin Family Of Poquoson*, 1994, nor this volume would have been possible.

Judge G. Duane Holloway of Williamsburg for his help on the Holloway family lineage.

Deanna Hunt, of 84 Browns Neck Road, Poquoson, Virginia, for her editing, proofreading, patience and many contributions on the Forrest, Carmines, and Weston families.

Frederick G. Morgan of Hayes, Gloucester County, Virginia, for his help with the Holloway, Forrest, and Carmines families.

Sally Mason Napier, Poquoson, Virginia, for her help on the Huggett family.

Vincent Watkins for his life long study of early Poquoson records.

Diane Willett, wife, for retyping the entire original *Poquoson Waterman* manuscript into a current computer language and scanning the photographs which illustrate this volume.

And lastly, to my mother, Mrs. Mamie Rose (Gilbert) Willett, through who I share ties of blood and kinship to the various Messick, Poquoson families.

POQUOSON GRADUATES OF THE VIRGINIA MILITIA INSTITUTE LEXINGTON, VIRGINIA

1951   G. Duane Holloway, York County Judge

1955   John William ("Billy") Wainwright, LTC Air Force

1962   William Cartier Ward, Newport News Shipbuilding and Dry Dock Company, Manager of Engineering Department

1981   John Early Holloway, Law Partner with the firm of Hunton and Williams, Norfolk, Virginia

1984   Robert Earl Turner, Old Point National Bank

1984   William Hunt, Dentist, Poquoson

1995   John Wayne Holloway, Jr., U. S. Secret Service

INDEX

ACKISS
Claire, 40
David Lansing, 40
Tommy, 40
William Leonard, 40
William Leonard, Jr., 40

AMBROSE
Evan Henry, 113

AMORY
Anna Charline, 101, 107
Eudora, 115
Evelyn, 101, 107
Helen F., 101
Mary Jane, 203
William Herbert, 100

ANDERSON
Blake Gordon, 177
Cooper Forrest, 177

ASHBURN
Everett, 161
Judy, 161
Joyce, 161

BACKUS
Jonathan Duane, 109

BARNETT
Juanita, 86

BARON
John, 64

BLOXOM
Betty Ann, 42

BRAD
Hattie, 213

Lola Florence, 121

BURCHER
Amy Carol, 76
John Barry C., 76
Mack C., 76
Tyler, 76

BURKE
Janice Gail, 229

BURZYK
Andrea, 106

CALLIS
Mary E., 185
Susan, 138

CANNELLA
Richard Thomas, 178
Richard Thomas, II, 178
Travis Ryan, 178

CARL
Amory Anne, 117

CARMINES
Edna L., 228
Grace Matilda, 213
Harry Linwood, 120
Jeffrey, 121
Lisa, 121
Mary Emma, 85
Mary Virginia, 194
Robert Lee, 121
Virginia Lee, 121

CASE
Amanda, 229

CHESSER
Martha Imogene, 164

CLARKE
Henry Stewart, Jr., 107

Henry Stewart, Sr., 107
Nanette, 107
Robert, 107

COOK
Lella Ellen, 124

COX
Barbara Dee, 117
Betty Milla, 117
Eva Constance, 39
Richard Gordon, 116
Richard Gordon, Jr., 116
Van Forrest, 117

CROSS
Debra, 57
Edward, 57,
Roy, 57

DAVIS
Ruth F., 212

DEAL
Mary E., 223

DEAN
Lillian, 186

DIGGS
Cotha C., 137
Ruby, 78

DIXON
Rosa, 128

DRYDEN
Gertrude, 219

ELLYSON:
Cheryl Lynn, 121
Elizabeth Ellen, 121
Lee Ann, 121

EVANS
Bernice L., 99
Erma H., 99
Eva Irene, 99
Fannie Lee, 159
Lemuel Vaden, 99
Mattie, 46
Osborne, 99
Raven Nicole, 67
Sarah Lacy Sue, 67
William Albert, 98

EVERETT
Donald Glenn, III, 228

FERGUSON
Martha Louise, 53

FIGUENICK
Elizabeth Anne, 169
Vincent Anthony, 169

FIRTH
Albert McHenry, 191
Albert Nelson, 209
Albert Nelson, Jr., 209
Alvin, 192
Andrea Dee, 209
Beulah, 33, 182
Carolyn Forrest, 182
Charlotte Temple, 182
Cora Lee, 182
Elijah Frank, 182
Eura A., 192
John Lemuel, 192
Mattie Lee, 192
Michael Lynn, 209
Mollie L., 48
Virgie Belle, 192
Virginia T., 192

FORBES
Pearl, 54

FORREST
Abraham, 1, 2, 3, 14,

131, 138
Aldrich, 210
Alice B., 191
Alfred S., 205
Alice Nell, 206, 209
Alma Lee, 73
Alvon N., 75, 78
Andrew I., 224
Amelia H., 32
Andrea, 58
Andrea Lee, 113
Andrew C., 190, 193
Andrew I., 224
Angela, 229
Ann, 8
Ann Elizabeth, 201, 215
Ann Temple, 33
Ann Thomas, 44, 45
Ann Watkins, 127
Anne, 140
Anne Virginia, 55
Annie, 190
Annie Geneva, 85
Annie J., 191
Annie Jeannette, 68
Annie Laura, 132, 134
Annie Marie, 94
Arenthia Susan, 96, 98
Asa, 186
Ashley, 77
Ava Alline, 136
Barbara Ann, 100
Barry Jay, 129
Beamon Taylor, 81, 85
Beamon Taylor, Jr., 85
Beamon Taylor, III, 85
Becky Sue, 109
Benjamin Franklin, 52, 65
Benjamin T., 26, 73
Bertha 185
Bertha Maud, 157
Bertram Ellsworth, 166, 178

Bessie Viola, 166, 168
Bethany Estelle, 159
Bette P. Woodson, 221
Bettie Taylor, 173, 174
Betty Ann, 78
Betty Sue, 227, 228
Betty Violet, 211
Billie Dove, 187
Blanche M., 212
Bonnie Faye, 43
Brandon, 77
Brenda, 68
Bunevista, 140
Candace Maureen, 67
Carlton Page, 172
Carmen Lee, 77
Caroline, 168
Carrie Elaine, 122, 206, 207
Carroll Fay, 227, 229
Carroll Mark, 124
Carroll Thomas, 122, 119
Cassie Etta, 155
Cathy Susan, 67
Cecelia, 49
Charles Franklin, 36
Charles W., 23, 35
Charlotte Elizabeth, 115
Chris, 58
Christina Sue, 67
Christine Evans, 160
Chrystal L., 137
Clarice Jean, 55
Claytor C., 185, 187
Clinton Lemuel, 110
Clinton Lemuel, Jr., 110
Cora A., 212
Corie Michele, 118
Crissy Mae, 111
Crystal, 159
Dana Kay, 48
Daniel Wilson, 48
David J., 187
David James, 179
David Lee, 57

David Neil, 58
David T., 187
David Warren, 178, 179
David Warren, II, 179
Dennis, 220
Diane, 78
Dolly E., 70, 78
Donald Lee, Sr., 53, 66
Donald Lee, Jr., 67
Donald Lee, III, 67
Doris, 188
Dorothy Maria, 190, 191
Dorothy Susan, 141
Dyland Riley, 172
Earnest Linwood, 226, 227, 228
Edith, 32
Edith Charlene, 38
Edith Florence, 52, 62
Edna Earl, 111
Edna June, 228
Edward Spencer, 55
Elaine Grey, 125
Eleanor Dale, 170, 171
Eleanor Hartness, 166, 175
Elijah Sterling, 108, 109
Elijah V., 97, 108
Elizabeth, 55, 140
Elizabeth Ann, 76, 77, 124, 167, 168
Elizabeth S., 152
Emily, 55
Emily Jean, 44
Emma, 218
Emma A., 93
Emma J., 134
Emma James, 95
Ersie, 157
Essie C., 158
Estridge James, 157, 158
Ethel, 32

Ethel J., 225
Ethelbert Lee, 224
Eudora Belle, 115, 116
Everett, 220, 221
Fannie Leone, 37
Fannie Virginia, 52, 56
Felton, 49
Florence Fae, 173
Flossie, 75
Floyd M., 75
Francis, 229
Frank Lee, 22, 30
Frank Lee, Jr., 31
George S., 204, 210
George S., Jr., 210
Gertrude, 221
Gladwyn Hartley, 81, 85
Gladwyn Hartley, Jr., 85
Gladys Louise, 47
Grace Virginia, 156
Gracie Mae, 214
Greg, 58
Gregory, 172
Gwendolyn Moore, 114
Harold, 227
Harriet, 202
Harry Calvin, 112
Harry Calvin, Jr., 113
Harry Grey, 122, 124
Harvey T., 136
Hattie A., 72
Hazel Inez, 108
Helen, 198
Helen S., 49
Henderson, 170
Henry, 8, 68
Henry Cornelius, 151, 189
Henry D., 141, 144
Henry Harry, 8, 149
Henry Milton, 205, 206

Henry Milton, Jr., 206, 209
Henry Nathaniel, 199
Henry Nathaniel, II, 201, 202
Henry Stephen, 25, 46, 47
Henry Stephen, Jr., 47, 48
Henry Stephen, III, 48
Henry Thomas, 204, 205
Henry Vernon, 52, 53
Herman Taylor, 166, 173
Hester J., 72
Hettie Leone, 160
Hilda V., 213
Howard Garland (Sr.), 98, 115, 116
Howard Garland, Jr., 115, 117
Howard Garland, III, 115
Howell Sinclair, 193
Hursena James, 156
Imogene Hall, 114
Indiana, 140, 146
Ira Bledsoe, 119, 121
Irene Sevilla, 133
Isaac H., 202, 218
Izora, 204
Jack Nathan, 33
James A., 140, 146
James Blanchard, 98, 113
James H., 190
James Osborne, Jr., 109, 112
James Osborne, III, 112
James Sife, 201, 203
James Thomas, 151, 152, 165, 167
Janet Muriel, 159
Janice Marie, 128
Jennifer Carol, 194
Jessie Faye, 122, 127
Jessie Miller, 159
Joanna, 23, 34
John, 33
John Andrew, 70, 80, 86
John B., 33
John Braden, 66
John Bunyan, 32, 33
John Bunyan, Jr., 33
John Cleveland, 137
John Crevasser, 222, 225
John Elwood, 81, 88
John Franklin, 201, 212
John H., 212, 213
John Healy, 134
John Henry, 11, 15, 24, 76, 167, 184, 185
John Lemuel, 111
John Magruder, 52, 58
John Messick, 221
John Messick, Jr., 221
John Samuel, 155, 164, 178, 179
John Samuel, II, 179
John Thomas, 26, 51, 95, 126, 149, 227, 229
John Thomas, Jr., 229
John W., 97, 111
John Wilkins, 186
John Wilkins, Jr., 186
John William, 166, 170
Joyce Anne, 222, 230
Joyce L., 225
Joshua, 229
Judy Reed, 229
Judith Lane, 44, 45
Judith Lynne, 88
Julia, 108
Julia Frances, 113

Julie Lynn, 209
Kara Janine, 113
Karen Nicole, 109
Kelli Renea, 118
Kenneth Ernell, 214
Kenneth Ernell, Jr., 214
Kenneth Melvin, 118
Kenneth Wayne, 111
Kenneth William, 113
Kevin D., 67
Kimberley, 172
Kory Laurene, 42
Kymberly Ann, 42
Kurt Moore, 41
L. E., 152
Lavenia Elizabeth, 76, 166
Lavinia Anne, 155, 182
Lavinia Elizabeth, 160
Leamond Lankford, 73
Leman T., 221
Lemuel, 190
Lemuel E., 32
Lemuel Mansfield Duncan, 93, 95
Lemuel Vaden, 97, 110
Leo Carl, 193, 194
Leo Carl, Jr., 194
Leroy P., 184, 187
Leroy Thaupe, 36, 42
Lillian C., 224
Lillian Ronelda, 213
Lillie Beatrice, 81, 110
Linda Layne, 88
Linnie Lee, 43
Lisa, 111
Lloyd, 26, 68, 81, 85
Lorenzo Charles, 39
Louis Anne, 159
Louise, 32
Lue Ceal, 47
Lyman Dan, 158
Madison McKenzie, 179

Maggie, 224
Malvina Jane, 204
Marie Annette, 84
Mark Leaven, 41, 42
Margaret A., 32
Margaret H., 100
Martha Louise, 23, 29
Margaret Sylvester, 94
Maria, 152
Marie Annette, 87
Marilyn Louise, 53
Marion Lillian, 114
Martha Ann, 11, 129, 172
Martha Jane, 132
Martha Louise, 22
Marty Louise, 179
Marvin, 100
Mary, 2, 3, 151
Mary Adlena, 94
Mary Celestia, 184
Mary Elizabeth, 136
Mary Emily, 138, 139, 140
Mary F., 22, 26
Mary Ilene, 42
Mary Jane, 70, 71, 154
Mary Jeanette, 10
Mary Linda, 114
Mary Lorene, 52, 59
Mary Lou, 115
Mary M., 205
Mary Margaret, 47, 112
Mary Susan, 119, 120
Mary T., 49, 50
Mary V., 26, 27
Mary Vergie, 187
Mary Virginia, 31, 38
Mason, 160
Matilda, 139
Maud Louise, 36, 39
Maylon Page, 43
Maywood, 47
Melanie Ann, 38
Melissa, 125

Melvin, 100, 136
Mildred, 188, 193
Minnie E., 100
Missouri Frances, 133
Missouri Jane, 184
Mollie Jane, 81, 82
Murdie Maud, 156
Myra Gail, 170
Nancy, 8
Nancy F., 210
Nancy Jeanne, 65
Nancy Lee, 88
Nannie, 49, 75, 85
Nannie Moore, 221
Naomi, 78
Nellie Geneva, 81, 206
Nellie Gray, 38
Nettie Ellis, 226
Nettie Leone, 85
Nonie Elizabeth, 118
Nowida Lulu, 23
Orville H., 47, 48
Osborne, 97, 111
Paige, 68
Pauline, 43
Pearl, 32
Pearle J., 75
Rachel Anne, 42
Raymond B., 158
Raymond E., 160
Rebecca, 224
Rebecca Susan, 201
Regina Rollins, 109
Reginald, 213
Reginald F., 214
Rhoda, 26
Robert, 68, 229
Robert Blanchard, 114
Robert Brian, 38
Robert Claytor, 36, 37, 87
Robert Craig, 77
Robert Dolby, 152, 197
Robert Edgar, 127, 128
Robert Elkanah, 137

Robert H., 78, 94, 96
Robert Hartness, 37, 38
Robert Hartness, Jr., 38
Robert Henry, 99
Robert James, 11, 70, 73, 89, 94
Robert L., 190
Robert Lee, 94, 118, 133, 137, 159
Robert Mead, 186
Robert Samuel, 76, 77
Robert Sterling, 109
Robert T., 25, 46
Ronald Dan, 158
Rosanna, 22
Rosanna Sue, 85
Rose Doloris, 171, 172
Roxanna Elizabeth, 155, 180
Roy Wilbur, 43
Ruby E., 137
Russell, 110
Ruth V., 193
Sallie E., 31
Sallie Lucille, 38
Sally, 78
Sally Margaret, 75
Samuel, 202, 219, 220
Sandra H., 210
Sarah, 94, 188
Sarah Anne, 127
Sarah F., 184
Sarah Fimiah, 152, 195
Sarah L., 157
Sarah M., 156
Sarah Margaret, 10
Sarah Maria, 140
Sarah Matilda, 155
Sarah Sylvester, 14, 132
Savannah D., 155
Savannah J., 155
Savannah Leigh, 179

Shelly, 55
Shellie B., 157
Sonya Lee, 194
Steven Wayne, 110
Stewart M., 190
Talmadge Bunyan, 33
Tammy Ann, 85
Taylor Nicole, 179
Ted Moore, 128
Thelma Wilma, 157
Theresa Delia, 194
Thomas Cornelius, 159
Thomas Dale, 129
Thomas Edwin, 168
Thomas Henry, 140
Thomas Humphrey, 2, 9, 12, 222, 223
Thomas Laurens, 32
Thomas Lee, 155, 159
Thomas Ward, 55
Thomas Warren, 87
Thomas Wilfred, 128
Tim Ray, 128
Tina Marie, 229
Travis, 77
Tyler James Calvin, 113
Vandelia Lee, 41, 112
Vergie E., 191
Vergie Griggs, 227
Vernell, 40
Viola, 32, 226
Viola Mae, 87
Virginia, 119
Virginia G., 140, 142
Virginia Viana, 151
Vivian, 220
Vivian Marcella, 221
W. K., 211
Wallace Fayette, 110
Wallace Fayette, Jr., 110
Wallace Jerome, 85
Walter Haywood, 160, 163
Walter Leon, 159
Warren Smith, 81, 87
Warren Smith, Jr., 87
William, 187, 201
William B., 25, 48
William Bryan, 172
William Crosby, 74
William Henry, 36, 39, 154, 156
William Hope, 220
William Hugh, 40, 41
William Hugh, Jr., 41, 42
William I., 151, 183
William John, 188
William Jennings, 160
William King, 204, 211
William Melvin, 108
William Otis, 52, 54, 197, 198
William Otis, Jr., 55
William Taylor, 186
William Thomas, 11, 43, 44, 70, 72, 73, 133, 135, 158, 184
William Thomas, Jr., 69
William W., 190, 193
William Warren, 170, 172
Winnie Colber, 74
Zachery, 77

FREEMAN
Carrie R., 205
Joseph Elvin, 83, 84
Joseph Elvin, Jr., 84
Joseph Elvin, III, 84
Mollie, 158
Mollie Jane, 83
Mollie Mae, 83
Wade Forrest, 83, 84
Wade Forrest, Jr., 84
William Taylor, 82
Yvette Holloway, 84

GARDY
Katelyn Elizabeth, 125

GARRETT
Dorothy Alexander, 85

GIBBONS
John Garland, 169
Thomas Page, 169

GIBBS
Mary Margaret, 108

GRAHAM
Ginger, 64
John B., 225
Matilda Elizabeth, 170

GREEN
Mark, 55
Michael, 55

GRIER
Roma Patricia, 103

HALL
Lois, 48

HACZEWSKI
Jennifer Renne, 209

HAMPKER
Christopher Michael, 83
Mollie Katherine, 83

HERB
Edward Charles, 177
William Preston Daniel, 177

HODGES
Robert Lee, III, 117

HOFFMAN
Mary Milton, 47

HOLLOWAY
Agnes V., 142
Andrew McCabe, 106
Ann Deborah, 94
Anna Marie, 102
Arthur, 230
Birdie, 170
Eva J., 231
Florence, 84
Gordon Duane, 102, 103
Gordon Grier, 106
Harrison Joyner, 106
Harry Elam, 162
Hugh G., 231
Jackie, 100
James, 29
James Stuart, 104
Jennie, 231
John Early, 104, 106, 141
John Wayne, 111
Joseph, 30
Julie, 100
Marvin, 100
Mary Ann, 24
Martha Lucy, 30
Mary Elizabeth, 30
Mary M., 142
Melissa Lee, 118
Melvin, 100
Melvin Lee, 100
Nancy Ada, 230
Pinkey, 142
Robert Abram, 141
Robert Forrest, 106
Robert M., 230
Robert Scott, 100
Robert Stephen, 101, 102
Robert T., 230
Robert Taylor, III, 176

Shannon, 111
Steven, 142
Steven Frank, 104, 106
Teresa, 100
Thomas Lee, 100
Victoria Annie, 231
Virginia, 202
Virginia Ann, 158
William Grier, 104

HOLZER
Paul Ward, 107

HOPKINS
Charles Wesley, 39
Emma, 30
Louise Forrest, 39
Sarah W., 225
Sarah Wesley, 721
Virginia Emeline, 189
William E., 216
William Eldridge, 39
William Thomas, 39, 71

HUDGINS
Barbara Jane, 176
Diane Lynne, 176
Thomas, 175
Thomas Clifton, 175

HUFF
Eunice, 102

HUGGETT
Bessie J., 71
Bethany Ann, 196
Edward Franklin, 195
Eliza Ann, 73
Henry Cole, 71
Henry J., 71
John H., 196
Josiah M., 196
Josiah Maxwell, 195
Mary Jane, 196
Matilda A., 71

Polly, 196
Robert Lee, 196
Sadie E., 71
Sarah Margaret, 196
William M., 71
William T., 196

HUNT
Buford Dwight, 60, 61
Buford Raymond, 59
Deanna Elaine, 60
Mary Susan, 60, 61
Rita Moore, 116
Robert Graham, 61
Todd Forrest, 61

INSLEY
Emily Virginia, 44
Ethelyn, 161
Garnett, 161, 162
Gilbert B., 26
Gilbert C./L., 28
John Sydney, 28
Lemuel J., 158
Lloyd F., 29
Mahala Louise, 28
Margaret M., 28
Mary R., 28
Raymond, 161
Sarah E., 28
Sudie Viola, 227
Virginia Bell, 187
William J., 28
William James, 83, 160

JARVIS
Mary Virginia, 112

JENKINS
Frances, 84

JOHNSON
Charles J., 45
Kimberley Ann, 45

JOYNER
Patricia, 106

KAUTZ
Kelly Nicole, 87

KENNEDY
Christina Ann, 170
Shane Gordon, 170

KRUSZEWSKI
Leah Jean, 214
Michael Joseph, 214
Reginald Thomas, 214

LAWSON
Mary Irella, 148
Susanna Elizabeth, 135

LEWIS
Virginia, 38

LOZAW
Alyssa Ashley, 117
Christopher Douglas, 117

MANN
Charlotte Ronelda, 214
Leslie Suzanne, 214

MARTIN
Anna Cecilia, 43
Ann Elizabeth, 216
Charles Frederick, 216
Danny Lee, 64
David, 64
George W., 215
Henry D., 215
Isaac, 216
Jacob Elwood, 108
Jacob Elwood, Jr., 109
John, 216
John Linwood, 180
Joyce, 222

Laura Beatrice, 180
Lavina, 152
Martha J., 216
Nan Carey, 109
Samuel C., 216
Thomas D., 180
William Colbert, 180
William D., 178

MCBRIDE
Cathy Arlene, 61

MCCLELLAND
Heather, 228

MCLAIN
Adam C., 107

MEADOWS
Joan, 179

MELTON
Clinton, 77
Derek, 77

MERCHANT
Charles Michael, 177
Kimberly Anne, 177
Michael Anthony, 177

MESSICK
John Thomas, 78
John Thomas, Jr., 80
Lettie Jane, 80, 220
Mary E., 80
Minnie B., 77

MILLER
Jeanne, 65

MINGEE
Margaret A. B., 86

MONTGOMERY
Jessica, 65

Susanna Forrest, 214
Ryan, 65

MOORE
Coretta Dawson, 41
Gladys Elizabeth, 128
James Sterling, 109
Justin Morton, 109
Mary Lillian, 113
Sarah, 221
Starkey, 109

MUNGO
Amos Jefferson, 173
Eric Thomas, 173
Erin Carol, 173
Steven Keith, 173
Scott Jefferson, 173

NEIL
Norma, Jr., 58
Tina Ann, 58

OUTLAW
Christopher Tyler, 65

PAGE
Dennis Gordon, 170
Emma, 42
Eric Gordon, 170
Harriet Lane, 172
Henry Gordon, 168, 170
Henry Gray, 168
Jean Gray, 169
Jill Ann, 169
John D., 130
John Fay, 168
Lewis Skidmore, 130
Margaret Ann, 170
Monroe, 130
Nancy, 69
Stephanie Ann, 169
Thomas Curtis, 127
Victor Fay, 169
Victor Garland, 168

William, 129, 131
William Wesley, 130

PARISE
Patricia, 177

PARRON
James Blanchard, 114
Penelope Ann, 114

PAULS
Margaret Indiana, 111
Mary Viola, 111

PHILIPS
Evelyn Louise, 53

POWELL
Martha Emma, 225
Minnie M., 80
Pauline E., 79

QUINN
Benjamin F., 14
Beulah Forrest, 120
Buena Vista, 72, 73, 148
James Sledd, 118
John Harwood, 14
John J., 14
Joseph J., 14
Maggie J., 156
Margaret Lee, 120
Martha A., 12
Mary A., 12
Mary O., 14
Rebecca I., 14
Rosalie Virginia, 120

REVELEY
John Gibson, Jr., 50
John Gibson, III, 50
Marianne, 50
William Forrest, 50

THE FORREST FAMILY

RIDDICK
Kim Laurene, 42

RIDEOUT
Florence, 178

RIGGINS
Maggie L., 193

ROBERTS
Brady, 77
Heidi, 77

ROBINS
James, Jr., 57
Neal, 57

ROBINSON
Ashley Carol, 76
Courtney Anne, 76

ROLLINS
Alice Geneva, 80
Barbara Ann, 57
Bessie, 135, 198
Bethany Elaine, 207
Betty Marie, 208
Bonnie Ellen, 208
Clara B., 143
Clara Belle, 144
Coretta, 109
Daniel James, 208
David Forrest, 207, 208
David Nicholas, 208
Elisha Mitchell, 143, 144
Ellen O., 143
Gabrila, 144
Henry C., 135
Holly Jane, 208
Ida Sue, 65
Jack Nathan, 56
Janet Sue, 576
Jeffrey Brent, 114
John A., 135
John Bailey, 144
John W., 134
Joseph Lee, 208
Judith Fae, 58
Kelly Eilene, 115
Laura, 167
Lawrie Leigh, 208
Martha Ann, 199
Mary Elizabeth, 143
Mary M., 135
Melanie, 57
Milford Buren, 144
Rhoda, 144
Rhonda, 57
Robert, 57
Robert Mitchell, 114
Roland Randolph, 56
Roland Royall, 144
Roman Elmore, 143
Ruhemma, 197
Scott, 58
Shawn, 58
Susan Kathryn, 207, 208
Thomas Milton, 208
William Gene, 115
William Melvin, 207
William Melvin, Jr., 207
William Randy, 56

SAGER
Elizabeth Obed, 162
Mary Louise, 162
Harry, 162

SAUNDERS
Annie Virginia, 51
Edna Louise, 47
Sallie Clyde, 35

SCHOTT
Kylene, 66

SELLERS
Neil, 57
Randy, 57
Timothy, 57

SHARP
Terry, 174

SHAW
Curtis Warren, Jr., 67
Jennifer Adelle, 67

SHIFFLETT
David Lee, 61
Heather Marie, 62
Kimberly Ann, 62

SIBBERS:
Don Wesley, 107
Linda M., 107
Lisa, 107

SIKARA
Sharlene Ann, 208

SIMPSON
Mary Rogers, 149

SMITH
Ashby Marie, 194
Esta, 58
Esther, 211
Misty Lee, 194
Nettie, 210

SOUTHALL
Charles Macon, 44
Charles Thomas, 44
David Sidney, 44

SPENCER
Thomas Edward, 115

STEELE
Betsy Marie, 63, 64
John Thomas, 64
John Thomas, Jr., 64
Kory Lee Elliott, 63
Paul Edward, 65
Robert Elliott, 63, 64
Ronald Ervin, 63, 65
Sharon Ellen, 65
Thomas Elliott, 62
Tina Margaret, 63

STEWART
Robert K., 45
Stacey Annette, 45
William Keith, 45

STONE
Jackie, Jr., 111
Parker, 111
Tarek, 111

TAYLOR
Donald Mark, 114
Kent Van, 114

THOMAS
Catherine, 131
Mary Elizabeth, 218

TOPPING
Charles Grayson, 35
Hattie, 35
John Oliver, 34
Lulu M., 35
Mary Augusta, 37
Oliver Cromwell, 34
Sarah Elizabeth, 131
Sarah L., 34

TRACEY
Gerald, 161

TUCKER
Elizabeth Kate, 208
Harry Keith, 208
Harry Keith, Jr., 208
James Milton, 208

TYNDALL
Carole, 87
Patricia, 87

VANDERVORT
Catherine, 125
Jennifer, 125

WALKER
Ashley Loren, 174
James, 174
James Cole, 174
James Taylor, 174
Logan Alayna, 174
Shannon Luv, 174
Taylor Anne, 174

WALTERS
Edith, 84

WARD
Anna Elizabeth, 107
Anna Marie, 107
Henry Stephen, 107
Jeannine, 107
Josephine Simpson, 168
Michael Duane, 114
Richard Dennis, 114
Teresa Lynn, 114
William Nathan, 107

WATKINS
Annie Forrest, 68
Basil, 133
Elsie E., 147
Eva Irene, 173
Henry W., 146
Missouri Hall, 93
Nolan, 147
Nolian, 147
Oren, 37
Randall, 137
Sarah Elizabeth, 126
Sarah Frances, 183
Sidney D., 146
Sidney V., 147
Spencer, 147
Tommie L., 147

WATSON
Ian Trevor, 172

WECHSLER
Bethany Michelle, 170
Jason Franklin, 170
Terri Lynn, 170

WELLS
Dayton Thomas, 194
Michael Eugene, Jr., 194
Steffi Joyce, 194

WESTON
Louisa, 15
Mary 9
Mary Frances, 89

WHITE
Donna Lee, 61
Esther Marie, 211
Wallie Gene, 211

WHITFIELD
Gladys, 81

WHITLOW
Kimberly Anne, 176, 177
Lauren Marie, 177
Megan Elizabeth, 177
Natalie Lynne, 176, 178
Paul Anthony, 176
Paul Anthony, Jr., 176, 177
Toni-Anne, 177
Victoria Lynne, 177

WILLIAMS
Kathryn Louise, 53

WILSON
Roselyn, 50

WINDER
Sarah Laney, 72

WOODS:
Kristin, 111

WRIGHT
Amanda, 228
Cathy Viola, 228
Drew, 228
Herbert, 228
Herbert, Jr., 228
James, 228
Tiffany, 228
Wanda Jane, 228

WOODS
Kristin, 109

ZADODNY
Eva C., 48

Heritage Books by Albert James Willett, Jr.:

Abraham Willett (c1735–c1805) of Onondaga County, New York

The Martin Family of the Poquoson District, York County, Virginia
Albert James Willett, Jr. and Dr. Fred William Martin, Ph.D.

*Poquoson Families, Volume I: The Forrest Family
of the Poquoson District, York County, Virginia*

*Poquoson Families, Volume II: The Holloway, Messick, and Linton Families
of the Poquoson District, York County, Virginia*

*Poquoson Families, Volume III: The Topping, Rollins, and Carmines Families
of Poquoson District, York County, Virginia*

*Poquoson Families, Volume IV: The Amory, Insley, Firman, and Firth Families
of the Poquoson District, York County, Virginia*

*Poquoson Families, Volume V: The Gilbert and Hopkins Families
of the Poquoson District, York County, Virginia*

*Poquoson Families, Volume VI: The Patrick, Evans and Lawson Families
of the Poquoson District, York County, Virginia*

CD: *Willett Family of Pennsylvania*

Willett House Collection [Willett Family of Pennsylvania]

www.ingramcontent.com/pod-product-compliance
Lightning Source LLC
Chambersburg PA
CBHW070728160426
43192CB00009B/1358